IVAN MYACHIN
VLADIMIR CHERNOV

MOSCOW

tourist guide

USSR
1917 - 1967

NOVOSTI PRESS AGENCY PUBLISHING HOUSE
MOSCOW

FIFTY YEARS

Only half a century separates us from those glorious days that, to quote John Reed, "shook the world." Yet the changes that have taken place in this country are astounding. As the years rolled by, the Soviet Union, in spite of innumerable harships (military intervention by fourteen imperialist states in the post-revolutionary period, invasion by Hitlerite fascist hordes during the Second World War) made spectacular economic, social and cultural advances.

Moscow is an old city and a fascinating one. Its 820 year-old history is rich in events, its numerous museums are crowded with relics of a long and tempestuous past. Yet it is the last fifty years that account for the city's unusual rate of development, and diversity of sights.

—During this period Moscow has gained particular fame and, first of all, as the chief centre of a new state—the Union of Soviet Socialist Republics.

—It has become a modern city with a multitude of plants and factories.

—The hub of the country's transport service with eleven railroad ter-

The Spasskaya Tower clock

minals and four airports. It is a great cultural centre, its museums and exhibitions presenting a rich chronicle of the history of architecture, literature, painting and music.

—A city where science and engineering are forging ahead.

—There are hundreds of colleges and scientific institutions, schools and kindergartens.

—And some of the country's finest theatres and concert halls.

Visitors to Moscow fall under the spell of its spacious squares and prospects, its numerous boulevards and embankments, picturesque by-streets and parks. And there are also the Muscovites, industrious, energetic and cordial folk who have made the city what it is today and who are determined to make it the fine city they need and want for the morrow.

Realizing that tourists may have only a very short time at their disposal - occasionally just one or two days—this booklet has been written to make a point of "the most interesting sights." It starts off with a general picture of Moscow and then concentrates on the city's districts with different Metro (subway) stations as the starting points.

If, as you read these pages, you come to have a fuller appreciation of the capital's great heritage, where history has been carefully preserved and is in the making, you, too, will risk leaving a bit of your heart here.

Moscow is growing younger

Moscow morning

Everything is new!

Everyday Moscow

Waiting hall at Domodedovo Airport

Visitors to Moscow

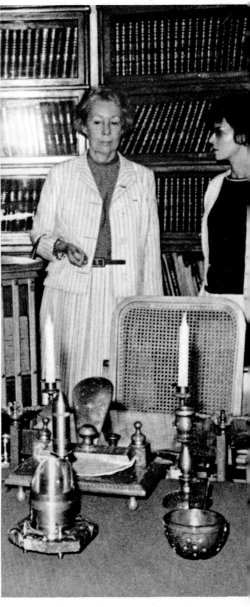

Lenin's study in the Kremlin 15

Moscow "gold"

Moscow skyline

Moscow "Swans"

Moscow windows

Muscovites like to read

In a café

In the world of science

Winter flowers

Radio messages from all over the world are received here

View from the Ukraina Hotel

MOSCOW TODAY AND TOMORROW

A Sketch of the City

The broad, straight highway with a belt of greenery down the centre disappears in the distance beyond the horizon. But it only appears to be straight, so imperceptible are its gradual, smooth bends. Actually there is no beginning and no end to this circular highway known as the *Moskovskaya Koltsevaya* (Moscow Ring Road). It marks the city limits, encircling Moscow at an average of 9.2 to 11.2 miles from the centre of town.

When completed (1962), this Ring Road accentuated the characteristic features of the city's layout: concentric rings cut through by rays radiating out from the centre.

In the middle of the 12th century, Prince Yury Dolgoruky set up fortifications consisting of several structures surrounded by a palisade, on the high bank of the Moskva River where it is joined by the Neglinnaya. That is how the Kremlin came into being.

The present Kremlin brick walls with some twenty towers were erected by the year 1500. About 30 years later a brick wall with 12 towers and a length of more than 1.5 miles was built to fence in *Kitai-Gorod*—an ancient *posad* [1] adjoining the Kremlin on the east. Remnants of this wall can be seen to this day in the centre of the city.

At the end of the 16th century, a similar wall 5.6 miles long with about 30 towers enclosed the Kremlin and *Kitai-Gorod,* and also *Bely Gorod* (the White City) which spread out to the north of the Moskva River. Nothing remains of that wall today. In its place a green boulevard encircles the city.

It was approximately at that time that the

---

1) Posad—the area settled by craftsmen in earlier days under the walls of a castle or monastery.

city was girded by an earthen rampart and a strong wooden wall with scores of towers and a deep moat in front. This line of fortifications crossed over to the right bank of the Moskva River forming the contours of the present *Sadovoye Koltso* (Garden Ring Road).

In the middle of the 18th century an earthen rampart was erected about 24.9 miles long, which served as the customs boundary of the city. The present Okruzhnaya Circular Railroad runs along the original route of this rampart in a number of places.

The walls of the circular fortifications were pierced by radiating streets, which started from the centre and eventually became highways leading to distant places.

That is how Moscow acquired its radial ring layout, which has much in common with Paris, Vienna and several other big cities.

Before too, Moscow was one of the biggest cities on the globe: in 1917 it occupied an area of 90 square miles, in 1939, 115 square miles. But it became much larger when the city limits were pushed back in August 1960 to include the towns of Babushkin, Kuntsevo, Lyublino, Perovo and Tushino, and also workers' and summer cottage settlements and rural inhabited points.

This extended Moscow to nearly 347 square miles, approximately a two-and-a-half-fold increase. Before the October Revolution there were 1,500 streets and by-streets in Moscow. Today, the Soviet capital has over 5,000 streets, avenues, by-streets, public squares, shoreline drives and highways.

A protective forest park belt stretching for 444,780 acres surrounds the Soviet capital, serving as a nearby recreation zone for Moscow's residents.

Moscow Weather

If you were to ask whether it is cold or hot in Moscow, you would probably be told it is neither one nor the other. The climate is temperate and the average precipitation is appreciable, the prevailing winds being westerly. Moscow's mean annual temperature is 39.9°F. The coldest months are December, January and February. The first snowfall is usually registered about the middle of October, but a lasting blanket of snow forms much later. The last snow falls towards the end of March and remains until the beginning of April.

The warmest months of the year are June, with an average temperature of 61.5°F, July and August. Next come May and September. October is often a dry, pleasantly cool and colourful month. Autumn and winter in Moscow and its suburbs have a distinctive charm of their own.

Mean annual precipitation in Moscow is 620 mm, which is slightly higher than in Paris (590 mm) or in San Francisco (562 mm) and a little less than in Vienna (680 mm). The most "productive" months in this respect are June, July and August. Then come September, October and November. March, April and May are drier, with December, January and February in the last place.

Muscovites

There are 6.5 million people living in Moscow today (1.8 million in 1917). The Soviet capital is one of the biggest cities in the world, next only to such giant metropolises as New York, Tokyo and London.

Russians make up nearly 94 per cent of the city's population. Then come Ukrainians and Jews, comprising over 100,000 each.

Moscow is the capital of a multinational state and this has noticeably affected the composition of the city's population. Of the nationalities numbering from 10,000 to 100,000 the most numerous are the Tatars and the Byelorussians, then come Armenians, Mordvinians and Poles. Georgians, Chuvashes, Letts, Lithuanians and Estonians number from 2,000 to 6,000.

The pattern of settlement of the Soviet capital by different nationalities is quite distinctive. Even insofar as large nationality groups are concerned, they live here and there and everywhere intermingled with Rus-

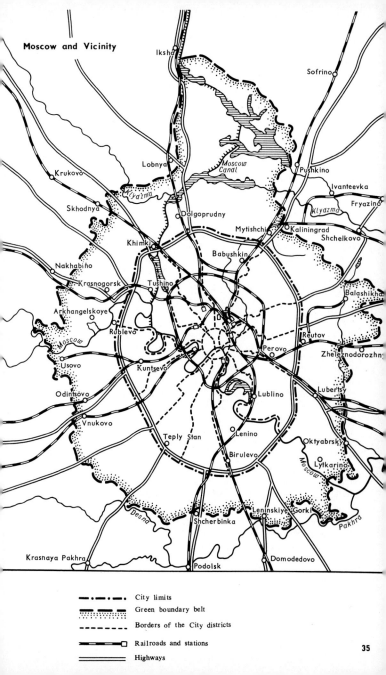

Moscow and Vicinity

Iksha

Sofrino

Krukovo

Lobnya

Moscow Canal

Pushkino

Ivanteevka

Skhodnya

Klyazma

Dolgoprudny

Fryazino

Klyazma

Khimki

Mytishchi

Kaliningrad

Shchelkovo

Nakhabino

Babushkin

Krasnogorsk

Tushino

Balashikha

Arkhangelskoye

Rublevo

Reutov

Moscow

Perovo

Zheleznodorozhny

Usovo

Kuntsevo

Odintsovo

Lublino

Lubertsy

Vnukovo

Lenino

Oktyabrsky

Teply Stan

Lytkarino

Birulevo

Moscow

Desna

Leninskiye Gorki

Pakhra

Shcherbinka

Krasnaya Pakhra

Domodedovo

Podolsk

sians and not in definite blocks or districts such as in New York, for instance.

Four-fifths of the able-bodied inhabitants (men from 16 to 60 and women from 16 to 55) work. The rest are college students, schoolchildren and women who remain at home. There are also quite a number of pensioners.

Muscovites, like all Soviet citizens, are friendly, attentive, exceedingly hospitable, good-natured, and have a discreet sense of humour. They are energetic and eager to lead a full life.

The Country's Heart

Moscow is both the capital of the Union of Soviet Socialist Republics and capital of the largest of these republics—the Russian Soviet Federative Socialist Republic (RSFSR).

Sessions of the USSR Supreme Soviet and RSFSR Supreme Soviet (the parliament of the country and republic respectively) are held in Moscow where the state and government offices and headquarters of the Central Committee of the Soviet Communist Party are located.

The USSR Communist Party convenes its congresses in Moscow, and Party and Government leaders meet there with workers, collective farmers, experts in the economy, and people engaged in science, culture and arts.

The Soviet capital is the seat of the executive bodies of various voluntary mass organizations, societies, and cultural associations.

Moscow is a hub of friendly international contacts between people in science, technology and culture, the gathering place of people of good will working for peace, social progress, and equality of peoples, for the happiness of all people.

Moscow heads a state in which over 120 large and small nationalities have united of their own free will. And to all of them Moscow is a parental home which always gives them a cordial welcome.

City of Toilers

More than three-fifths of Moscow's residents are wage and salary earners. The city has numerous modern industrial enterprises, primarily engineering and metal-working plants with a wide range of output which includes programme-controlled machine tools, automatic production lines, motor cars, cranes, bearings, pumps of all kinds, transformers, electric motors, television sets, watches, transistorized instruments, computers, and highly complex radioelectronic and telemetric equipment, etc. Moscow is also a major centre of the chemical industry. On the whole, output of the city's big-scale-industry has outstripped the pre-revolutionary level 100 times. There probably isn't a single settlement in the Soviet Union that doesn't use the products of Moscow textile, footwear, clothing, perfume and other light industry enterprises; the city's consumer goods enterprises account for nearly a half of its total industrial output.

All sectors of the municipal economy are staffed with more than 750,000 experts with a higher and specialized secondary education.

Moscow products enjoy a good reputation on the world market. Some 300 of the city's plants and factories export their products to about 70 foreign countries. Many of these goods have won high awards and diplomas at international exhibitions and fairs.

Transportation Hub

Spreading out far and wide along the banks of the Moskva River, Moscow has long since dissected the Russian Plain with radial roads. Today some two dozen highways and railways connect the Soviet capital with the most distant parts of the country. Air lines connect Moscow with points within the country and abroad. Following the construction of the Moscow Canal (linking the Volga and the Moskva River) and the Volga-Don Canal, the Soviet capital became the port of five seas: the White, Baltic, Caspian, Azov and Black Seas. One and a half million people stream into Moscow every day through the city's railroad terminals and airports.

The first suburban electric railroad line, covering a distance of 11.2 miles from Moscow to Mytishchi, went into operation in the late 1920's. Today not a single steam locomotive is to be seen at the capital's railroad junction. Moscow has become the centre of the country's electrified railroad system, which now has far more track than any other country.

Cultural Centre

Moscow may rightly be called a city of students. More than half a million students are enrolled at its higher educational establishments, and 1,200,000 at technical and general secondary schools. This means that just under a third of the population are studying. Every year Moscow alone graduates more than half the number of engineers trained in all higher educational establishments of the United States.

The oldest and best known higher educational establishments include *Moscow State University* named after Mikhail Lomonosov, the *Bauman Higher Technical School,* the *Timiryazev Agricultural Academy,* and the *First Medical Institute.* And the new *Patrice Lumumba Peoples' Friendship University* is becoming equally well known. More than 4,000 young men and women from nearly 80 countries in Asia, Africa and Latin America are studying at the Peoples' Friendship University, Moscow University and other higher educational establishments in the city.

Moscow is the seat of the *USSR Academy of Sciences* and several specialized academies, among them the academies of medicine, pedagogics, arts and municipal economy. It also has more than 550 research institutes, designing offices and laboratories. These institutions are staffed with over 100,000 scientific workers, including one-fifth with post-graduate degrees.

The *Bolshoi Theatre* of the USSR is world renowned. Its opera and ballet stars have been enthusiastically welcomed in the United States, Belgium, Japan, France, Great Britain and Italy.

Universal recognition has been won by

the *Art, Maly, Vakhtangov, Mossoviet,* and *Mayakovsky* theatres.

Besides the dozens of professional theatres, there are over 300 clubs and excellent cultural centres at factories, plants, higher educational establishments, offices and societies with amateur drama, dance and choral groups.

Moscow has some 3,000 libraries with a total book fund topping 160,000,000 volumes.

Thousands upon thousands of tourists make it a point to visit the *Central Lenin Museum,* the *Tretyakov Art Gallery, Pushkin Museum of Fine Arts, History Museum, Oruzheinaya Palata* (Armoury), and the *National Economic Achievements Exhibition.*

Many films have brought Soviet cinematography world fame, and the finest foreign films are shown on Soviet screens. No wonder the 130-odd Moscow moving picture theatres are always full.

Rich and varied programmes are given at Moscow's best concert halls—the Grand and Small Halls of the *Conservatoire, Tchaikovsky Hall,* and the *Hall of Columns,* Trade Union House.

The *USSR State Symphony Orchestra* was founded thirty years ago. During this quarter of a century, it has played works by Mozart, Beethoven, Grieg, Saint-Saens, Ravel, Mahler, Stravinsky, Hindemith, Prokofiev and Shostakovich to audiences totalling about six million.

The birch tree—the symbol of Russian nature—is always charming, fresh and poetic. And so are the dances of the *Beryozka* (birch tree) *Dance Company,* which has triumphantly borne this name throughout many countries of the globe. But there are many other groups that are equally popular, among them the *USSR Folk Dance Company* directed by Igor Moiseyev, the *Soviet Army Song and Dance Company* and the *Pyatnitsky Russian Folk Song Choir.*

Heroic City

In the Autumn of 1941, the peoples of the USSR and the fascist hordes of Nazi Germany met in mortal combat at the walls of the Soviet capital.

Moscow Districts

1. Sverdlovsky
2. Baumansky
3. Kirovsky
4. Frunzensky
5. Leninsky
6. Kievsky
7. Krasnopresnensky
8. Leningradsky
9. Timiryazevsky
10. Dzerzhinsky
11. Kuibyshevsky
12. Pervomaisky
13. Kalininsky
14. Zhdanovsky
15. Proletarsky
16. Moskvoretsky
17. Oktyabrsky

New Districts of Moscow under Construction

1. South West (districts 32-33, 34-35, 37-38 and Experimental District)
2. Michurinsky Prospekt
3. Matveevskoye
4. Fili-Mazilovo
5. Kuntseva-Rublevskoye Chaussee
6. Testovsky Poselok
7. Khoroshevo-Mnevniki
8. Shchukino
9. Tushino
10. Khimki-Khovrino
11. Vsekhsvyatskoye
12. Verkniaya Maslovka
13. Koptevo
14. Degunino
15. Medvedkovo-Beskudnikovo
16. Babushkin
17. Maryina Roshcha-Ostankino
18. Prospekt Mira-Alexeevskoye-Rostokino
19. Bogorodskoye
20. Otkrytoye Chaussee
21. Shcherbakovskaya Ulitsa
22. Izmailovo-Shchelkovskoye Chaussee
23. Perovo-Novo-Gireevo
24. Vyazovka
25. Veshnyaki
26. Kuzminki-Tekstilshchiki
27. Lublino
28. Simonovsky Val-Dubrovka
29. Kozhukhovo
30. Novinki-Nogatino
31. Kolomenskoye-Sadovniki
32. Kashirskoye Chaussee
33. Lenino
34. Volkhonka-ZIL
35. Chertanovo
36. Nagornaya Streets and Zuzino
37. Cheryomushki
38. Belyaevo-Derevlyovo
39. Kalinin Prospekt (New Arbat)

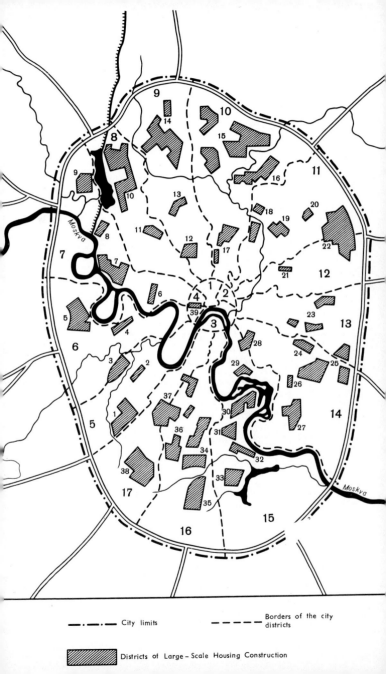

City limits

Borders of the city districts

Districts of Large-Scale Housing Construction

Until the Battle of Moscow, many American and British statesmen and military leaders doubted whether the Soviet Union could be victorious. And indeed, nothing could halt the advance of the German war machine over the fields and roads of many West European countries. Hitler concentrated 75 divisions, including 14 tank and 8 motorized divisions, and about a thousand aircraft on the approaches to Moscow. But the enemy was routed. There, in the city's suburbs, the German-fascist forces suffered their first big defeat in the Second World War. The myth of the invincibility of Hitler's armies was dispelled.

Moscow stood its ground; Moscow was victorious. The Soviet capital sent more than 700,000 of its sons and daughters to the front; more than half the city's Communists fought at the front. Twelve Moscow divisions of volunteer corps fought side by side with them. Divisions from Siberia and the Urals came to the defence of the city. Ukrainians and Georgians, Kazakhs and Letts, Azerbaijanians and Byelorussians, Armenians and Mordvinians, the sons of all the peoples of the Soviet Land defended their capital.

The residents of Moscow and its suburbs turned their native town into an impregnable bastion, belting it with reliable defence structures. Within a short period they dug out 395 miles of anti-tank ditches and 16,500 entrenchments for infantry sections, organized 27,640 machine-gun and artillery emplacements, raised 32,260 hedgehogs, put up 792 miles of wire entanglements, and slashings were made over an area of some 40,000 hectares.

Muscovites displayed bravery and valour on the battle-fields of the Great Patriotic War (1941-1945): hundreds of thousands of them were awarded military decorations, more than 800 received the Gold Star of Hero of the Soviet Union, the country's highest military award, and five of them were twice given this signal honour.

Moscow men and women, young and old, contributed more than 500,000 litres of their blood to save the lives of wounded soldiers. Muscovites helped smash the enemy with their savings too. During the war years, they voluntarily donated 2,600,000,000 roubles to the defence fund.

Valiant warriors and tireless workers, the Muscovites brought well-merited glory to their city: today a Gold Star and a second Order of Lenin—symbols of a heroic city—adorn Moscow's banner.

Symbol of the City

The city is building and rebuilding.

Until the Great October Socialist Revolution, Moscow lacked a unified plan of development and grew haphazardly.

Old Moscow was a city with narrow, crooked streets; blocks dissected by numerous by-streets and blind-alleys; an unevenly built-up centre and outskirts; a centre jammed with warehouses and small enterprises; low buildings (90 per cent of the structures were one and two-story high).

In the last 50 years Moscow has changed beyond recognition.

Now rid of all unnecessary encumbrances, the squares in the centre of town, at the intersections of ring roads and radial thoroughfares, and the railroad terminal squares, have become much more spacious. The main thoroughfares were made several times wider, paved, built up with new apartment houses and beautified.

The banks of the Moskva River have been faced with granite (more than 42 miles of stone embankments have been added to the original four) and the river itself, which could no longer satisfy the greater requirements of the rapidly growing city, became a deep waterway replenished by water from the Volga channelled to Moscow htrough a 80-mile canal used by large passenger boats and barges. Per capita daily water consumption is now 570 quarts (70 quarts in 1913).

Besides the many new avenues, entire new districts have been built up, each equal in size to many a city.

Here are a few of the relatively new structures:

the huge skyscraper edifice of Moscow State University;

the Palace for Young Pioneers and Schoolchildren;

a sports complex that has completely changed the face of Luzhniki, and the buildings of the Patrice Lumumba Friendship University—all in the Yugo-Zapadny (South-Western) District;

the grounds and premises of the National Economic Achievements Exhibition and the exhibition premises in Sokolniki—in the Northern part of the city;

Moskva Hotel, the House of the Council of Ministers (Government House), the Moskva Swimming Pool, the Kremlin Palace of Congresses and Europe's biggest hotel, *Rossiya* —all in the centre of town;

the Battle of Borodino Panorama on Kutuzovsky Prospekt;

the Moskva Department Store and AUCCTU [1] Hotel on Leninsky Prospekt;

the International General Post Office and the Railway General Post Office with helicopter landing facilities on the roof—both on Komsomol Square;

the modern *Minsk Hotel* on Gorky Street;

the Dynamo Stadium, swimming pools and the skyscraper premises of the Hydro-Designing Institute—all on Leningradsky Prospekt;

the over 1,700-feet-high tower and the All-Union TV Centre in Ostankino.

Passengers are already enjoying the facilities at the new Moscow air terminal and the new buildings at Vnukovo, Sheremetyevo and Domodedovo airports.

New bridges have been thrown across the Moskva River.

The city has been beautified with many trees, new squares and parks, new monuments, and a 328-foot obelisk commemorating the conquest of space by Soviet people.

In 1917 the total dwelling space in Moscow amounted to over 13 million square yards, these for the most part lacking modern conveniences.

Moscow has been growing progressively: in 1947, 155,000 square yards of floor space were made available to Muscovites, in 1955 about 1,200 thousand; since 1960 more than 3,500 thousand square yards of space have been commissioned each year.

Intensive housing construction in Moscow in fifty years of Soviet rule has made

---

1) ACCTU—All-Union Central Council of Trade Unions.

44

the city four times as big as before the October Revolution.

More than 90 per cent of the city's housing has all modern conveniences. Muscovites are much better supplied with gas, hot water, baths and sewerage than the inhabitants of London, Paris and Rome.

The pace of housing construction in the Soviet capital is constantly increasing. Regardless of which railway or highway you use to enter the city, everywhere you'll see housing construction going on—cranes, cranes, and more cranes. And indeed, there is no better symbol for the ever growing city of Moscow than the image of a crane.

Moscow Tomorrow

The realization of a master municipal development plan is now under way in Moscow.

The bounds of the capital will remain within the Moscow Ring Road which marks off a total area of 341.7 square miles. Moscow's population will be stabilized at 6.5-6.8 million.

In Moscow it is prohibited to build new plants and factories or to expand those in operation, as well as to build new scientific research and designing institutions, experimental bases, higher educational establishments and technical schools. Exception is made for enterprises concerned with public services and housing construction.

The growth of industrial output at Moscow plants and improvement of its quality must be attained without additional employment by raising labour productivity and the technical level of production, introducing new machines, expanding mechanization and automation of production, modernizing or discarding obsolete equipment.

In the last 10 years 50 plants and 100 workshops, that were detrimental to the city from the standpoint of hygiene and sanitation, have been transferred from Moscow. Two hundred more enterprises will soon follow, and 340 will undergo reconstruction for the same reasons. This will free a large labour force for work in the spheres of culture and public amenities and help reduce air pollution.

Nearly three million Muscovites have moved into new flats between 1959 and 1965. To provide each resident with a 12-15 square yards room it is expected to build within 20 years (1961-1980) 66 million square yards of dwelling space, or 112 million square yards of useful floor space.

Houses with nine, twelve, sixteen and more storeys will be built. This will provide for more efficient use of the capital's area leaving sufficient room for parks and sports grounds, and make Moscow's skyline more expressive.

Extensive housing construction will be continued in the new outlying districts of the capital.

The reconstruction of the central districts in the vicinity of the Sadovoye Koltso (Ring) is a particularly complex and responsible job.

First of all, these districts will be cleared of all enterprises. The residential distincts will be preserved, but all dilapidated and worthless buildings will be removed. The area around the Kremlin, when cleared of old houses, will be covered with greenery and lakes.

The future centre will become the site of some 600 historical and architectural monuments. Monumental works of art—memorials and frescoes—will beautify the central thoroughfares, parks and squares and other districts.

The chief radial thoroughfares including Dimitrov Street, Chekhov Street, Sretenka, Dzerzhinskaya Street, Ulyanovskaya, Internatsionalnaya, Pyatnitskaya, Bolshaya-Ordynka, Bolshaya Polyanka will be reconstructed and broadened.

Novokirovsky Prospekt will run from Dzerzhinsky Square to Komsomol Square. The semi-circular boulevard chain in downtown Moscow will be continued to Zamoskvorechye (district of Moscow on the left bank of the Moskva River to the south of the Kremlin). Highway bridges along the circular boulevard chain and the Sadovoye Koltso will eliminate traffic congestion and Kitay-Gorod will be closed to all transport.

In the near future a monument to Lenin, a new Moscow University building for the humanities (already under construction) and a Youth Centre are to be erected on Lenin Hills.

The extensive construction of new schools and establishments for children by 1970 will put an end to the two-shift system of studies at schools and provide all children with nurseries and kindergartens in the immediate neighbourhood of their homes.

The green area will be more than doubled. The network of public amenities will be ramified thrice as much as it was in 1960. The number of shops will increase by two and a half times and public catering by six and a half times. Hotels will cater to four times as many persons.

Gas and electricity consumption will go up by four times. Each flat will have a telephone.

The number of stadiums will increase threefold. New skating rinks, swimming pools, track and field and other sports grounds will be able to admit regularly two-thirds of Moscow's residents.

New bridges will span the Moskva River to connect the districts in the vicinity of Bolshaya Pirogovskaya Street and the Lenin Hills, Solyanka and Lenino.

Hundreds of miles are to be added to the overall length of trolleybus lines. The outskirts will receive dozens of miles of tram lines. The Moscow Metro will be still further ramified and will be extended by more than 100 miles. It will account for 40 per cent of the city's passenger turnover.

It is planned to cut the time it takes Muscovites to get to work to a maximum of 30-40 minutes, to provide transit with maximum speed and convenience between residential and industrial districts, business sections and recreation zones.

In the future rapid transit lines will connect districts that are today still considered remote. Monorail roads and helicopters will provide rapid transportation between the town and Vnukovo, Sheremetyevo, Domodedovo and Bykovo Airports.

EXCURSION **1**

STARTING POINT:
**BIBLIOTEKA LENINA
(LENIN LIBRARY),
KALININSKAYA
AND ARBATSKAYA**
METRO STATIONS

THROUGH THE ANCIENT KREMLIN

AFTER visiting Moscow and seeing the sights, the historical monuments and places of interest, Emile Verhaeren, the eminent Belgian poet, said:

"The whole city seems like a huge open-air museum to me, and the most perfect, the most unique and the most attractive sight is the Kremlin.

"Walled in by a huge crenelated parapet, the Kremlin, with its hundreds of protruding cupolas looking for all the world like the golden bills of birds stretching their long necks up towards the light, remains in my mind's eye the most beautiful of all the fairy-land scenes on Earth.

"As soon as I stepped out of the train, the first thing I did was to set off for the Kremlin. ."

Emile Verhaeren visited Moscow back in 1913, but today too, hundreds of thousands of tourists do exactly as he did upon arriving in the Soviet capital: they hurry off to see

The Kremlin Palace of Congresses

THE KREMLIN

1. Spasskaya Tower; 2. Tower of the Senate; 3. Nikolskaya Tower; 4. Corner Arsenal Tower; 5. Intermediate Arsenal Tower; 6. Trinity Tower; 7. Trinity Bridge; 8. Kutafya Tower; 9. Commandant's Tower; 10. Armoury Tower; 11. Borovitskaya Tower; 12. Vodovzvodnaya Tower; 13. Tower of the Annunciation; 14. Tainitskaya Tower; 15. Ist Nameless Tower; 16. 2nd Nameless Tower; 17. Petrovskaya Tower; 18. Beklemeshevskaya (Moskvoretskaya) Tower; 19. Konstantino-Yeleninskaya Tower; 20. Nabatnaya Tower; 21. Tsarskaya Tower; 22. Cathedral of the Assumption; 23. Cathedral of the Annunciation; 24. Cathedral of the Archangel; 25. Granovitaya Palata; 26. Bell Tower of Ivan the Great; 27. Tsar Bell; 28. Tsar Cannon; 29. Cathedral of the 12 Apostles; 30. Palace of Congresses; 31. Former Arsenal; 32. Building of the USSR Council of Ministers; 33. Obelisk to the Officers and Cadets of the Kremlin Military School; 34. Seat of the Presidium of the USSR Supreme Soviet and Kremlin Theatre; 35. Great Kremlin Palace; 36. Oruzheinaya Palata.

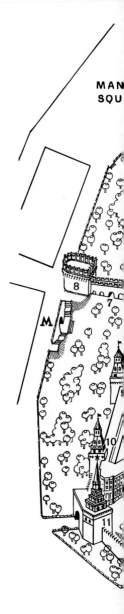

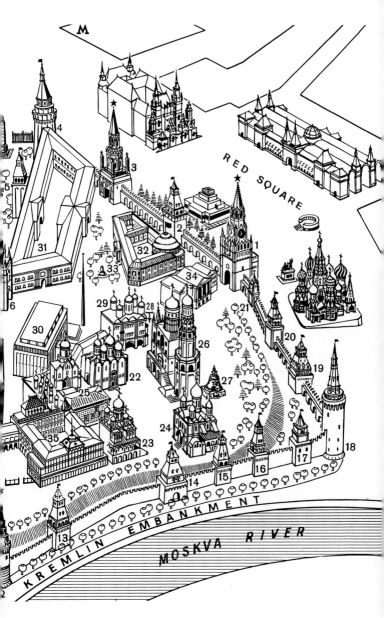

M

RED SQUARE

KREMLIN EMBANKMENT

MOSKVA RIVER

51

52

Walls and towers of the ancient Kremlin   53

the *Kremlin,* which stands on a steep elevation overlooking the left bank of the Moskva River.

Moskvoretsky Bridge is the best place to take in and admire the sweeping panorama of the Kremlin—a vantage point providing an excellent view of its cathedrals, Grand Palace, wall and towers.

The Moscow Kremlin is the ancient historical and architectural centre of the city; ancient annals tell of the meeting between Prince Yury Dolgoruky of Rostov-Suzdal and Prince Svyatoslav of Chernigov-Seversk on Borovitsky Hill (now called Kremlin Hill) back in the year 1147. This is the first time Moscow was mentioned in chronicles. However, remnants of ancient structures discovered during recent excavations in the Kremlin induce us to believe that people had settled on that territory back in the 11th century, long before the generally accepted date of the city's foundation.

In 1156, Prince Yury Dolgoruky ordered a wooden fortress to be built atop Borovitsky Hill, which subsequently became the centre of the Moscow Principality.

This fortress was burned to the ground in 1238 during a Tatar invasion. But Moscow continued to live and grow. In 1326-1339 oaken walls were erected around the Kremlin. At that time, two stone cathedrals —the *Arkhangelsky* and the *Uspensky*—were built, forerunners of the present Kremlin cathedrals. The Kremlin became the residence of the grand dukes and the metropolitans of Moscow.

The oaken walls gave way to white stone walls and towers in 1367-1368 and Moscow began to be called the white-stone city.

During the reign of Ivan III, the Kremlin grounds were extended to their present area and the white-stone Kremlin walls, which had survived many a conflagration and siege in 100 years, were replaced (in 1485-1495) by new, brick walls and towers. These are still standing to this day.

Skilled craftsmen were brought from all corners of the Russian state—from Pskov and Vladimir, Novgorod and Tver—to put up new cathedrals in place of the old ones built more than a century before. By the decree of Ivan III, such famous Italian architects as Aristotle Fioravanti of Bologna, Pietro Antonio

Solari, Marco Ruffo and Aleviso Novy—were invited to work in Moscow. Russian craftsmen worked with these renowned masters to create the magnificent structures that up to this day amaze all who set eyes on them.

The 17th century ushered in a new period in the history of the Kremlin. Consolidation of the Russian state was accompanied by a flourishing of Russian art and architecture. This was reflected in the new structures that appeared in the Kremlin. In 1712, the capital was moved from Moscow to St. Petersburg. The Kremlin became a temporary residence of the tsar's court. Russian emperors and empresses came there to be crowned and pay their respects to their ancestors and the "holy places" of the Kremlin.

In 1737 a devastating fire destroyed all the wooden buildings still standing in the Kremlin. The Kremlin also suffered wanton destruction in 1812. In September of that year, Napoleon's armies marched into Moscow, which had been abandoned by the inhabitants and the Russian Army. The French troops were quartered in the Kremlin for a month. When they retreated from Moscow, the soldiers, on Napoleon's orders, attempted to blow up the Kremlin. The French were foiled in this. At the risk of their lives, Russian Cossacks and city dwellers extinguished many burning fuses. But several explosions caused considerable damage.

After the Patriotic War of 1812, all the historical monuments in the Kremlin were restored.

In the 19th century, new structures were added: the *Grand Palace* and new premises for the *Oruzheinaya Palata* (the Armoury).

On March 11, 1918, the Soviet Government moved from Petrograd to Moscow. Ancient Moscow became the capital of the world's first socialist state. In 1918, Lenin signed the decree on the protection of artistic and historical monuments. In keeping with this decree, all cultural and artistic monuments of the past, including the Moscow Kremlin, were placed under state protection. Restorations began in the Kremlin.

Massive ruby stars were mounted on the five highest Kremlin towers in 1937.

Large-scale restoration work was resumed

Cupolas ►

in the Kremlin in 1945, immediately on the conclusion of the Second World War. Sections of the walls and towers which had begun to crumble were restored to their original state. The ornamental spire-shaped super-structures on the towers were reroofed with new tiles and sheet copper and the walls were coated with a durable water-proof covering to protect them from the destructive action of atmospheric precipitation.

By 1955 the cathedrals and the *Granovitaya Palata* (the name *Granovitaya* comes from the many small, faceted stones in the façade) had been fully restored, the ancient stone pavement of Cathedral Square had been returned to its original state, and the cupola topping the belfry on the *Bell Tower of Ivan the Great* had been re-gilded.

Today the Kremlin is not merely a treasure-house of masterpieces of Russian culture. It is also the residence of the Soviet Government, and sessions of the USSR Supreme Soviet, the Soviet Parliament, are held there.

The Kremlin has been open to the public since July 1955.

Which is the best way to see the Kremlin? One way would be to make the round along the crenelated walls stretching for 7,331 feet. Or one could begin with a view of the Kremlin as seen from the Maurice Thorez Embankment, the Moskvoretsky Bridge or the Bolshoi Kammeny Bridge. There is also a good view from Red Square or Manège Square, or from the windows of the *National Hotel*. By following all these suggestions you would see the Kremlin from many aspects. And, of course, nothing can take the place of a stroll through the Kremlin itself. Time permitting, the best thing would be to devote two days to the Kremlin.

The *Troitskaya Tower* is recommended as the starting point of your sightseeing tour. It is not far from Biblioteka Lenina (Lenin Library), Kalininskaya and Arbatskaya Metro Stations.

You come face to face with an impressive scene the moment you step out of the Metro. An ancient high tower of red brick with a white-stone battlement stands next to a light and graceful structure in glass and concrete, that rises above the Kremlin walls. This edifice is the Palace of Congresses—the newest building in the Kremlin architectural group.

But let's enter the grounds. The first structure we pass on the way is the white-stone *Kutafya Tower,* built at the beginning of the 16th century. Surrounded by a moat at that time, which was crossed by draw-bridges, it served as a bridge-head watch-tower. From this tower, we walk along a stone bridge with a crenelated parapet, at one time spanning the Neglinka River. In 1821, the river was diverted into a sub-terranean aqueduct and the original channel was landscaped into a beautiful park, known as the *Alexandrovsky Gardens.* These shady gardens, stretching along the Kremlin wall from the Moskva River practically up to Red Square, have become a favourite haunt of Muscovites.

The *Troitskaya Tower,* whose gates are hospitably flung wide open, was erected in 1495. It is six stories high and has deep two-story basements, where the ammunition for defending the Kremlin was stored in old times. In the 16th and 17th centuries these basements were used as a prison. It was through the gates of the Troitskaya Tower that the tsar and military commanders return-ing from campaigns would ride into the Kremlin. It was also through these gates that Napoleons's troops entered the Kremlin and later fled, pursued by the Russian Army. The Troitskaya is the tallest tower. It is 262.4 feet to the top of the ruby-red star above it.

To the right of the Troitskaya Tower, on the far side of the Kremlin wall, is the *Palace of Congresses.* This monumental building was erected on the site of several subsidiary service structures of no historical value.

In 1961, a building with expressive and severe lines was erected out of Ural marble, glass and aluminium according to the design of a group of Soviet architects and engineers working under Mikhail Posokhin. White marble pylons and glass panels lend a light-ness and festive, imposing air. At the same time, the building combines well with its historical surroundings.

This very complex structure both from an architectural and engineering aspect was erected in record time—a little over a year.

Foreign tourists in Cathedral (Sobornaya) Square inside the Kremlin

In one of the Kremlin Cathedrals ▶

The work was highly rated by the Government. Orders and medals were bestowed on a number of people responsible for the building. The group of designers and engineers that headed the projet were given the Lenin Prize, the country's highest award.

The Palace of Congresses has an overall volume of 400,000 cubic metres. To keep the building from towering above the rest of the Kremlin structures, it was sunk 49.2 feet into the ground. It has a total of 800 rooms. The five floors are connected by wide stairways and 14 escalators.

Good taste, ingenuity and inventiveness are apparent in the interior decoration. The walls and columns are faced with marble and various kinds of tuff from Georgia, Armenia, Siberia and the Urals.

From the glass-walled entrance hall, the visitor takes an escalator either down to the spacious cloak-room in the lower lobby, whose mirrored walls add to the impression of vastness, or up to the auditorium. The lobby adjacent to the auditorium is decorated with the emblems of the 15 Union Soviet Socialist Republics made of variegated smalt, the work of Alexander Deineka, a well-known Soviet artist.

The huge auditorium 164 feet deep, 65.6 feet high and 114.8 feet wide has a seating capacity of 6,000. The decorative stage-drop is made of chased metal, according to a sketch by Professor Mylnikov: a monumental bas-relief of Lenin against the background of a crimson banner fluttering in the rays of the rising sun. The hall fittings are simple and elegant. Silvery aluminium bands across the ceiling follow the pattern of the rows of chairs. Four thousand five hundred lighting fixtures in the ceiling in combination with indirect luminescent lighting coming from behind the aluminium bands produce a unique lighting effect.

The acoustics are perfect. A complex amplification system carries the sound to all corners of the huge hall, providing ideal conditions for performers. Powerful installations change the air in the building every 12 minutes.

The "Tsar-cannon"

Exhibits in the Armoury (Oruzheinaya Palata)

Speeches can be translated simultaneously into 29 languages. The giant stage (one and a half times larger than the Bolshoi Theatre stage), 131 feet wide and 75.5 feet deep, is equipped with the latest techniques. On the floor above the auditorium there is a banquet hall seating two and a half thousand. It is quite unique, "floating," as it were, on steel springs, which improves sound insulation.

The adequate refreshment facilities in this hall take care of large audiences. There is a splendid view of Moscow and the ancient Kremlin cathedrals from its huge glass windows.

The Palace of Congresses is used by the Bolshoi Theatre, to stage opera and ballet productions there. It is also used for Soviet Communist Party and Trade Union congresses, various international conferences and festivals, and mass public meetings of Muscovites.

Along the Kremlin wall to the left of the Troitskaya Tower are the long two-story premises of the former *Arsenal*. This building, ornamented with a carved white stone frieze, is more than 98 feet high. The few and far-between deep-set windows placed in pairs accentuate the thickness of the walls. The Arsenal is a splendid monument of early 18th century architecture. Work on it began in 1702 on the instructions of Peter I and was only completed in 1736. Architects Dmitry Ivanov and Mikhail Choglokov are believed to be the principal designers.

Lined up along the façade of the Arsenal are 875 guns captured by the Russian troops from Napoleon's army in 1812. Here, too, you can see ancient Russian ordnance used in battle.

A memorial plaque is mounted on the wall of the building to the right of the entrance in commemoration of the revolutionary soldiers who were brutally shot by White Guard Cadets on October 28, 1917.

Beyond a small square, opposite the Arsenal, there is a three-story building with a high socle crowned by a pompous white stone cornice with pilasters between the second and third floor. This is the former *Senate* designed by Matvei Kazakov in Russian classical style and completed in 1788. Its eastern façade faces Red Square, and the Soviet flag fluttering above its dome is plainly visible from there.

Since March 1918, it has been the seat of the *Soviet Government*. Vladimir Lenin lived and worked there. His study and apartment on the third floor have been turned into a museum. Everything there is exactly as it was during Lenin's lifetime. The furnishings of the study and apartment of the great revolutionary are very simple and modest. In the room where Lenin lived, there is a small desk with a simple desk set and school penholder. It was here, already gravely ill, that Lenin wrote his five last works: "Pages from a Diary," "On Co-operation," "Our Revolution," "How We Should Reorganize the Workers' and Peasants' Inspection," and "Better Fewer, But Better," which are his political will to the Communist Party and the Soviet people.

On the third floor of this building there is a hall where the USSR Council of Ministers —the Soviet Government— sits. An armchair that was used by Lenin stands near the chairman's seat. It has been preserved as a sacred relic, for Lenin presided over the meetings of the first Soviet Government in this hall from 1918 through 1922.

Immediately beyond and to the right of the Palace of Congresses there is the small five-dome *Cathedral of the Twelve Apostles* and the *Palace of the Patriarch* built in 1635-1656.

The former Palace of the Patriarch consists of a number of halls, rooms, passages and stairways built inside the walls. Many of these have come down to us in their original appearance. They have all been fundamentally restored during the past few years. There is now a museum of applied art and 17th century life in the premises of the Palace of the Patriarch and the Cathedral of the Twelve Apostles. Over 700 works of art include unique copper, tin and silver articles, fabrics and jewelry. There is an interesting display of rare books, both printed and manuscript copies. The interior of a 17th-century dwelling is shown in two of the halls, and every exhibit can be well considered as a work of art.

There is a display of ancient Russian gold brocade and embroidery.

The Spasskaya Tower of the Kremlin

In front of the Cathedral of the Twelve Apostles one can see the *Tsar Cannon,* an extraordinary example of 16th-century military engineering and foundry skill. The biggest caliber gun in the world, it was cast in bronze by master craftsman Andrei Chokhov in 1586. The Tsar Cannon weighs 40 tons, has a 17.5-feet-long muzzle and a caliber of 890 millimetres. This gun was never fired. In the opinion of experts, it was made for case shot and the cannon balls beside it are for purely decorative effect. They were made in the 19th century.

There is a splendid view of the south-eastern part of the Kremlin grounds from the spot where the Tsar Cannon stands. You can see the *Tainitsky Garden* located in the angle formed by the junction of the eastern and southern Kremlin walls. Moscow children hold winter New Year parties there. It is plainly visible from the brow of the Kremlin Hill, the spot you should visit after seeing the Tsar Cannon. It is very pleasant to relax admist the bright flowers and green lanes.

From the garden you get a good view of the *Spasskaya* (Salvation) *Tower,* the gates of which open onto Red Square. A building designed by engineer Ivan Rerberg and érected in 1932 stands in front of the tower. This is where the *Presidium of the USSR Supreme Soviets* sits. In 1958, a 1,200 capacity theatre, called the Kremlin Theatre, was opened in the building. It does not have its own company and productions are staged by other Moscow companies and visiting artists.

A small tower can be seen immediately to the right of the Spasskaya Tower. This is the *Tsarskaya Tower,* built in 1680, which is topped by a pyramidal tent-like structure. White stone decorations, a gilded weather vane, and small conical structures along the edges lend the tower the appearance of a fabulous little *terem*. In old days, a wooden tower stood in its place, from where, legend tells, Ivan the Terrible watched executions, hence the name Tsarskaya, or Tsar's Tower.

Still further to the right, a 151.5-feet-high round tower built in 1487 by the Italian architect Marco Ruffo can be seen down

70 *Part of cast-iron grille in the Tomb of Tsarevich Dimitry in the Archangel Cathedral in the Kremlin*

below. This tower (formerly called the Beklemishevskaya, and now the *Moskvoretskaya*) was the first to bear the onslaught of the Tatar hordes advancing on the Kremlin. In the 17th century, it was topped by a four-story super-structure that lent it well-proportioned architectural lines, doing away with the grim appearance of a fortress it had previously.

From the Kremlin Hill you get a good view of the new *Rossiya Hotel* (to the right of St. Basil's Cathedral) and the tall 568-feet-high apartment house built in 1949-1952 on the Kotelnicheskaya Embankment.

The Kremlin walls extending along the Moskva River embankment are also plainly visible from there. The walls and their 19 towers served as a strong defence works. They are from 16 to 62 feet high and from 11 to 21 feet thick. Surmounting the battlemented parapet are double-pronged merlons, 1,045 of them all in all from 5.6 to 8.2 feet high. When the Kremlin was besieged by an enemy, its defenders plugged up the crenals with wooden shields and fired at the hostile forces through narrow slit-shaped loop-holes, which have remained to this day. In days of old the walls had a protective wooden roofing that sheltered the defenders in bad weather. This roofing was destroyed by fire in the 18th century and never restored.

In the centre of the Kremlin stands one of the most remarkable structures of the 16th century—the *Bell Tower of Ivan the Great*. This is a three-story pillar in the shape of elongated octahedrons, one on top of the other, each progressively smaller in diameter than the one under it. Bells (21 in all) hang in the arched bays of each of the octahedrons. These are splendid monuments of Russian foundry. They are all richly ornamented and each one bears an inscription giving its history: the date it was cast, its weight, and the name of the founder who cast the bell.

The white-stone bell tower is crowned by a gilded cupola with an inscription in Slavic ligature below noting that the edifice was erected in 1600 during the reign of Tsar Boris Godunov.

Cathedrals of the Assumption and the Annunciation in the Kremlin ▶

Actually, however, work on the Bell Tower of Ivan the Great was begun back in 1505-1508. An Italian by the name of Bon Friazin was the first architect to tackle the job. Then a belfry was added by architect Petrok Maly in 1532-1543. In its central embrasure you can see the huge Uspensky Bell weighing some 70 tons. During the reign of Boris Godunov the Bell Tower of Ivan the Great was added to and crowned with a gilded cupola. This gilding was renewed during restoration work undertaken in 1955. The tower, rising to a height of 265 feet, was for many years the tallest structure in Moscow. In bygone days, it was the main watch tower of the Kremlin, providing a good view of the city's surroundings within a radius of up to 18.6 miles.

As they retreated in 1812, Napoleon's soldiers tried to blow up the Bell Tower. But they failed to do so. Only the belfry and an extension on the northern side of the tower were wrecked. They were later restored by the architect Gilardi.

The Bell Tower of Ivan the Great served as a model for many pillar-shaped churches built in ancient Russia which, by their grandeur, personified, as it were, the might of the centralized Russian state.

On a stone pedestal at the foot of the Bell Tower there proudly stands the *Tsar Bell*—the world's biggest bell. It weighs 200 tons, is 20 feet high and over 21.6 feet in diameter. Next to it stands a fragment weighing 11.5 tons, which split off during a great fire in 1737. The Tsar Bell is an extraordinary example of Russian casting art. The surface is decorated with a delicate design bearing the images of Tsar Alexei and Tsarina Anna, and also five icons and two inscriptions telling the history of the bell. It was cast in 1733-1735 by two Russian craftsmen, Ivan Motorin and his son Mikhail, and lay in its deep moulding pit for over a hundred years. It was only in 1836, under the supervision of the eminent architect Auguste Monferran, that the bell was raised from its pit and placed on the granite pedestal where it now stands.

The square stretching from the Tsar Bell to the Spasskaya Tower was called Ivanovskaya in bygone days. That is where the *prikazi* (ministries) of justice and the treasury were located. On this square the guilty were mercilessly beaten and *dyaki* (officials) shrilly proclaimed the tsar's decrees. That is how the Russian saying *Krichat na vsiu Ivanovskuyu* (To shout across the whole Ivanovskaya Square) arose.

The Bell Tower unites all the ancient cathedrals in the Moscow Kremlin in a majestic architectural group. These edifices face *Cathedral Square,* the most ancient square in the Soviet capital. It dates back to the beginning of the 14th century, and ever since has been the Kremlin's main square. This is where the ceremonial processions took place when tsars were invested, emperors were crowned and foreign ambassadors were received.

On the northern side of Cathedral Square there is the five-dome *Uspensky* (Assumption) *Cathedral,* built in 1475-1479 by Russian craftsmen under the supervision of Aristotle Fioravanti, an Italian architect. A native of Bologna who was invited to work in Moscow by Grand Duke Ivan the Third, Fioravanti made a profound study of the finest examples of Russian church architecture, visiting Vladimir, Pskov and Novgorod. He modelled the cathedral after the Uspensky Cathedral in Vladimir. That is why motifs of Vladimir-Suzdal architecture were used so extensively in the Uspensky Cathedral in the Kremlin.

The walls of the cathedral are made of white stone, and the arches and cupola supports, of brick. Its painted portals are framed with decoratively finished white stone. The architectural proportions of this temple are perfect. It is 124.5 feet high, 8.7 feet wide and 116.4 feet long. Inside we find a spacious, lofty and bright hall with arches supported by round pillars. The interior decorations are festive. The cathedral's first murals were painted by Russian artists in 1514. The frescoes and temperas are of exceptional artistic and historical value. Most of them are the work of 14th-17th century Russian artists. Among them is the 12th-century "Georgy" Icon, an outstanding monument of ancient Russian painting, and the 13-14th-century "Troitsa." One of the cathedral's most ancient relics is the "Vla-

Bell Tower of Ivan the Great

Bell Tower of Ivan the Great seen through a loophole in the Spasskaya Tower

▶

This shadow is 400 years old

The Kremlin (ancient engraving)

dimirskaya Bogomater" Icon, an example of 11th-century Byzantine painting. It is now on display in the Tretyakov Art Gallery. The ancient murals in the Uspensky Cathedral were covered over several times with layers of oil paintings. In 1949-1950, Soviet experts undertook major restoration work in the cathedral, bringing to light and revonating the old, original murals.

There are many examples of the applied art of ancient Russia in the cathedral, among them the southern doors plated with black-lacquered copper sheets with twenty scenes on biblical themes done in gold. Near this entrance stands the throne of Ivan the Terrible, the first Russian tsar. This is a unique monument of the craftsmanship of Russian wood carvers. It was made in 1551. In an open-work bronze shrine lies the coffin of Patriarch Germogen, who was tortured to death by the Polish interventionists in 1609 and was proclaimed a Saint. The shrine was skilfully cast in 1627 by a Russian craftsman, Dmitry Sverchkov.

Daylight penetrates into the cathedral through narrow windows disposed in two rows. Twelve 17th and 19th century church-chandeliers, eleven of gilded bronze and the one in the centre of silver and bronze, provide an additional source of illumination. It is interesting to note that the silver used to make the central chandeliers was recaptured in 1812 from Napoleon's troops. When Napoleon seized the Kremlin, he turned the Uspensky Cathedral into a stable. The French soldiers ransacked the cathedral and stole some 300 kilograms of gold and more than 5 tons of silver.

The architectural lines and magnificent appointments of the Uspensky Cathedral, the main temple of ancient Russia, reflected the might and majesty of the centralized Russian state. It was the coronation church of the Russian tsars and emperors. Important state decrees were proclaimed and all solemn ceremonies were held there. And that was where Moscow metropolitans and patriarchs were buried.

Next to the Uspensky Cathedral there is a small single-dome temple called the *Church of Rizopolozhenie* (Ordination of Priests). Built by Russian craftsmen from Pskov in

1484-1486, it was the private church of the patriarchs. The iconostasis, attributed to painter Nazary Istomin (1627), is of great artistic value.

The *Granovitaya Palata* stands to the left of this church. This is one of the oldest civil edifices in Moscow. It was built in 1487-1491 by Russian craftsmen working under the direction of Italian architects Marco Ruffo and Pietro Solari.

On the inside, the palata consists of one huge hall with arches resting on a central pillar. The hall is 29.5 feet high and has 5,325 square feet of floorage. In the second half of the 16th century, the walls and arches were covered with paintings on church and biblical themes. Work on these murals was resumed in 1668 by an outstanding Russian painter, Simon Ushakov. The latest restorations of the wonderful murals were carried out in 1949.

As in the past, official ceremonies and Government receptions are held in the Granovitaya Palata. In the 15th and 16th centuries, foreign ambassadors were received there. That is where Tsar Ivan the Terrible celebrated the conquest of Kazan in 1552 and Emperor Peter I marked the victory of the Russian troops at Poltava in 1709. Today the Council of Elders of both chambers of the USSR Supreme Soviet meets there.

On the same side of Cathedral Square and somewhat closer to the Moskva River stands another remarkable monument of 15th century architecture—*Blagoveshchensky* (Annunciation) *Cathedral* with its nine cupolas. It was erected in 1484-1489 by Russian craftsmen from Pskov. After the fire in 1547, the cathedral was restored in two years during the reign of Ivan the Terrible. At that time a porch was added to it (on the south-eastern side), which was called *Groznenskoye* (the Porch of Ivan the Terrible). The terrible tsar must have climbed the steps of this porch more than once, for this cathedral was the private church of Russian princes and tsars. For that reason the architecture and internal appointments of this cathedral are of a more intimate nature than those of the Uspensky Cathedral.

The frescoes of the Blagoveshchensky Cathedral are majestic. First executed in 1508, they were renovated many times throughout the centuries and covered with oil paintings. For a long time it was thought that the ancient frescoes had been irretrievably lost. It was only in 1947 that Soviet artists specializing in the restoration of paintings completely cleared the murals, bringing to light the ancient paintings. The frescoes of the cathedral in the main are themes from the Apocalypse.

The iconostasis, which was transferred to the cathedral from the temple of the Annunciation which once stood on that site, is of exceptional artistic and historical value. It was covered with paintings in 1405 by such outstanding artists as Theophanous the Greek, Andrei Rublyov and Prokhor of Gorodets. The icons created by these masters of the brush testify to the splendid skill of 14th and 15th century Russian painters.

On the pilasters of the walls in the gallery near the porch of Ivan the Terrible there are portraits of Moscow princes, and philosophers and poets of ancient Greece and Rome: Aristotle, Plato, Homer and Virgil, among others.

This cathedral faces a third Kremlin temple —the *Arkhangelsky* (Archangel) *Cathedral*. Five cupolas crown this well-proportioned white-stone edifice, which was built in 1505-1509 under the direction of architect Aloisio Novy. Shortly afterwards the walls were covered with murals. In 1652, however, the paintings were removed together with the plaster.

The present murals date from 1652-1666. The Russian icon-painters depicted certain aspects of Russian life and effectively portrayed the struggle of the Russian people for their national independence. The murals were restored in 1953.

A gilded iconostasis 32.8 feet high separates the central part of the cathedral from the altar. It is covered with wonderful icons —splendid relics of 15th-17th century Russian painting. Outstanding in beauty and perfection is the icon "Archangel Mikhail," attributed to the brush of Andrei Rublyov (15th century).

The Arkhangelsky Cathedral contains the burial vaults of the Moscow grand dukes and tsars. There are 46 tombs with white tombstones bearing inscriptions in old Slavic script. Ivan the Terrible and his sons were buried in the cathedral. The tomb of Prince Ivan Kalita, who died in 1341, is the most ancient.

An interesting monument of early 17th-century applied art is the gilded white-stone canopy covered with carvings over the tomb of Ivan the Terrible's son Dimitry.

The Arkhangelsky Cathedral was especially revered by the grand dukes and tsars, who came there to pay their respects to their ancestors.

After making the rounds of Cathedral Square, we can go in the direction of the Blagoveshchensky Cathedral. Immediately beyond it is the sprawling structure of the *Great Kremlin Palace,* erected in 1838-1849 (architect—Konstantin Ton). The building, which is 410 feet long, faces the Moskva River. The best view of this magnificent edifice is from the Maurice Thorez Embankment across the river. The palace seems to be a three-story building, for there are indeed three rows of windows along the façade. But nowadays it has only two stories. The arched windows on the first floor are separated by narrow piers. The double row of windows on the second floor is separated by pilasters and decorated with carved white-stone window frames the way it was done in 17th-century Russia. The tallest central part of the building is crowned by a gilded balustrade and a flagstaff. Sessions of the Supreme Soviets of the USSR and the RSFSR are held in the Great Kremlin Palace and during sessions the national flag of the USSR or the RSFSR is flown.

The Great Kremlin Palace was erected on the site of a ducal mansion the ancient halls of which were included in the huge new rectangular structure. It served as a temporary residence of the emperor's family during visits to Moscow.

There are several spacious halls, the *Georgievsky* being especially well known. This hall is 199 feet long, 57.4 feet high and 67.24 feet wide. It is magnificently ornamented with stucco mouldings and adorned with eighteen spiral columns topped by sculptured figures with laurel wreaths. All decorations commemorate victories of Russian arms in the 15th-18th centuries.

Marble tablets in niches high up on the longitudinal walls bear the names, engraved in gold, of military units and soldiers and officers decorated with St. George's Cross. The gala hall is lighted by six bronze chandeliers with three thousand electric bulbs. The parquet flooring is laid out with twenty species of precious woods. The Georgievsky Hall is used for state receptions and official ceremonies.

The celebration to mark the victory over Hitler's Germany was held there in 1945. Here Yury Gagarin, the world's first astronaut, was presented with the Gold Star of Hero of the Soviet Union in 1961. And every year, during the winter school holidays, New Year parties for children of the Soviet capital are held there.

Next to the Georgievsky Hall is the circular *Vladimirsky Hall*, which leads into the *Teremnoi Palace*, the *Zolotaya Tsaritsina Palata* (Tsarina's Golden Hall) and the *Granovitaya Palata*. The Teremnoi Palace was built in 1635-1636 under the direction of Bazhen Ogurtsov, Antip Konstantinov, Larion Ushakov and several other Russian architects. It is a highly interesting monument of 17th-century Russian architecture and life. The *terems* are rooms with low vaulted ceilings; the walls and ceilings were covered with multicoloured paintings in 1837; the windows are glazed with coloured sheets of mica and there are tiled stoves in the corners. Formerly the private chambers of the Russian tsars, the *terems* recreated distant, fabulous times. The *Prestolnaya Palata* (Throne Hall), which used to be the tsar's study in the 17th century, is very interesting. The middle window was called the "petition" window: a box would be lowered from this window and anyone could submit a petition in writing to the tsar. Among the common people this box was called *dolgy* (one in which things were shelved), for the petition would lie around for a long time without being read by anyone. And that is how the

View of Moscow through a loophole in the tower of the Kremlin ▶

saying *Ne otkladyvai delov dolgy yashchik* (Don't put things off) arose.

The largest hall in the Great Kremlin Palace with a seating capacity of 3,000 is the hall where the sessions of the USSR Supreme Soviet are held. Adjacent to the Georgievsky Hall, its two rows of windows open onto the Moskva River. A sculpture of Lenin by Sergei Merkurov stands in a niche behind the seats of the presiding committee. Solemn and majestic, yet unusually simple, this hall was reconstructed in 1934 from two 19th-century halls. The Constitution of the USSR was adopted in this hall on December 5, 1936.

To the right of the main entrance on the first floor there is a suite of rooms that used to be the emperor's private apartments. All the rooms—the antechamber, drawing-room, study, bedroom and reception room—are richly finished with marble, stucco mouldings and paintings and furnished with statues, chinaware, and beautifully incrustated gilded furniture. These rooms are preserved as relics of the skilled art of unknown 19th-century Russian craftsmen.

Next to the Great Kremlin Palace stands the *Oruzheinaya Palata* (Armoury), which was built in 1851 (architect—Konstantin Ton). But it actually dates back to the 16th century. At that time it consisted of shops where armour and weapons for warriors were made and kept. Later military trophies and regalia of the tsars were kept there. In 1720, by decree of Peter I, the shops were reorganized into a museum. The Armoury's exhibits include very rare relics of Russian and foreign applied art, royal regalia, gifts from ambassadors, collections of 13th-18th century arms and accoutrements, the world's only collection of 14th-19th century fabrics and clothing, and highly artistic articles by goldsmiths and silversmiths from the 12th to the 19th century.

Among the royal regalia there is the famous golden *Cap of Monomakh,* used to crown all Russian tsars until Peter I; the first Russian imperial crown of Catherine I, made of gilded silver; the diamond-studded diadems of Ivan and Peter (1682); the throne of Ivan the Terrible; the wedding dress of Catherine II, of exquisite silver brocade; and other interesting exhibits. The museum also has on display very rare and highly artistic articles of gold, silver, precious stones, ivory and porcelain, and fabrics embroidered with pearls and adorned with precious stones. There too you will see one of the biggest collections of royal ceremonial carriages, each one being a work of art.

Special show cases display gifts from the embassies of Turkey, Austria, Poland, Denmark, Holland, Sweden and Great Britain. The richest of these collections are the gifts presented by Swedish ambassadors, totalling some 200 valuable items; valuable gifts from Karl XII include rare works of art by Stockholm craftsmen brought to Russia in 1699.

The exhibits include the world's finest collection of old English silverware, made by London silversmiths of the 16th-17th centuries.

The Oruzheinaya Palata is a world famous treasure-house containing unique works of decorative and applied art. Most of these are closely bound up with the history of Russia and the Moscow Kremlin. These priceless collections are of exceptional interest as evidence of the inexhaustible creative forces and artistic gifts of the Russian people.

As we leave the Kremlin, we see two more towers crowned with ruby stars. One is the *Vodovzvodnaya* (Water-raising), the best proportioned and most beautiful of them all, which rises 200 feet high to our left, in the extreme south-west end of the grounds. It was first erected in 1805 and, after being wrecked by the French troops in 1812, was restored in 1819 according to a design by the architect Osip Bove.

The second is the *Borovitskaya Tower* (from the Russian word *bor,* meaning grove) erected in 1490 (architect—Pietro Solari). It is pyramidal in shape, structurally conceived as three-stepped, tapering tetrahedrons, one on top of the other, crowned by a tall stone spiral shaped structure.

About 985 feet from the Borovitskiye Gate is the Lenin Library Metro Station. You can get to it by walking along Alexandrovsky Gardens which run parallel to the Kremlin wall.

EXCURSION **2**

STARTING POINT:
**PLOSHCHAD REVOLUTSII
(REVOLUTION SQUARE),
PLOSHCHAD SVERDLOVA
(SVERDLOV SQUARE)
AND PROSPEKT MARXA**
METRO STATIONS

RED SQUARE

TO Muscovites and many others *Red Square* is one of the most beautiful squares in the world. Spreading out along the eastern wall of the Kremlin, this huge plaza covers an area of over 785,300 square feet: it is 2,280 feet long and has an average width of 426 feet. Many momentous events in the country's history are connected with Red Square. It is first mentioned in annals of the 15th century. Nearly all the roads leading to Moscow from all corners of the Russian land converged there. By that time it was both a "great market place and what the forum was for ancient Rome." Idlers and buyers thronged the square from morning to evening. It was a place to learn the news and the starting point of popular demonstrations and mass action against the power of the rich. A deep moat running along the Kremlin wall separated Red Square from the Kremlin. The square got its name in the 17th century from the Russian word *krasnaya*, which meant *krasivaya*, or beautiful.

The architectural ensemble facing Red

*Red Square.
View of the Kremlin from the
Spasskaya Tower*

RED

RED SQUARE

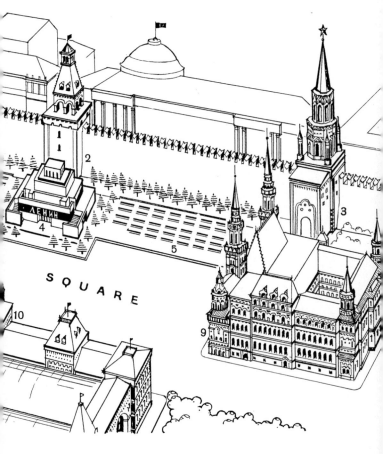

1. Spasskaya Tower; 2. Tower of the Senate; 3. Nikolskaya Tower; 4. V.I. Lenin Mausoleum; 5. Stands; 6.
Pokrovsky Cathedral (St. Basil's Cathedral); 7. Memorial
to Minin and Pozharsky; 8. Scaffold; 9. History Museum;
10. State Department Store (GUM).

Square was erected gradually, reaching completion at the end of the 19th century.

St.Basil's (Pokrovsky) *Cathedral*, a masterpiece of Russian architecture, is on the south side of Red Square. It was erected in 1555-1561 by order of Tsar Ivan the Terrible to commemorate Russia's annexation of the Khanates of Kazan and Astrakhan.

The names of the builders had been forgotten for over three centuries. Only in 1896 was mention found for the first time in ancient manuscripts of two Russian architects, Postnik and Barma, who produced this masterpiece of world architecture. In 1957, however, other ancient records were discovered which lead us to assume that Postnik and Barma stand for one architect, Postnik Yakovlev, nicknamed Barma.

Russian craftsmen created a marvel of architecture—a picturesque temple formed of nine pillar-shaped chapels, closely interconnected by a single artistic idea yet totally unlike in appearance. The tallest of these chapels, rising to a height of 154 feet and topped by a bright spire-shaped structure, is in the centre of the group.

A small, tenth chapel was erected next to the cathedral in 1588 over the grave of *Yurodivy Vasily* (God's fool Vasily), a well-known beggarly and weak-minded devotee at the time in Moscow. And ever since then Pokrovsky Cathedral began to be called the Temple of Vasily the Blessed in his honour.

Built of stone in traditional Russian style, the Pokrovsky Cathedral at the same time skilfully incorporated elements of ancient Russian wood architecture. Restoration work begun by Soviet experts in 1954 has revealed remarkable 16th-century frescoes inside.

The interior decorations of each of the ten chapels are just as distinct as their external appearance. One has an icon, "Entering Jerusalem," considered one of the finest 16th-century Russian icons. This cathedral has one of the most ancient works of Russian applied art that has been preserved: the iconostasis in the Church of Troitsa (Trinity Church).

Restoration is still going on. By now, most of the treasures of ancient Russian paintings, hidden for ages under much later layers of oil paintings, have already been restored to their original appearance. Splendid frescoes dating back to the time of Ivan the Terrible once again amaze and gladden the eye.

The beauty and splendour of the temple gave rise to the legend that Tsar Ivan the Terrible asked the creators of the cathedral whether they could build something finer or at least duplicate what they had already constructed. And when he heard them say they could, he was furious and ordered them to be blinded, so that there would never be anything finer than St. Basil's.

A branch of the Museum of History has now been opened in the temple with exhibits tracing the history of the creation of this remarkable monument of Russian architecture and Ivan the Terrible's campaign against the Khanate of Kazan.

Just outside the grilled fence surrounding the temple there is the monument to Minin and Pozharsky. This is the first civilian monument to be erected in Moscow and one of the finest in Russia. Until 1930 it stood in the centre of Red Square, opposite the Kremlin wall.

This statue, by Ivan Martos in classic style, depicts the historic meeting of Kuzma Minin, a Nizhny-Novgorod merchant, with prince Dmitry Pozharsky. Under the leadership of these two heroes of the war of 1612, the people's volunteer corps drove the Polish invaders out of Moscow and upheld the independence of the Russian state. No portraits made of Kuzma Minin and Dmitry Pozharsky in their lifetime had remained, so the sculptor gave them the typical features of the finest Russian people of that day, people of strong will, courage, and boundless love for their country, reflecting in his sculptural group the staunch readiness of the Russian people to defend Moscow and drive the enemy out from their native land.

An inscription on the pedestal reads: "To citizen Minin and prince Pozharsky from a grateful Russia, summer, 1818."

Erected with public funds, collected by subscription, Martos's statue became a real national monument.

To the right of St. Basil's Cathedral rises the main Kremlin tower, the *Spasskaya*, which has become the emblem of Moscow. This

Red Square (old engraving) ▶

95

St. Basil's Cathedral

The Nikolskaya Tower of the Kremlin

98 *The guard of honour outside
the Lenin Mausoleum, Red Square*

Grandfather and grandson

majestic and graceful tower was erected in 1491 by Russian craftsmen working under the supervision of Italian architect Pietro Solari of Milan. But it acquired its present appearance in 1624-1625, when a Russian architect by the name of Bazhen Ogurtsov erected the octahedral multi-story stepped superstructure that now tops it.

Ceremonial processions of the clergy used to pass through the Spasskaya Tower Gate, and the tsars, emperors and foreign ambassadors rode into the Kremlin through it. It was forbidden to ride through on horseback or pass through with covered head—even the tsars had to remove their head-dress.

The first clock was presumably mounted on the Spasskaya Tower in 1491. In 1851-1852, the *Kremlin Chimes*—ten bells cast in the 17th and 18th centuries—were installed. The chime mechanism occupies three floors. The face of the clock is 21 feet in diameter. Each figure is 2.36 feet high. The hour hand is 9.74 feet long, and the minute hand 10.76 feet long. The clock weighs 25 tons.

When the Kremlin was stormed during the October Socialist Revolution of 1917, the clock was damaged by artillery fire. The following year (1918) it was restored on the instructions of Vladimir Lenin. The Kremlin chimes are broadcast daily by Radio Moscow.

In 1937, five of the Kremlin towers, including the Spasskaya Tower, were crowned with ruby stars. The span between the spires of the biggest stars (on the Spasskaya and the Nikolskaya Towers) is 12.3 feet and there is a span of 9.84 feet between the spires of the smallest star (on the Vodovzvodnaya Tower). Incidentally, the stars weigh as much as 1.5 tons each, but thanks to special ball bearing mountings, they turn freely with the wind.

Not far from St. Basil's Cathedral is the so-called *Lobnoye Mesto,* an enclosed elevation built of white stone. It is more than 400 years old. In old times the tsar's *ukases,* imperial edicts, were proclaimed there, and nearby was the place for public executions. That was where Tsar Ivan the Terrible executed unruly boyars. And that was where the body of the Impostor, the False Dmitry, lay—the Polish henchman, pretender to the Russian throne at the beginning of the 17th century.

To the left of the cathedral, and beyond the confines of Red Square, you can see the outlines of the twenty-story *Rossiya*, the largest hotel in Europe, (architect—Chechulin). It has over 3,000 rooms and can accommodate some 6,000 persons.

The hotel building covers 9.9 acres and stretches along the Moskva River embankment for 820 feet. There is a garden with a theatre seating 3,000.

At the other end of Red Square, on the north side, there is a turreted red brick building. This is the *State History Museum*, established in 1883. The edifice was designed by Academician Vladimir Sherwood (artist) and the architect Semyonov and built in 1878-1883 on the site of the former two-story building of the Moscow University founded in 1755 by Mikhail Lomonosov, the great Russian scholar. Before the revolution, the museum was supported by private donations. Only half a million persons visited it during the first 35 years of its existence. Today, the State History Museum is a depository of documents and monuments of the history of the peoples of the USSR. More than 25 million persons have visited it in Soviet times.

There are over 300,000 exhibits concerning the history of the country from the Stone Age up to the end of the last century. They include a unique collection of coins and medals, collections of precious ornaments and household articles, a valuable collection of old manuscripts and books, and many original copies of historical documents. There you will see clothes worn by Tsar Ivan the Terrible, the bed abandoned by Napoleon during the flight from Russia, and the first number of the famous magazine *Kolokol* (The Bell).

To the left of the History Museum another of the Kremlin towers can be seen. This is the well-proportioned, three-story *Nikolskaya Tower* (architect—Pietro Solari), erected in 1491. It was through this tower that the people's volunteer corps led by Minin and Pozharsky fought their way into the Kremlin in 1612 to oust the Polish interventionists who had firmly entrenched themselves. And it was through this same gate that the revolutionary forces broke into the Kremlin

Red Square on a fête day

in 1917 and crushed the resistance of the White Guards.

An outstanding architectural feature of the Nikolskaya Tower is its Gothic superstructure (architect—Ruska) with white-stone elements covered with tracery and the tall spire, erected at the beginning of the 19th century. The spire was wrecked in 1812 by Napoleon's retreating troops but in 1816 was restored (architect—Osip Bove). Together with its star, the Nikolskaya Tower is 230.9 feet high.

In the centre of Red Square there is the *Lenin Mausoleum*, a striking example of Soviet architecture in red granite and black labradorite (architect—Alexei Shchusev). A constant procession files past the crystal sarcophagus with the body of Vladimir Lenin, the great revolutionary and founder of the Soviet Communist Party and the Soviet state, who passed away on January 21, 1924.

Originally, a wooden mausoleum was designed in one night and built in two and a half days. In May of that same year it was reconstructed and remained that way until 1930 when it was replaced by a granite mausoleum of exactly the same shape. The interior is faced with polished black and grey labradorite, crossed by a bright-red zig-zag band of smalt.

A large oblong monolith over the main portal bears the name "Lenin," incrustated in dark purple. For more than forty years now, all who come to Moscow, including numerous visitors from abroad, invariably wend their way there. A guard of honour stands at the entrance. It is changed regularly, the accompanying ceremony always attracting many onlookers by its solemnity and precision. Stately spruce trees stand motionless on both sides of the Mausoleum like sentinels.

Along the Kremlin wall, where stately blue firs stand motionless in mournful silence, there are the common graves of workers and soldiers who fell fighting for Soviet power in October 1917. Sculptured portraits of Yakov Sverdlov, Felix Dzerzhinsky, Mikhail Frunze, Mikhail Kalinin and Andrei Zhdanov by sculptor Merkulov stand on granite pedestals before their respective tombs behind the Mausoleum. Here, too, Joseph Stalin is buried. Urns with the remains of

Maxim Gorky, Sergei Kirov, Nadezhda Krupskaya (Lenin's wife), Georgy (Sergo) Orjonikidze and other distinguished Soviet leaders, and also of the outstanding foreign communists Clare Zetkin, Sen Katayama, John Reed, and Fritz Heckert are immured in the Kremlin wall.

A two-story building with plate-glass windows stretches along the entire length of the square opposite the Kremlin. This is *GUM,* one of the Moscow's large department stores. The building, erected in 1890-1893 (architect—Pomerantsev), was formerly the upper trading emporium. Until the revolution, it had up to 200 small stalls. The building was fundamentally remodelled in 1953. There are some 1.5 miles of counters and 3.1 miles of storage shelves. GUM handles as many as 85 million customers a year.

On the corner of Red Square between GUM and the History Museum there is a building, erected at the beginning of the 18th century, which used to house the former Provincial Administration. In those days there was a "pit"—a debtor's jail—in the yard where Radishchev, a well-known Russian writer and revolutionary, was confined in 1790 on his way to exile in Siberia. Radishchev was the author of the famous book *A Journey from Petersburg to Moscow,* which Pushkin called "a summons to rebel."

If ancient Red Square could speak, it would be able to tell us about many historical events. In 1671, Stepan Razin, the leader of a peasant uprising, about whom many songs have been written, was brutally put to death there by the tsar's executioners. And it was there that Peter I in 1698 executed the *streltsy* [1], who had mutinied against the young tsar in favour of his older sister princess Sophia. In October 1917, fierce fighting broke out on Red Square between the forces of revolution and reaction. The place was stained with the blood of the heroic revolutionary fighters. Since then, the name of the square has acquired a new, deep-felt meaning. It became the symbol of the battle standards of the revolutionary people. On March 12, 1918, at Lenin's

---

1) Irregular troops in Russia before the regular army was created by Peter I.

orders, the red banner was raised over the Kremlin: red became the colour of the national flag of the Soviet Union. And ever since, for nearly half a century, it has been fluttering over the cupola of the building housing the USSR Council of Ministers.

Lenin made many speeches on Red Square. His addresses to the people were infused with ardent calls to defend the Socialist Revolution, the freedom and independence of the Soviet Land, to defend it from foreign intervention, to put an end to wars between nations, to build a new, communist society.

In November 1941, when the German fascist forces had already approached very close to Moscow, the traditional military parade was held on Red Square on the seventh of that month, on the anniversary of the Great October Socialist Revolution.

There, in front of Lenin Mausoleum, Soviet soldiers vowed to defend their native city, Moscow, and went straight into battle from Red Square.

On June 24, 1945, a triumphant Victory Parade was held on Red Square to mark the defeat of Hitler's Germany. Back from the front, Soviet soldiers, to the roll of drums, cast down at the foot of the Mausoleum hundreds of enemy standards captured from the fascist troops on the battlefields. Hitler's personal flag was the first to be cast down on the cobblestones of the square.

Every May 1 and November 7, military parades and popular processions of Moscow working people are held on Red Square.

Here, too, the people honour their heroes. Muscovites joyously welcomed Yury Gagarin, the world's first astronaut, Valentina Tereshkova, the world's first woman astronaut, and their fellow-astronauts on Red Square. Every year in June high school graduates wind up their graduation ball by coming to Red Square with flowers and guitars, and the ancient square sounds with songs and laughter until dawn.

Military parade, Red Square

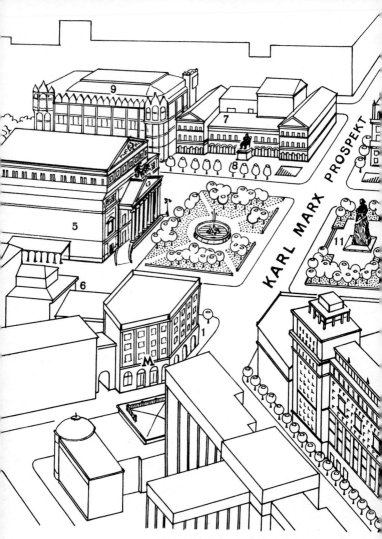

SVERDLOV AND REVOLUTION SQUARES

KARL MARX PROSPEKT

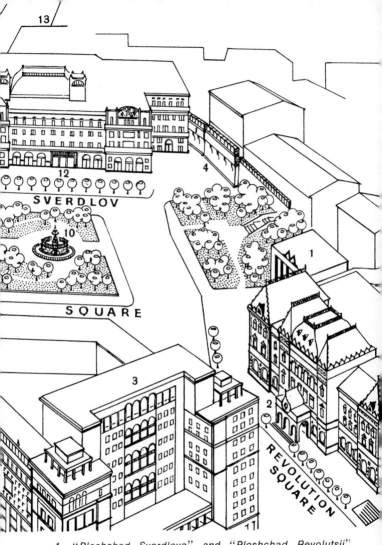

1. "Ploshchad Sverdlova" and "Ploshchad Revolutsii" Metro Stations; 2. V.I. Lenin Museum; 3. Moskva Hotel; 4. Kitai-Gorod Wall; 5. Bolshoi Theatre; 6. Children's Theatre; 7. Maly Theatre; 8. Alexander Ostrovsky Monument; 9. Central Department Store (TSUM); 10. Fountain, designed by Ivan Vitali; 11. Karl Marx Monument; 12. "Metropole" Hotel; 13. Memorial to Ivan Fyodorov.

and the theatres open, the crowds taper off and the hustle and bustle on the streets dies away.

The Metro stations here disgorge the biggest masses of people. Two of them have a common surface foyer with signs *Ploshchad Sverdlova* and *Ploshchad Revolutsii* indicating the respective underground stations. The squares themselves also merge at the entrance to the metro. When you step into the street, Sverdlov Square is straight ahead to your right, and Revolution Square to your left. We'll begin our tour of this section of the city with the latter.

A large brick building in pseudo-Russian style topped by silvery tent-like structures stands out to the left of the station. It was erected more than 70 years ago, and until the October Socialist Revolution housed the City Duma (Council). During the revolutionary uprising in October, White Guards established themselves in this building and resisted furiously. But finally their resistance was overcome and the building was seized by revolutionary detachments of workers after it had been subjected to artillery fire from the direction of the Bolshoi Theatre and outflanked by way of 25th of October Street.

Today this is the main branch of the *Central Lenin Museum,* opened in May 1936 on the decision of the Central Committee of the Communist Party of the Soviet Union.

The museum's more than 20 halls contain numerous photographs of Lenin and of his family and comrades-in-arms, newspapers, leaflets, maps, the finest works of Soviet painters and sculptors, original copies of first editions of Lenin's works, photographs of Lenin's manuscripts, letters, documents, gifts from working people, Lenin's personal belongings, and many other exhibits reflecting the life and work of the founder and leader of the Soviet state and the Communist Party of the Soviet Union.

Several halls opened during the past few years contain exhibits concerning the efforts of the Soviet people, led by the CPSU, to carry out Lenin's behests, denoting the triumph of his ideas, the persistent struggle of the Soviet Union for peace among all nations.

The Lenin Museum

Grille on the Lenin Museum building

An exact reproduction of Lenin's study in the Kremlin is of particular interest to visitors. Documentary films about Lenin are shown in the large conference hall.

Since its foundation, upwards of 27 million people from all over the Soviet Union and many foreign countries have visited the museum. It has branches in Leningrad, Ulyanovsk, Kiev, Lvov, Tbilisi and Baku.

An old five-story building with large balconies occupies almost the entire opposite side of Revolution Square. This is the former *Grand Hotel,* now part of the adjacent *Moskva Hotel.* Before the revolution the hotel boasted of such frequent visitors as composers Nikolai Rimsky-Korsakov and Pyotr Tchaikovsky, writers Anton Chekhov, Vladimir Korolenko and Maxim Gorky, and Ilya Repin, the painter. In Soviet times, Theodore Dreiser, Stefan Zweig and Rabindranath Tagore stayed there.

To the right of the Metro station, a public garden has been laid out. In the summer time its bright green carpet blends effectively with the dark red medieval brick wall surmounted by a low crenelated battlement. This wall extends over half the southern side of Sverdlov Square and joins up with a massive, squat tower on Karl Marx Prospekt. These are the remains of a line of fortifications that embraced *Kitai-Gorod,* which adjoined the Kremlin on the east. The fortifications built in 1535-1538 under the direction of Petrok Maly were 1.6 miles long and had 12 towers. The remnants of the wall and the towers were removed thirty years ago during reconstruction of the squares and the streets in the centre of town.

From any point on Sverdlov Square you can see the tall massive white columns of an impressive building surmounted by four rearing steeds harnessed to the chariot of Apollo. This is the building of the *USSR State Academic Bolshoi Theatre.* It stands on the site of the Petrovsky Public Theatre, which was opened in 1780 and burned down in 1805. Commenting on the conflagration, a contemporary wrote: "Many are absolutely convinced that the theatre burned down because a performance of "Rusulka" with all its devilry was billed for Sunday..."

Nearly twenty years later, a new theatre (architects—Osip Bove and Andrei Mikhailov) was built on the same spot. However, it subsequently suffered the same fate. The walls and portico that remained standing after the fire formed the framework of the new, remodelled building (architect—Albert Kavos) erected in 1856.

Shortly after the new theatre opened, Richard Wagner conducted a series of performances there. He introduced something new that amazed the public at the time: he stood facing the orchestra instead of the audience, as was the practice in Russia until then. Subsequent generations of opera conductors followed the example of the famous composer in facing the orchestra and the stage.

A two-year reconstruction job was completed in November 1958, and a complex air-conditioning system was installed operating from a new extension in the rear of the building. The system gets its constant supply of low-temperature water from deep artesian wells that were specially drilled nearby.

Many glorious pages in the history of Russian music and ballet are connected with the Bolshoi Theatre. Many leading personalities of the opera stage—singers Fyodor Shalyapin, Antonina Nezhdanova and Leonid Sobinov and ballerina Yekaterina Geltser—have performed there. The theatre stages classical operas and ballets by Russian and West European composers and works by Soviet composers.

Before the Kremlin Palace of Congresses was built, the country's finest theatrical and concert-stage companies frequently performed in the Bolshoi Theatre. There is never an empty seat in this huge red and gold six-row auditorium holding over 2,000.

In the first few years after the October Revolution, Party congresses and all-Russia and all-Union congresses of Soviets were held in the Bolshoi Theatre.

The Fifth All-Russia Congress of Soviets, held there in July 1918, unanimously adopted the First Soviet Constitution—the Constitution of the Russian Soviet Federative Socialist Republic (RSFSR)—established on the basis of a voluntary union of free nations. On December 30, 1922, the First Congress of Soviets of the USSR was held at the Bolshoi

Sverdlov Square ▶

Outside the Bolshoi Theatre

Boxes in the Bolshoi

Ballet in the Bolshoi

and confirmed the pact for the formation of the Union of Soviet Socialist Republics with Moscow as its capital.

Vladimir Lenin addressed many meetings, conferences and congresses at the Bolshoi Theatre beginning with 1918.

In December 1920, the Bolshoi Theatre was the scene of the Eighth All-Russia Congress of Soviets.

Ending his report to the Congress, Lenin said: "We have before us the results of the work of the State Commission for the Electrification of Russia... In my opinion it is a second programme of our Party... We need it as first draft, which will be submitted to the whole of Russia as a great economic plan designed for a period of not less than ten years and indicating how Russia is to be placed on the real economic basis which is required for communism."

At its second session, the Congress heard the report of the head of the Commission, Gleb Krzhizhanovsky. Each time he named one of the contemplated electric stations a bright luminous point would flash up on the map. The decree on the electrification of Russia was unanimously approved by the Congress.

Here, too, in the Bolshoi Theatre, on November 20, 1922, Lenin made his last public address, which he concluded with the following words: "Socialism is no longer a matter of the distant future... NEP Russia will be transformed into Socialist Russia."

For many years, the auditorium of the Bolshoi Theatre was the traditional place for large meetings of the Moscow Soviet and public organizations of the capital to mark important national events. With the completion in 1956 of the Luzhniki Sports Palace seating 17,000 these rallies were held there. In the autumn of 1961 the meeting place shifted once more, this time to the newly completed Kremlin Palace of Congresses, which seats 6,000.

To the left of the Bolshoi Theatre is the *Central Children's Theatre,* and to the right, the *Maly Theatre,* built in 1821. The latter is more modest, as to size and appearance. A monument to Alexander Ostrovsky, the great Russian playwright, unveiled in May 1929

The Metropol Hotel

Monument to Ivan Fyodorov,
first Russian printer

Dzerzhinsky Square viewed through grille-work on the roof of the Metropole Hotel

(sculptor—Nikolai Andreyev), stands at the entrance. The Maly Theatre is frequently called Ostrovsky House because of his plays which brought the theatre fame. It is also called Shchepkin House for it was in this theatre that the great actor, Mikhail Shchepkin, who firmly established realism on the Russian stage, developed his great gifts. The theatre stages plays and dramatizations of works by Soviet writers, and foreign authors, including William Shakespeare, Johann von Schiller, Gustave Flaubert, William Thackeray, Henrick Ibsen, George Bernard Shaw, Oscar Wilde, John Steinbeck, and Heila Vuulioki.

In April 1844, Clara Schumann, who had come to Moscow with her husband, Robert Schumann, performed in the Maly Theatre. And a year before, Franz Liszt played there.

Next to the Maly Theatre stands the *TSUM* (Central Department Store), one of the best known in Moscow. Built back in 1909 it is now being remodelled.

Two public gardens adorn Sverdlov Square. One of them is laid out in front of the Bolshoi Theatre. There is a beautiful fountain in the centre, spouting 70 litres of water a second, surrounded by many fruit trees. In the spring, these trees are laden with blossoms. The tulip beds are a beautiful sight.

The other public garden, covering a greater area, occupies the centre of the square. Laid out shortly after the war, it today has luxuriant foliage. Here, too, is a beautiful fountain (sculptor—Ivan Vitaly), erected in 1835, and a sculptural group in bronze on a stone pedestal fenced in with a cast iron railing.

On May 1, 1920, Vladimir Lenin arrived on Sverdlov Square at two o'clock in the afternoon to take part in the ceremony of laying the cornerstone of the monument to Karl Marx. He made a speech from a low improvised wooden rostrum.

With a sharp-pointed wire, Lenin engraved his name on a metal scroll—protocol for a stone-laying ceremony—then representatives of workers' delegations from Moscow enterprises followed. Lenin laid the first stone in the base of the monument; after that the metal scroll, enclosed in a brass box, was immured in the foundation and covered with a marble slab.

A *Monument to Karl Marx* was unveiled on this spot in October 1961, during the 22nd Congress of the Communist Party of the Soviet Union, in the presence of many delegates and foreign guests. Carved out of a huge monolith of grey granite, it rises over the centre of the square, amidst the greenery of the public garden, facing Karl Marx Prospekt.

Sculptor Lev Kerbel, who was awarded the Lenin Prize for the monument, has depicted the great teacher and leader of the proletariat as though he were standing on a rostrum passionately affirming the idea of Communism. Inscribed on the plinth of the monument is the famous slogan "Workers of all countries, unite!" Pylons flank the monument on either side. The one on the left is inscribed: "His name and work will endure through the ages! Engels" and the pylon on the right, reads: "Marx's teaching is all powerful since it is true. Lenin."

More than 170 years ago, the Neglinka River used to flow through what is now Sverdlov and Revolution Squares. By damming it, a large pond was formed in days gone by over what is now Sverdlov Square. The water from this pond was directed into a deep ditch that ran across Red Square. By 1791 the waters of the Neglinka were flowing through a specially dug canal (the old bed was filled up). In the early part of the 19th century it was channelled into an underground conduit. Not so many years ago in winter the river's "breath" could be seen on Revolution Square when trucks would dump snow into open manholes, which would belch forth dense white vapour on frosty days. And no matter how much snow was dumped in, it would vanish without trace, rapidly carried away by the swift current of the Neglinka, which can be seen pouring into the Moskva at the *Bolshoi Kamenny Most* (Large Stone Bridge).

However, the Neglinka's old underground channel became inadequate, for the city is growing and the flow of water has greatly increased. A new subterranean canal has been dug in the centre of town, to channel the Neglinka waters into the Moskva River in the vicinity of the *Rossiya Hotel.*

Another interesting building in this area is the *Metropole,* which faces Sverdlov Square and Karl Marx Prospekt. This hotel for foreign tourists was built in 1903 (architect—Valkot). The building contains a moving picture theatre with three viewing rooms, with a show beginning every 30 or 40 minutes. The central mosaic panel on the façade of the hotel, designed by the eminent Russian painter Mikhail Vrubel, is based on the play "Princesse Lointaine" by the French playwright Edmond Rostand.

A high relief of the *Metropole* depicting the offensive of the revolutionary forces is mounted on the Karl Marx Prospekt side of the building.

Right after the October Socialist Revolution, when the *Metropole* was used as the premises of the Second House of Soviets, Lenin made many reports and speeches there at congresses, Party conferences and sessions of the All-Russia Central Executive Committee of Soviets of Working People's Deputies and had talks with Petrograd workers concerned with food supplies. In 1918-1919 the All-Russia Central Executive Committee functioned there, under the chairmanship of Yakov Sverdlov. And, in 1919, the name of the outstanding Soviet statesman was given to this square, which up to now had been called Teatralnaya (Theatre) Square.

If you walk up Karl Marx Prospekt towards Dzerzhinsky Square, next to the *Metropole* you will see another tower of the already familiar Kitai-Gorod wall. Somewhat further, on a slight eminence in a public garden, there is a *Monument to Ivan Fyodorov,* the founder of book printing in Russia and in the Ukraine.

The monument was erected in 1909 with funds collected by nationwide subscription. It was restored at the beginning of 1957. The name Ivan Fyodorov is carved on the front of the stone pedestal, and below it, a reproduction of his colophon (book plate) and the date when the printing of the first Russian book began—April 19, 1563. On the opposite side of the pedestal are Fyodorov's words: "For the sake of my brothers and my near ones..." Together with Pyotr Mstislavets, Ivan Fyodorov published the *Acts of the Apostles*, the first dated printed Russian book, kept in the Lenin Library. The monument was erected not far from the *Gosudarev Pechatny Dvor* (State printing house), the printshop of Tsar Ivan IV, which was located on what is now House No. 15, October 25th Street.

Russian book-printing has traversed a long road since March 1, 1564, the day the first book was printed. No more than 50 different books were published in Russia in the 16th century, and as many as 500,000 in the 19th century. But in the first 45 years after the Revolution, 1,748,000 books were printed, totalling upwards of 26,000,000,000 copies.

Today books are published in the Soviet Union in the languages of more than 120 nationalities inhabiting the country, among them 40 nationalities which before the revolution did not have a written language of their own. One fourth of all books printed in the world are Soviet books.

From the elevated position of the side of Karl Marx Prospekt where the monument to Ivan Fyodorov stands, you get a good view of a large part of the avenue and Sverdlov Square. It is a particularly pleasant sight in the evening when the street lights are on, the traffic signals wink gaily with their red, yellow and green lights and the continuous stream of oncoming cars look like so many glow-worms. No wonder there have been so many pictures of "Moscow Lights" from precisely this vantage point. It is also a favourite spot for professional and amateur photographers.

GORKY STREET

THE first thing that strikes your eye as you step out of the Mayakovskaya Metro Station is the monument in the spacious square before you. This is the bronze figure of Vladimir Mayakovsky, a distinguished Soviet poet, bard of the October Socialist Revolution.

The statue was unveiled in the summer of 1958. Alexander Kibalnikov, the sculptor, was awarded a Lenin prize.

Vladimir Mayakovsky (1893-1930) lived in Moscow many years. He produced his best works here, dedicating many poetic lines to the Soviet capital.

Before 1935, this square that now bears his name was called Triumphalnaya Square because of the wooden Triumphal Gates there, lavishly adorned with sculptures, paintings and fabrics. The gates were erected in the 18th century. The tsars used to ride through them on coronation and other ceremonies.

This square could well be called Teatralnaya (Theatre) Square, for it is the site of four theatres, a motion picture house and a

Gorky Street o
New Year's night

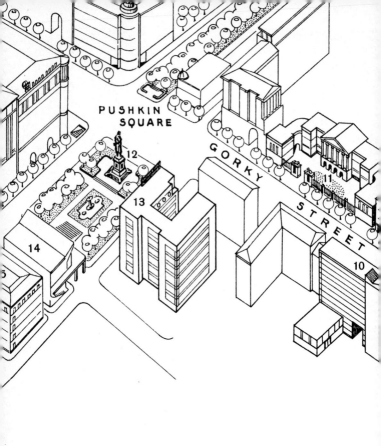

PUSHKIN SQUARE

12

13

14

GORKY STREET

11

10

**GORKY STREET
FROM MAYAKOVSKY SQUARE
TO PUSHKIN SQUARE**

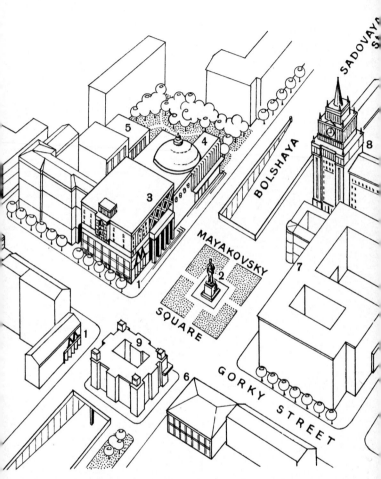

1. "Mayakovskaya" Metro Station; 2. Vladimir Mayakovsky Monument; 3. Tchaikovsky Hall; 4. Satire Theatre; 5. Mossoviet Theatre; 6. Central Puppet Theatre; 7. "Moskva" Cinema; 8. "Peking" Hotel; 9. "Sofia" Restaurant; 10. "Minsk" Hotel; 11. Museum of the Revolution; 12. Alexander Pushkin Monument; 13. "Izvestia"; 14. "Rossiya" Cinema; 15. "Novosti" Press Agency.

Gorky Street

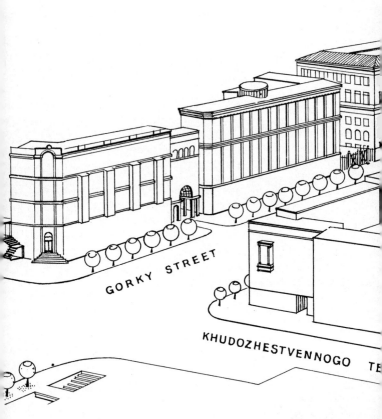

GORKY STREET

KHUDOZHESTVENNOGO TE

**GORKY STREET
FROM PUSHKIN SQUARE
TO MARX AVENUE**

16. Central Actors' Club; 17. Food Store No. 1 and Nikolai Ostrovsky Museum; 18. "Druzhba" Book Store; 19. Mossoviet; 20. Vladimir Lenin Monument; 21. Yury Dolgoruky Monument; 22. Art Theatre (MKhAT).

concert hall named after Pyotr Tchaikovsky, the great Russian composer. The main entrance to Tchaikovsky Hall is on the square, with another entrance in Gorky Street. The entrance to Mayakovskaya Metro Station is on the corner.

Tchaikovsky Hall (architects—Dmitry Chechulin and Konstantin Orlov) was built in 1940. It is shaped like a three-tier amphitheatre so that every spectator, no matter where he sits, has a good view of the entire stage, which projects into the hall. An 8-metre Czechoslovak organ with 7,800 pipes weighing more than 20 tons, one of the biggest organs in Europe, was installed there in the autumn of 1959.

Next to Tchaikovsky Hall there is the *Moscow Satire Theatre* and behind that, amidst the Aquarium Garden, the *Mossoviet Theatre,* to which was given the title of Academic Theatre.

The third theatre is located diagonally across the square from Tchaikovsky Hall. This is the *Central Puppet Theatre,* founded by that remarkable master of puppetry, Sergei Obraztsov. It will shortly move to a new premise on Sadovaya-Samotyechnaya Street.

A new austere-looking building stretches the length of Mayakovsky Square. To be more exact, it is an entire complex of buildings. The building occupying the big block between the Moskva Motion Picture Theatre and the *Peking Hotel* has the offices of the Moscow Central Architectural and Planning Administration, the Moscow Designing Institute—the centre for settling all matters related to reconstruction of the Soviet capital.

Erection of this building has practically rounded out reconstruction of Mayakovsky Square. However, there still is a small old structure in front of the square used by the *Sovremennik* (Contemporary) *Theatre Studio.* It will shortly be replaced by a more up-to-date building. Extensive remodelling of the building with the *Sofia Restaurant* is under way. On completion this restaurant will occupy all floors in the building and be the biggest in the Soviet capital.

The construction of a traffic underpass on Gorky Street *(Ulitsa Gorkogo)* and two pedestrian tunnels, one connected with Mayakovsky Metro Station, has considerably relieved traffic congestion in the square.

Facing Mayakovsky Square, in front of Tchaikovsky Hall the street to your left is Bolshaya Sadovaya. On the opposite side, where it joins the square, there is a building with a ten-story tower topped by a spire: that is the *Peking Hotel;* the street to your right is Sadovaya-Triumphalnaya, and the street straight ahead is Gorky Street, running in the direction of the Byelorussian Railway Terminal and Leningradsky Prospekt. Our route takes us along Gorky Street towards the centre of town. A short way down the street is house number 27/29. There is a large polished gray granite memorial slab on it with a sculptured portrait and the inscription: "Writer Alexander Alexandrovich Fadeyev lived and worked in this house from 1948 to 1956."

Across the street, not far away, you will see the new ten-story *Minsk Hotel* with more than 350 rooms. It was assembled from prefabricated reinforced concrete elements. The street level is walled in with huge floor to ceiling plate glass windows framed in aluminium.

Back on the right side of the street, an old building (No. 21) with a colonnade and sculptured lions over the gates can be seen a bit farther on behind a high wrought iron fence. At one time this was the English Club; now it is the *Museum of the Revolution.*

The museum has exhibits right out in front: a gun that shelled the Kremlin when it was seized by Cadets, and the pylon of an overhead electric tram feed line that had been twisted by a shell during the armed insurrection in October 1917 and placed in front of the museum following the reconstruction of Pushkin Square (1936).

The museum has materials telling about the first Russian revolution of 1905-1907, the period of the Stolypin reaction which followed and the new revolutionary upsurge, the First World War and the February bourgeois-democratic revolution, the preparations for the Great October Socialist Revolution and its victorious consummation, the triumphant advance of Soviet power and the subsequent stages in the history of the Soviet state.

There are new exhibits concerning recent

events: a copy of the emblem that the second Soviet Lunik delivered to the Moon in September 1959 and a model of the atomic icebreaker *Lenin*.

Continuing down Gorky Street, we come to spacious *Pushkin Square*, where the street intersects the Boulevard Ring. There is a bronze *Monument to Alexander Pushkin*, cast in 1880 by Alexander Opekushin and restored several years ago by the Mytishchi Art Castings Works. It was erected with funds subscribed by the population. The unveiling ceremony was attended by many notables, including Ivan Turgenev, Fyodor Dostoyevsky and Alexander Ostrovsky.

The great Russian poet was born and grew up in Moscow; here he spent his early years, nearly a third of his short life. In the last period of his life, the poet paid many long visits to Moscow. Alexander Pushkin loved his native town. Who in Russia does not know his verses dedicated to Moscow:

> *How often, sick with separation,*
> *My thoughts in exile turned to you,*
> *Oh, Moscow, Moscow: I would view*
> *You in my fond imagination...*

The monument stands in a fairly new public garden with a large fountain. There is rarely a day in spring or winter when bouquets of flowers have not been placed at the foot of the monument; there are always admirers of the "sun of Russian poetry" here, both old and young. The words of Vissarion Belinsky, a well-known Russian critic of the last century, involuntarily come to mind: "He was not only a great Russian poet of his times but a great poet of all peoples and all ages, a genius of Europe, a poet of world-wide fame."

Vladimir Mayakovsky loved Alexander Pushkin's poetry. At the age of nineteen, he stood on a precipice in Kuntsevo (then a Moscow summer suburb) reciting "Eugene Onegin." Later, as a mature poet, Mayakovsky remarked:

> *After death we'll stand*
> *almost side by side*
> *you under "P"*
> *and I*
> *under "M".*

Mayakovsky Square

142

*Monument to
Alexander Pushkin*

This prophecy has come true in a way. Pushkin Square is next to Mayakovsky Square. No poet in bronze stands as close to the carved image of Pushkin as Vladimir Mayakovsky, a great Soviet bard.

A tall building with large windows faces the square to the left of the Pushkin Monument. It is the editorial office and printshop of the newspaper *Izvestia*. At the far end of the square there is a large building with an all-glass façade. This is the *Rossiya Motion Picture Theatre,* the largest in the country. It was opened in the summer of 1961 in time for an important event: the Second Moscow International Film Festival.

The theatre has three viewing rooms: the main one with a large screen (111.5 feet wide and about 46 feet high) seating 2,500 and two with a seating capacity of 250 each. The small viewing rooms are intended for showing shorts and newsreels.

To the back of the Rossiya Motion Picture Theatre there are the editorial offices of the magazine *New Times.* A few steps beyond that the *Novosti Press Agency,* established by mass public organisations, is installed in a newly remodelled four-storey building. Sergei Rakhmaninov, the renowned Russian composer and pianist, once lived for several years in an apartment of the fourth floor of this house.

From Pushkin Square, Gorky Street continues to Karl Marx Prospekt. This stretch of the thoroughfare has been almost completely rebuilt. Only a few structures have remained from pre-revolutionary times. Most of the tall, bright, new buildings were put up before the Second World War. During reconstruction, the former Tverskaya Street (the name of the street until 1935) was widened to more than twice the previous width.

Lined with linden trees and richly dressed store windows topped by neon signs that are especially colourful at night, this beautiful, spacious central thoroughfare is always thronged with people—Muscovites, visitors from other Soviet cities, and tourists from abroad.

In the first corner building on the left,

Gorky Street on a week-day ▶

Minsk Hotel in Gorky Street

which also faces Pushkin Square, you will find the All-Russia Theatrical Society at the Central House of the Actor. Next to it (house number 14) is *Gastronom* (Food Store) No.1 (formerly called Yeliseyevsky), with its large glistening plate-glass show windows, huge lavish chandeliers, and tracery-covered interior. Until recently the biggest food store in the Soviet capital, there are now several others to vie with it.

Nikolai Ostrovsky, author of *How the Steel was Tempered* and *Born of the Storm,* novels that are great favourites with Soviet youth, lived and worked in this house in 1935-1936. His apartment was turned into a state museum more than 25 years ago. Since then it has been visited by over two million persons.

The first floor of the building on the corner of Gorky Street and Soviet Square is entirely given over to a book store, which opened in 1958. Memorial plaques with bas-reliefs mounted on the façade remind us that composer Vladimir Zakharov, writer Vyacheslav Shishkov and poet Demyan Bedny lived in this house.

Another large book store was opened several years ago on the opposite side of the street. Called *Druzhba* (Friendship), it deals in books published in Poland, Czechoslovakia, Hungary, the German Democratic Republic and the other people's democracies.

A pedestrian tunnel has been made under Gorky Street between these two buildings. In the course of construction a very interesting find was made. At a depth of one and a half metres excavators came upon a timbered pavement with potholes made by carriage and cart wheels. This ancient city carriage way was a timbered road: longitudinal oak logs were covered by pine pavement with a layer of thick boards on top. At the edge of the carriage way were the traces of a paling which had surrounded a country estate. This means that at one time there was not only a road but also a street there, which led the way to the Tver Principality. The regiments of Ivan the Terrible took this road to the shores of the Baltic, strings of traders' carts went along it, foreigners drove over it on their way to the embassies, and pompous cortèges of the Russian tsars rode along this road when coming to Moscow from Petersburg for coronation ceremonies and to celebrate military victories.

Now we have come to one of Moscow's main squares—*Sovietskaya*—which has been laid out anew. This is where the city hall is located—the *Moscow Soviet of Working People's Deputies*. The lower part of the building was erected in 1782 (architect—Matvei Kazakov). Before the revolution, it was the residence of Moscow's governor-general.

In October 1917, the house was occupied by the Central Military Revolutionary Committee—the headquarters of the armed insurrection in Moscow. Vladimir Lenin spoke there many a time from 1918-1921, addressing large gatherings in the street from the balcony of the building and meetings of active members of the Moscow Party organization. His name remains forever inscribed in the lists of members of the Moscow Soviet as a deputy of the working people of Moscow; credentials with the Number 1 are never assigned to other deputies.

When the street was being widened in keeping with the master plan for the reconstruction of Moscow, the building of the Moscow Soviet was moved back 44.3 feet and later two more stories were added. The main entrance is now adorned by sculptural bas-reliefs, and the high pediment by a large gilded State Emblem.

Sovietskaya Square was reconstructed before the Great Patriotic War: it was built up with tall apartment houses and a pleasant public garden was laid out in front of the building containing the archives of the Institute of Marxism-Leninism (erected in 1927), with a red granite monument to Lenin (sculptor—Sergei Merkurov) and a fountain. A *Monument to Yury Dolgoruky*, the founder of Moscow (sculptors—Sergei Orlov and others), stands in the centre of the square on a high rectangular pedestal of polished dark grey granite. He is in a coat of mail astride a prancing steed, reining it in and gesturing, as though indicating where Moscow should be sited. The ancient coat-of-arms of Moscow cover the face of the horseman's shield. The corner-stone was laid in 1947 to commemorate the 800th anniversary of the founding of Moscow and the statue was unveiled in 1954.

The building on the southern side of the square was once the *Dresden Hotel* where Robert Schumann, the composer, and his wife, Clara Schumann, the pianist, stayed in 1844. Nikolai Nekrasov, Ivan Turgenev and Anton Chekhov, famous Russian writers, and the renowned surgeon and scientist Nikolai Pirogov also stayed there occasionnally.

There is a splendid view of the lower part of Gorky Street, Manège Square and the Kremlin from Soviet Square. From here, the thoroughfare slopes down rather steeply to the underground Neglinka River. Large houses built in 1949 and 1950 line the right side of the street where it begins to slope down. The ground floors are faced with granite blocks and decorated with diverse polished granite elements. This building material had been prepared by the Hitlerites during the Great Patriotic War and intended for a monument to commemorate victory over the Soviet Union. After the rout of the fascist troops the granite blocks were brought to Moscow and used to build the river embankments.

Lower down the street beyond these houses, a grey building with large windows and a clock and a globe above the entrance, occupies the entire block. This is the *Central Telegraph Office,* built in 1930 (engineer—Ivan Rerberg). The offices of the Ministry of Communications are located there and also the offices for handling inter-urban and international telephone calls constantly used by foreign correspondents, diplomats and tourists.

On the other side of Gorky Street, directly opposite the Central Telegraph Office, there is a small side-street called *Proyezd Khudozhestvennogo Teatra* (Art Theatre Lane), where the *Moscow Art Theatre* is located. This world-renowned theatre, founded by Konstantin Stanislavsky and Vladimir Nemirovich-Danchenko, has been in existence for more than 70 years now. Plays by Anton Chekhov and Maxim Gorky were staged there when it first opened and are still part of its repertoire. "The Art Theatre is just

New administrative building under construction in the centre of Moscow

as fine and significant as the Tretyakov Art Gallery, St. Basil's Cathedral and all that is best in Moscow," said Maxim Gorky. "It is impossible not to love it."

The next side-street to the left going down Gorky Street (you enter it through a high archway) is Georgievsky. A house has been preserved here which belonged to the Troekurov *boyars.* It is a very interesting example of late 17th-century civil architecture. After restorations in 1961-1963, it was given over to *Glinka Central Museum of Musical Culture,* which was established more than 20 years ago, at the time of the Great Patriotic War.

The museum has more than 220,000 exhibits, including original manuscript copies of sheet music, archives, memoirs, letters, rare editions, sculptures, graphics, photographs, household articles and musical instruments, connected with the life and work of outstanding composers, performers and musicologists. Among the exhibits are materials pertaining to Mikhail Glinka, Pyotr Tchaikovsky, Nikolai Rimsky-Korsakov, Modest Moussorgsky, Hector Berlioz, Ludwig Van Beethoven, Franz Liszt, Wolfgang Amadeus Mozart, and Gioacchino Rossini.

The museum staff is enthusiastically collecting the musical heritage of Soviet composers: Nikolai Myaskovsky and Rheinhold Gliere, Sergei Prokofiev and Isaac Dunayevsky.

A very rich collection of books, sheet music and magazines is available in the museum library to music lovers and scholars. So is the exceptionally valuable collection of 2,000 musical instruments of the nationalities inhabiting the Soviet Union, and an unusually rich collection of records.

As you end up at the beginning of Gorky Street, on your right is the *National Hotel.* A new, 20-story annexe planned to accommodate over a thousand persons, is now going up next to the old building, which will be remodelled and refurnished and become taller and more beautiful.

From Mayakovsky Square, you have strolled all the way down to Karl Marx Prospekt, where the *National, Moskva* and *Metropole* Hotels are located. And there are several others in the vicinity (the *Berlin, Budapest* and *Armenia).*

Sovietskaya Square with monument to Prince Yuri Dolgoruky, the founder of Moscow

EXCURSION 5

STARTING POINT:
VDNKh
METRO STATION

THE NATIONAL ECONOMIC ACHIEVEMENTS EXHIBITION

VDNKh is the abbreviation for *Vystavka Dostizheny Narodnovo Khosyaistva* (National Economic Achievements Exhibition).

This is the country's biggest "museum." First opened in 1959, it now is a permanently functioning exhibition where some 100,000 displays are renewed annually, acquainting the visitor with the present level and achievements of industry, agriculture, transport, science and culture in the USSR. The grounds cover an area of 550 acres, larger than that occupied by the 1958 World's Fair in Brussels. There are some 300 structures and 78 pavilions on this extensive territory, which has been turned into a luxuriant garden of fruit trees. It is hardly possible

Big fountain in the grounds of the National Economic Achievements Exhibition

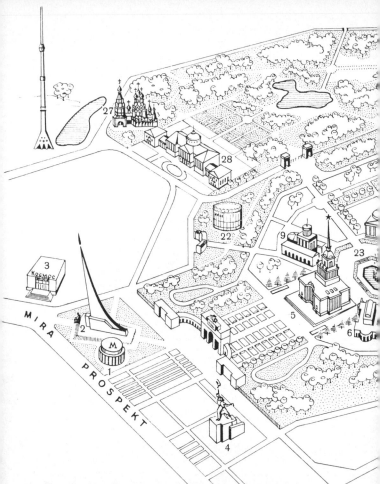

NATIONAL ECONOMIC ACHIEVEMENTS EXHIBITION

1. "VDNKh" Metro Station; 2. Obelisk in Commemoration of the Conquest of Space by the Soviet People; 3. "Kosmos" Cinema; 4. "Worker and Woman Collective Farmer" Sculptural Composition; 5. Central Pavilion; 6. "Atomic Energy" Pavilion; 7. "Agriculture" Pavilion; 8. "Soviet Culture" Pavilion; 9. "Space" Pavilion; 10, 11. "Transport of the USSR" Pavilions; 12. "Education" Pavilion; 13. "Health Services and Medical

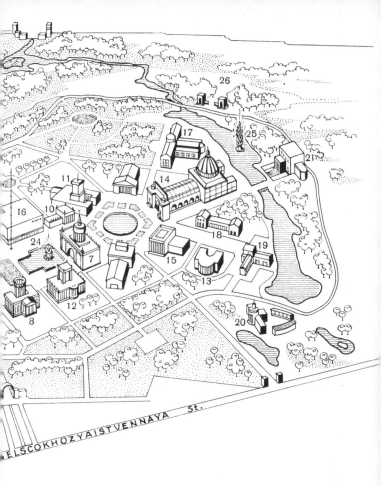

ELSCOKHOZYAISTVENNAYA St.

Instruments Industry" Pavilion; 14. "Engineering" Pavilion; 15. "Electrification of the USSR" Pavilion; 16. "Radio-Electronics" Pavilion; 17. "Floriculture and Urban Greenery" Pavilion; 18. "Cattle Breeding" Pavilion; 19. "Horse Breeding" Pavilion; 20. "Fur Animal Breeding" Pavilion; 21. "Irrigated Farming and Water Supplies" Pavilion; 22. Circorama; 23. "Peoples' Friend-ship" Fountain; 24. "Stone Flower" Fountain; 25. "Gold Ear" Fountain; 26. Botanical Gardens of the USSR Academy of Sciences; 27. Trinity Church; 28. Serf Art Palace-Museum.

to see everything in one day. A 3.1 mile trolley-bus line and open excursion car-trains are a convenience for visitors. In 1958, the subway was extended as far as the exhibition. The stop is called VDNKh.

You walk out of the Metro onto a vast stretch of parkland—the access to the exhibition. To the right of the station, the silvery shaft of an obelisk can be seen rising to a height of nearly 330 feet. The monument (architects—Mikhail Barshch and Alexander Kolchin: sculptor—Andrei Faidysh-Krandievsky), erected to commemorate the outstanding achievements of the Soviet people in the conquest of outer space, was unveiled in 1964.

The obelisk proper consists of a steel frame faced with sheets of polished titanium, a highly weather-resistant and durable metal.

Expressive reliefs with many figures cover both sides of the granite base of the obelisk. They depict those who made possible man's first flight into space, those who today boldly continue to discover the secrets of the Universe.

In front of the monument there is a sculpture of K. Tsiolkovsky, who predicted man's inevitable flight into space and laid down the principles of the theory of rocket engineering and cosmonautics. The statue is carved out of light-grey granite and stands out splendidly against the background of the shaft of the obelisk.

The base of the obelisk contains premises for a museum of the history of the conquest of outer space. There will be two halls. The first will contain documents, photographs, diagrams, drawings, and scale models to acquaint the visitor with the elaboration of the theory and practice of rocket flight. Models of sputniks and spaceships built in the Soviet Union will be displayed in the second hall, which is 52.5 feet high.

A huge portico with the sculptured figures of a man and woman collective farmer with a sheaf of grain high above their heads, marks the main entrance to the exhibition grounds. But before entering, you should have a look at another splendid monument— the *Worker and Woman Collective Farmer* by Vera Mukhina.

The monument stands some 1,640 feet to the right of the main entrance. This stainless steel statue is one of the best examples of Soviet monumental art. Made in 1937, it has since become the symbol of the Soviet Union for many people throughout the world. It is 82 feet high and weighs 75 tons.

The exhibition has been designed so as to familiarize visitors with Soviet industry and agriculture on a country-wide scale. The unique architecture of the pavilions reflects the national art traditions of the various Soviet republics.

A broad lane with multi-jet fountains in the middle and a double row of lamp-posts in the shape of ears of wheat lead from the main entrance to the *Central Pavilion,* where the exhibition begins. The 115-foot spire topped by a star and ears of wheat rising above this building is visible from any point on the exhibition grounds.

The tallest structure, 246 feet high, is the *Engineering Pavilion,* in which hundreds of exhibits of machines and machine tools give the visitor a good idea of the present level of Soviet engineering, including the auto- mobile industry.

There are certain pavilions which are al- ways crowded, including those of *The USSR Academy of Sciences—Space, Atomic Energy for Peaceful Purposes, Public Education in the USSR—Soviet Higher Schools,* and *Radio- Electronics and Communications.*

The exhibits in *The USSR Academy of Sciences—Space* pavilion indicate the latest Soviet achievements in various fields of natural and technical sciences. They acquaint the visitor with the work of Soviet scientists and engineers in the conquest of outer space and the mastery of controlled thermo-nuclear reactions, and also in practic- al application of the latest scientific achieve- ments in the national economy. A special section is devoted to the world's first sput- niks, made in the Soviet Union, the luniks, space rockets, and the *Vostok* and *Voskhod* spaceships.

Other displays in the pavilion include instruments for studying roentgen and ultra- violet radiation of the sun, the model of a silicon solar-battery with a cosmic-ray count-

The National Eco- nomic Achieve- ments Exhibition ▶

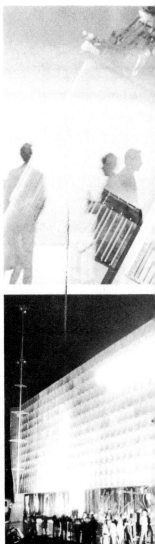

164   *Picture gallery at Ostankino Palace*

Ostankino, past and present

er, the nose-cone of a meteorological rocket with standard equipment, and so forth.

Special halls in this pavilion are devoted to the flights of Soviet astronauts, including Yury Gagarin, Valentina Tereshkova and Alexei Leonov, the first man in the world to "walk" in space. Dozens of exhibits acquaint the visitor with the training of an astronaut, the construction of the *Vostok* spaceship, and the orbits of the flights by space trail blazers.

A great many display stands, instruments, and diverse apparatus and installations tell about research being done by Soviet scientists in the physics of solids, low-temperature physics, the physics of elementary particles, chemistry, biology and other sciences.

A scale model of the world's first atomic icebreaker, the Lenin, is on view in the hall called *Atomic Energy for Peaceful Purposes.*

One of the sections in this pavilion tells about the experimental work being done in the USSR on an industrial scale to develop profitable types of atomic electric stations. There is a scale model of the world's first atomic electric station with a capacity of 5,000 kilowatts, commissioned in the USSR in 1954. Other exhibits acquaint the visitor with atomic electric stations in this country, in particular the first 100,000-kilowatt atomic electric station.

A section called *Safety Precautions and Protection Against Radioactivity* is concerned with ways and means of protecting the health of persons working with radioactive substances. Of special interest are the exhibits in the section called *Production of Isotopes,* and also those showing the application of radioactive isotopes in technology, agriculture, biology and medicine. One of the display stands gives some interesting figures. Today the Soviet Union produces 126 different kinds of radioactive isotopes and 630 tagged compounds, which are obtainable in 230 places in the country.

All in all more than 5,000 machines, machine-tools, instruments, and apparatus, or models of them, are on display in the industry and transport pavilions. Some 18,000 products of light industry are on view, including goods made of artificial and synthetic materials, and also many other consumer goods.

The exhibition grounds are one huge park with shady lanes, fruit orchards, and millions of flowers of all kinds. It is a fine place for recreation and relaxation. There are theatres, open-air concert stages, a motion picture theatre, circorama, restaurants, many cafés and a dance hall. Two fascinating fountains, really unique sights, are situated beyond the *Central Pavilion:* the *Peoples' Friendship Fountain,* with bronze figures of young women representing the nationalities of the USSR, and the *Stone Flower Fountain,* which is especially beautiful at night, when its many-coloured rocks light up, in fairy-tale splendour, in an emerald cascade of upward-spurting and falling water. The exhibition lights are all aglow and rowboats ripple the smooth surface of the lake until late into the night.

The admission fee, giving you the right to visit all the pavilions, is 30 kopecks.

Incidentally, the *Building Materials and Construction* pavilions of the exhibition are at the other end of town: at 30 Frunzenskaya Embankment (it can be reached by Metro: the stop is *Frunzenskaya).* There you will find 10 pavilions and 10 open-air demonstration grounds, which graphically indicate the progress that has been made here in construction, in particular housing, and tell about prospects for the future.

The gardens of the National Economic Achievements Exhibition merge with the *Main Botanical Gardens* of the USSR Academy of Sciences on the north and Dzerzhinsky Recreation Park on the west.

Here, in the grounds of this park, you will find the renowned *Ostankino Palace,* a remarkable monument of Russian architecture and decorative art. This palace, which belonged to Count Sheremetyev, was erected in 1792-1797 by serfs and designed by a group of architects, also serfs, under the supervision of a self-educated architect by the name of Pavel Argunov.

The edifice was built entirely of wood in the Russian classical style. Its façade is adorned with a high six-columned portico topped by a rotunda. On the garden side there is a portico with ten columns, it is executed in a less severe style, accentuating the intimacy of the garden.

"Troika" (at the All-Union Exhibition of Economic Achievements)

►

*Obelisk comme-
morating the begin-
ning of space ex-
ploration*

The interior—the foyer, halls, and galleries —is lavishly embellished. The delicate ornate wood carvings on the furniture, the doors and walls of the halls, the parquet mosaic floors of different species of wood, and also the very rich collection of cut-glass and bronze chandeliers, carved and gilded floor lamps and incense burners—everything is the highly artistic work of serf craftsmen. Of particular interest are the paintings, especially the work of the Argunovs who were serf artists, and also the rich collections of porcelain, pictures, prints and sculptures.

The entire central section of the palace served as a theatre, one of the finest in Russia at the time. The theatre's company was comprised entirely of serf actors and actresses, including the gifted Russian actress Praskovya Zhemchugova.

In 1917, the Ostankino estate was nationalized. Subsequently the palace was turned into a museum of serf art.

Next to the palace stands the Trinity Church, a fine examples of late 17th-century Russian architecture.

The All-Union Television Centre, the biggest in Europe, is under construction in Ostankino. When completed in 1968, its tower will be over 1,700 feet high.

Programmes will be broadcast on six channels (one of them coloured). The spacious, amply illuminated building will accommodate 18 studios, the two biggest of which will each be nearly 1,200 square yards in area. All the equipment will be Soviet-made.

The tower will have an observation platform and a restaurant, slowly revolving on the tower axis 1,082 feet from the earth's surface.

High-speed lifts will operate inside the tower.

LENIN HILLS

THE Moscow subway system has more than 80 stations, and 20 bridges span the Moskva River. But this station—*Leninskiye Gory*, on one of the bridges, is different from all the others. Nor can you mistake this bridge—the starting point of our next sightseeing stroll—with any of the others. It is the only two-level bridge across the river. The upper level is for motor car and trolley-bus traffic, and the lower one for the Metro. This bridge links the centre of town with Moscow's young, rapidly growing South-Western District.

Everything about this structure is unique. It spans the river at an appreciable angle. The bridge is nearly 3,936 feet long and has a slope due to the big difference in height of the river banks. The framework is made of prefabricated prestressed reinforced concrete, including the arched spans, which were assembled right on the bank and then floated on pontoons to the designated spot.

The Metro station has exits on both banks of the river: one down below at Luzhniki and the other up above on the Lenin Hills.

Moscow State University

172

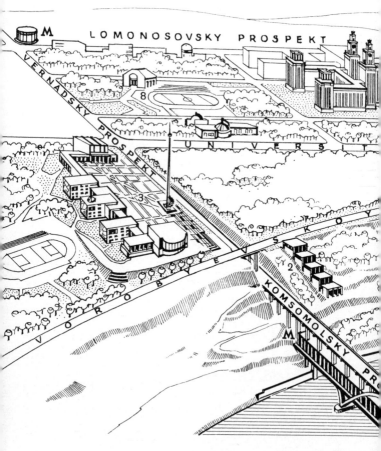

LENIN HILLS
MOSCOW STATE UNIVERSITY

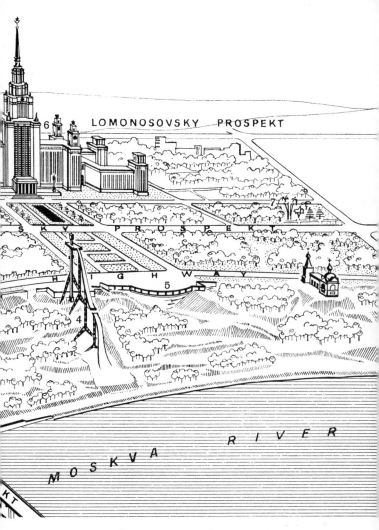

LOMONOSOVSKY PROSPEKT

SKY PROSPEKT

HIGHWAY

MOSKVA RIVER

1. Metro Bridge, "Leninskiye Gory" Metro Stations; 2. Escalator; 3. Young Pioneers' and Schoolchildren's Palace; 4. Ski Jump; 5. Observation Platform; 6. Moscow State University; 7. Botanical Gardens; 8. Sports Centre.

Our route begins at the upper exit; as you go up there by special escalator, you get a wonderful view of the surroundings through the glass walls.

Straight ahead facing the exit is the *Palace for Young Pioneers and Schoolchildren.* You can easily recognize this palatial club by its 180-feet arrow-shaped flagstaff topped by a large red flag fluttering in the breeze. The 140-acre grounds of "Pioneerland" are bounded by Vorobyevskoye Highway, Vernadsky and Universitetsky Prospekts.

Work on this big children's club began in 1958, and on June 1, 1962, Moscow's Young Pioneers were handed the symbolic key to the building, which was erected on the initiative and with the participation of the Moscow Komsomol (Young Communist League members), who put in more than three million hours of work on the job.

Inside the Young Pioneer's Palace there is a Lenin Hall for ceremonies when children are admitted to the Young Pioneer Organization; Museum of Young Pioneer Fame; an International Friendship Hall; winter garden; library and reading room; an art studio; film studio; sculpturing studio; observatory; planetarium; radioengineering laboratory; airplane and ship modelling section; glee clubs; and concert hall seating a thousand, to mention a few of the facilities. It is impossible to list them all here, for the palatial club has hundreds of rooms with a total floorage of 25,000 square metres and some 750 clubs, study and other groups, circles attended by 7,500 children. There is also a lake on the grounds and a stadium with grandstands seating 7,000.

The architects and artists who designed and decorated this club displayed a great deal of ingenuity. They skilfully utilized the relief of the locality and created a whole "Pioneerland" complex, with everything to bring out and develop the children's interests and talents. The entire locality has been attractively landscaped.

From the children's palace stroll down the shady lane of Vorobyevskoye Highway and along the brow of gullied and wooded Lenin Hills towards a distinctly visible ski jump. The road, which follows a bend in the

Moskva River and gradually ascends upward, leads, after about a 15-minute walk at a leisurely pace, to the central part of Lenin Hills.

This picturesque spot, open to the sun and air, is the highest point on the Moskva River's right bank, which drops abruptly to the blue ribbon of the water. From here, you can get an exceptionally good view of Moscow. That was why Peter I brought Kornelis Philander de Bruyn, a guest from abroad, to *Vorobyevy Gory* (as the Lenin Hills were called then) and showed him the best place from where to draw his panorama of the ancient city. Anton Chekhov, the great Russian writer, once said about the hills: "Anyone who wants to understand Russia should come here and admire Moscow..."

Lenin Hills leave an unforgettable impression. No wonder scores of Soviet and foreign tourists go on excursions to the hills; people go there in groups, in pairs, or single. Many Muscovites make a point of going there frequently.

On the brow of Lenin Hills there is an observation platform with a balustrade of polished granite. Here, from a 263-foot height you can get a splendid view of the city stretching out boundlessly down below.

The towers, gilded dome and white pillar of the Bell Tower of Ivan the Great, and, next to it, a green cupola topped by a red flag are plainly visible straight ahead in the distance on a clear day. That is the Kremlin. At the foot of the hills, a huge smooth curve of the Moskva River encompasses *Luzhniki* —a sports centre which was completed in 1956. The main structures include a *Large Sports Arena* seating 103,000 (in the centre), swimming pool (to the right), a *Small Sports Arena* (to the left), a *Sports Palace* seating over 17,000 (still further to the left) and a *Children's Sports Stadium* (by the river), besides dozens of different sports grounds and courts. To your right, you can see the two-level bridge where the excursion began; and the completely reconstructed Frunzenskaya Embankment beyond Luzhniki, along the opposite side of the Moskva River. Also to your right, on the bank where you are standing, you can see the extensive grounds

Moscow students ▶

Lenin Hills. Double-decker bridge for road and metro

of *Gorky Central Recreation Park* and the towers of the Moscow Television Centre on the horizon farther off to the right.

To the left of Luzhniki and the railway embankment you can see the *Novodevichy Convent,* a medieval fortress with a tall, well-proportioned belfry, and a cemetery which is the burial ground of prominent writers, poets, actors, painters, sculptors, scientists, architects, and military men. To the left of the Novodevichy Convent one can see a 31-story building of the Council for Mutual Economic Aid, located at the end of Kalinin Prospekt.

Here and there, tall buildings pierce the sky with their sharp spires. A vast mosaic of façades and roofs, walls and windows with glass glittering in the sunlight spread as far as the eye can reach. Three basic colours of the surrounding buildings stand out noticeably: the brick-red of pre-revo- lutionary structures, the dark-grey of edifices erected in the 20's and 30's, and the pale- yellow of more recent houses. But it is most gladdening to see the warm sunny tones making broad inroads everywhere in the old sections of the city that grew up in the course of many centuries. As for the new housing developments, bright tones are all you will find there.

That is how Moscow looks from the Lenin Hills in the daytime. And at night, too, one can stand on the observation platform for hours trying to pick out familiar places from the bright haloes and chains of lights.

Standing with your back to the Moskva River, you face a huge science centre (architects—Lev Rudnev, Sergei Chernyshev and others). This is the *Moscow State University* named after M.V. Lomonosov, one of Russia's greatest encyclopaedists.

A broad handsome avenue leads from the observation platform to the university. It is divided by a wide strip landscaped with trees, decorative bushes, lawns, flower beds, and with granite busts of distinguished Russian scientists placed along at intervals. In front of the main building there is an elongated pond 656 feet by 131.1 feet with fountains.

The bright buildings of Moscow University extend for some distance. To visit all its 45,000 rooms, you would have to walk 90.1 miles, and even if you only spent a minute looking at each one, it would take you 750 hours to make the rounds.

The main 32-story building with an impressive colonnade (bearing the dates: 1949-1953, when it was erected) is crowned by a nearly 196-foot spire. Towering 994 feet above the Lenin Hills, it is visible from various parts of the city. The central section has on both sides 18-story wings, flanked, in turn, by 12-story buildings. The latter contain dormitory facilities for students and post-graduates and apartments for the instructors and professors.

A steel frame of unique design weighing some 40,000 tons served as the skeleton for the building. Over 170 million bricks and nearly half a million cubic metres of concrete and reinforced concrete went into its construction. There are over a hundred elevators able to lift upwards 1,500 persons and 10 tons of freight at one time.

The *Assembly Hall* is a real credit to the university. You get to it through an attractive lobby finished in marble of different colours with artfully executed mosaic portraits of outstanding world scientists on the walls. At the entrance to the Assembly Hall there are statues of Dmitry Mendeleyev, Ivan Pavlov, Ivan Michurin and Nikolai Zhukovsky. Large chandeliers with fluorescent lamps hang from the stuccoed ceiling supported by 26 tall white marble columns. There are 1,500 soft chairs in the parterre.

The students have a fine club with an auditorium seating 800, a gymnasium and a swimming pool.

In a matter of a few seconds express elevators carry passengers up to the top floors, where the *Geography Museum* is located. The exhibits of the museum, which occupy seven floors, are grouped in three sections: the history of the natural and exact sciences in Moscow University and the history of geography; the history of the development of the Earth (general geography); and nature of the USSR.

The museum has newly acquired geological, mineralogical, soil, biogeographical and historical collections. On display are specially painted pictures depicting various landscapes of the country from a scientific angle, and also several dozen statues, drawings and photographs of distinguished geologists, geographers, pedologists and other scientists.

The floors below are occupied by Geography and Mechanics and Mathematics Departments, the Rector's Offices, Assembly Hall, and the Geology Department. All the numerous auditoriums and lecture halls are equipped with sound amplification installations and motion picture projectors. There is a library which is one of the largest in the country.

The university buildings are surrounded by a wide belt of greenery and flower gardens. More than 40 varieties of trees and shrubs have been planted there, among them silver fir, birch, maple, ash, apple, pear, jasmine, and acacia. The university's new Botanical Gardens are to the right, covering an area of 110 acres. There, too, you will find the premises of the Biology and Soil Department, which can easily be recognized by the two glassed roofs in the shape of a prism.

On the other side of the main building, near the students' summer sports centre, there is an observatory and a meteorological station where students do theoretical and practical work.

The Institute of Theoretical Astronomy has a laboratory in the observatory on Lenin Hills. Telegrams with the cable address "*Moscow. Cosmos.*" are sent there from hundreds of stations at home and abroad reporting visual and photographic observations of Soviet sputniks and spaceships. These telegrams are immediately deciphered and processed there, and then sent on to the computing centre.

There is another building on the observatory grounds—the *State Astronomical Institute* named after Pavel Shternberg. Here, in a tightly sealed basement deep down underground, there is a clock under a bell-glass that keeps exact time.

Two spacious edifices rise up behind the

Luzhniki ▶

Young Pioneers Palace on Lenin Hills

Market scene

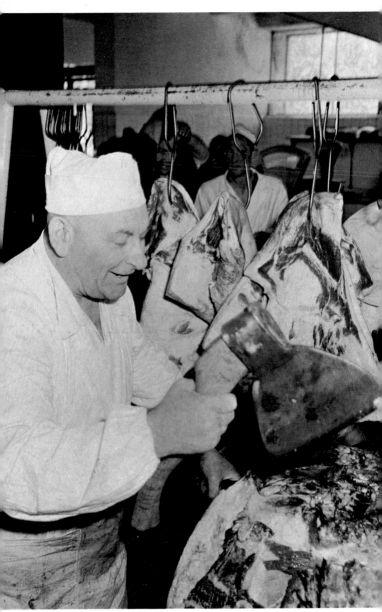

main building, one on each side. In front of one there are statues of Alexander Stoletov and Pyotr Lebedev, two distinguished Russian physicists; and in front of the other, the statues of Dmitry Mendeleyev and Alexander Butlerov, two great Russian chemists (the monuments were made by a group of Byelorussian sculptors under the direction of Zair Azgur). These are the physics and chemistry buildings.

In the long strip of lawn between the two buildings there is a statue of Mikhail Lomonosov (sculptor—Nikolai Tomsky) on a grey-granite cylindrical pedestal.

You will find full-length statues and busts everywhere: in front of the university and behind it, on the buildings and inside. They are the work of 70 sculptors.

Moscow State University recently acquired a large new building. It houses the Institute of Mechanics, where students and postgraduates of the Mechanics and Mathematics Department obtain practical training and do research.

A preparatory department was organized at the university several years ago. That is where foreign students study Russian, natural sciences and the humanities, and then specialize in the fields they have chosen either at the university or some other Soviet institution of higher learning. Some 2,500 students from 70 countries are studying at Moscow University.

Moscow State University today has 14 departments with a total enrolment of nearly 32,000 (including correspondence students). [1]

And so, within a relatively small area, there stand three unique structures: the Palace for Young Pioneers and School children, the huge sports complex in Luzhniki, and, finally, the vast science centre on Lenin Hills—Moscow State University.

Moscow University initiated a big development programme in the south-western section of the city. Hundreds and hundreds of large apartment houses have arisen there

---

[1] There is another Moscow higher educational establishment that has a still larger student body. It is the All-Union Correspondence Polytechnical Institute with an enrolment of more than 34,000.

Ski-jumping on the Lenin Hills

THE LUZHNIKI SPORTS COMPLEX

A S you step out of the subway station, the first thing that strikes your eye is a high embankment along which diesel locomotives are hauling long freight trains. This is the *Okruzhnaya* (Circular) *Railway Line,* which was laid in 1908 and now lies completely within the city limits. Some two hundred years ago a 25-mile-long earthen rampart with a deep moat in front was built on the site of the present Okruzhnaya Railway Line. Known as the *Kamer-Kollezhsky Val,* it had check-points with wooden gates where officials and noblemen passing through were registered, the quantity of

A sportswoman at Luzhniki

M O S K V A   R I V E R

K O M S O M O L S K Y   P R O S P E K T

LUZHNIKI

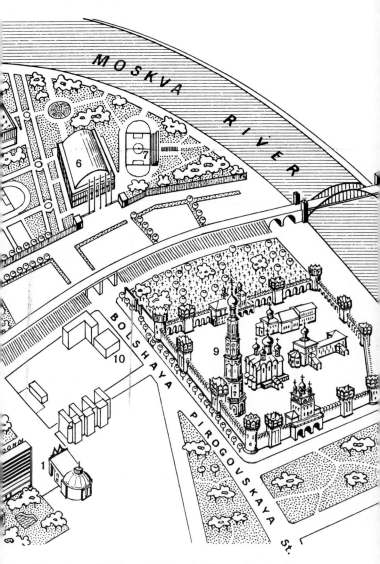

1. "Sportivnaya" Metro Station; 2. Large Sports Arena;
3. Vladimir Lenin Monument; 4. Swimming Pool; 5. Small
Sports Arena; 6. Sports Palace; 7. Children's Stadium;
8. "Yunost" Hotel; 9. Novodevichy Convent; 10. Jewellery
Store.

Luzhniki—township of sports

goods entering the city and live-stock driven in for slaughter were counted, and peasant carts were inspected to see if they were carrying vodka in violation of the state monopoly. More than a hundred years ago the check points lost their significance.

Beyond the embankment, the Moskva River makes a big bend. Not so long ago there were big empty lots and refuse dumps surrounding solitary squat structures on its low-lying bank. In the distant past, this whole locality, which was inundated meadowland, was flooded by spring waters. And it was from these meadows that the place got its name of Luzhniki (the Russian word for meadow is *loog*).

The *Lenin Central Stadium* in Luzhniki, Europe's biggest sports centre, was built in a little over a year, and officially opened on August 5, 1956, for the USSR National Sports Competition. A large group of architects were awarded the Lenin Prize for designing the project and solving a major city development problem involving the speedy reconstruction and modernization of the entire Luzhniki area.

To prevent the Luzhniki area from being flooded by high waters in springtime, its surface had to be raised up about five feet. This meant driving in 10,000 piles, hauling in and spreading nearly three million cubic metres of earth, laying 770,000 square metres of asphalt and concrete pavement, and covering 5,000 metres of vertical embankment slopes with granite and topping them with wrought-iron fencing.

The central structure of the sports complex is the *Large Sports Arena.* In April 1960, the statue of Lenin (sculptor—Matvei Manizer) that had been on view in the Soviet Pavilion at the World's Fair in Brussels, was erected in front of the stadium.

The 72 rows of seats of the grandstands have a total length of 25 miles and can hold 103,000 spectators. Eighty exits and nearly 50 stairways enable the grandstands to be cleared of spectators in less than 10 minutes.

Under the grandstands there are dressing

rooms; showers; rooms for judges, and referees; a track-and-field warm-up area; medical facilities; a post office; radio, TV, telegraph and telephone facilities; a sports museum and exhibition; training facilities for gymnastics, boxing, wrestling and various games; restaurants; two motion picture theatres; and a hotel for visiting athletes.

A 400-metre running track with automatic devices for registering results skirts the stadium's soccer field; there, too, you will find four grounds for athletic events.

The opening and closing ceremonies of the 6th World Youth and Student Festival, in July and August 1957, were held in the Large Sports Arena and the entire sports complex at Luzhniki was used for the 3rd International Student Games.

Beside the Large Arena there is an *open-air swimming pool* with grandstands seating 13,500, on one side, and a *Small Sports Arena* which seats 15,600, on the other. The small arena is used for volleyball and basketball games, fencing meets, boxing matches and weightlifting competitions in summer and hockey games and figure skating competitions in winter.

There is also a huge indoor *Sports Palace* near the Moskva River embankment; it is nearly 500 feet long and 300 feet wide and can hold over 17,000 spectators. The premises can be adapted for sports events, games and meets; concerts; youth balls; children's New Year's parties; meetings; and make a fine summer ice skating rink.

Next to the Sports Palace, right on the embankment, there is a Children's Stadium, with grandstands seating 3,000.

All in all, the Lenin Central Stadium has 19 gymnasiums and more than 90 open-air sports fields and grounds, soccer training fields, tennis courts and so forth.

Luzhniki takes up an area of 450 acres. More than half the territory is covered with lawns, flower beds, trees and shrubs. The Moskva River at this point is 820 feet wide.

New traffic arteries run to the Lenin

Novodevichy Convent

Black swans by Novodevichy Convent

Central Stadium and there are two subway stations with exits nearby: Sportivnaya and Leninskiye Gory. You can also get there by river boat.

Next to the *Sportivnaya* Metro Station there is a very attractive building among the tall new structures on Frunzensky Val in the vicinity of the Luzhniki sports complex. This is *Yunost Hotel,* with accommodation for 500.

Not far from Luzhniki, at the junction of the Okruzhnaya Railway Line embankment and the Moskva River, a well-proportioned belfry can be seen on the bank. Several stories high in the shape of octahedral prisms with columns at the corners, it has a very graceful appearance. This marks the site of the *Novodevichy Convent,* [1] founded in the first quarter of the 16th century, after Moscow Grand Duke Vasily III had returned Smolensk to Russia and vowed to build a new cloister. The bottom of the belfry is hidden behind thick red-brick walls with towers, which served to protect the convent and Moscow from enemy assault.

The Smolensky Cathedral at the convent is an historical monument of considerable artistic value. Outwardly it resembles Uspensky Cathedral in Moscow Kremlin. The interior is simple, yet majestic. Steps taken in Soviet times to clean the walls brought to light ancient, highly artistic murals on uniting the Russian lands, and also certain episodes from the personal life of Vasily III.

In the convent cemetery, you will find the graves of composers Alexander Scriabin and Sergei Taneyev; writers Nikolai Gogol and Anton Chekhov; singer Leonid Sobinov; actress Maria Yermolova; theatrical directors Konstantin Stanislavsky and Vladimir Nemirovich-Danchenko; artists Isaac Levitan and Valentin Serov; the Tretyakov brothers, Pavel and Sergei, who founded the gallery named after them in Moscow; sculptress Vera Mukhina; scientists Vladimir Komarov and Otto Schmidt; Soviet writers and poets, Vladimir Mayakovsky, Alexander Fadeyev among

---

1) The Novodevichy Convent is a branch of the History Museum.

them; heroes of the war against Hitler's Germany; many old Bolsheviks; famous military leaders; etc.

From the Novodevichy Convent you can get to the centre of town by Metro (Sportivnaya Station), motorbus or trolley-bus. But if time permits, the pleasantest way to get back is to board a river boat [1] and sail down the Moskva River, past picturesque Lenin Hills and Luzhniki, past Gorky Park, past the Kremlin, as far as the *Rossiya Hotel*.

---

1) The nearest wharf to board a river boat is close to the Children's Stadium at the Luzhniki sports centre.

TRETYAKOV ART GALLERY

THERE is a small street in Moscow which has nothing special as far as size and architecture are concerned but has something very precious to offer. The *Tretyakov Art Gallery*—the capital's priceless treasure-house of art—is located there, in *Lavrushinsky Pereulok* (by-street).

Vladimir Stasov, a prominent figure in the pre-revolutionary Russian cultural world, once wrote: "Whether a person comes to Moscow from Arkhangelsk or Astrakhan, from Crimea, Caucasus or Amur, he immediately sets the day and hour when he must go to a distant corner of Moscow, to Lavrushinsky Pereulok, to feast his eyes with delight, tender emotion and gratitude on that whole display of treasures which have been accumulated by this amazing person throughout his whole life." This "amazing person" was Pavel Tretyakov, after whom the gallery was named.

Many people who come to Moscow even for a short time consider the Tretyakov Art Gallery a "must." To be in the Soviet capi-

The Tretyakov Gallery. Icon by Rublyov: "The Trinity"

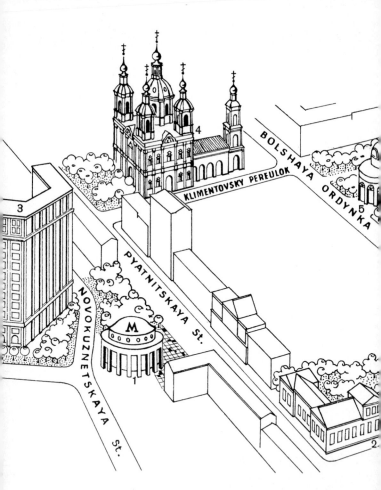

**FROM PYATNITSKAYA STREET
TO TRETYAKOV GALLERY**

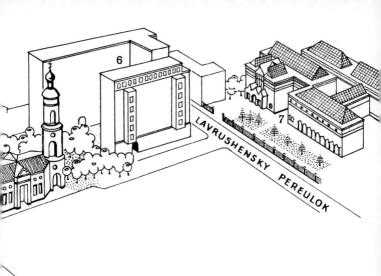

1. "Novokuznetskaya" Metro Station; 2. House where Lev
Tolstoi lived; 3. State Radio and Television Committee;
4. St. Kliment's Church; 5. Church of all the Pious; 6.
Writers' house; 7. Tretyakov Gallery.

tal and not go to the gallery is the same as being in Paris and not visiting the Louvre.

The best way to get to the Tretyakov Art Gallery is to take the Metro to *Novokuznetskaya Station,* which is on *Pyatnitskaya* Street. This street grew out of an old trade route at the beginning of the 15th century; in the 16th century the *Church of Praskovya Pyatnitsa* after which the street was named (in the 18th century) was built on the site of what is now the metro station.

On Pyatnitskaya Street there is still the modest one-story house where the great Russian writer Lev Tolstoi rented an apartment in the middle of the last century. At that time he had returned to Moscow after the famous defence of Sebastopol and was busy on his novel *The Cossacks* and other works. Not far from here, there is a two-story house (No. 6) which also bears a memorial plaque. That is where Soviet poet Vasily Lebedev-Kumach was born and lived. Songs written to his verses by composer Isaac Dunayevsky are very popular to this day.

Two former presidents of the USSR Academy of Sciences—Alexander Karpinsky, a prominent geologist, and Vladimir Komarov, a distinguished botanist—once lived at No. 33 Pyatnitskaya Street.

Near the entrance to the Novokuznetskaya Metro Station there is a new ten-story building faced with light-coloured slabs. For several years this has been the home of the *Committee on Radio and Television.* Soviet radio stations transmit in languages of the Soviet nationalities and over 50 foreign tongues.

If you go down Pyatnitskaya Street to the left of the subway station, you will see, on the corner of the first side street, one of the finest architectural monuments of mid-18th century Moscow. This is the *Church of St. Kliment,* after which the by-street on which it stands is named—*Klimentovsky Pereulok.* In 1612, at the fortifications that then stood there, the Russians gave battle to the Polish *szlachta* (nobility) invaders who tried to break through to the Kremlin. Reinforcements that arrived on the scene and also the bold attack of the detachment led by Kuzma Minin brought victory. At the decisive moment, he crossed the Moskva River and dealt the enemy a blow at Krymsky Bridge, now Krymsky Val (street). The routed troups of the foreign invaders beat a hasty retreat to positions beyond Vorobyevy Gory (now Lenin Hills) and then slunk off in the direction from which they had come, "much to their disgrace," as one eyewitness wrote.

A new square will be laid out in the near future on the broad expanse bounded by the Novokuznetskaya Metro Station, Radio House and St. Kliment's Church.

If you head for the Tretyakov Art Gallery along Klimentovsky Pereulok, you will come to a street running off to the left just beyond the church. This is *Ostrovsky Street,* where Alexander Ostrovsky (1823-1886) was born and lived in a small two-story wooden house (No. 9). Nearby, there is a public garden with a bronze bust of the great Russian playwright.

In his numerous dramas and comedies, Alexander Ostrovsky depicted the life and ways of the merchants, including the *Zamoskvorechye* [1] merchants he knew so well.

In Soviet times former mansions of merchants and manufacturers were turned over to kindergartens and nurseries, designing offices and medical institutions, music schools and pedagogical institutes, foreign embassies and art studios...

Klimentovsky Pereulok leads you to *Bolshaya Ordynka Street.* Long ago (beginning with the 14th century), a road ran along here from the Kremlin to the Tatar Golden Horde. Tatars settled in the vicinity and engaged in trade with the Russians. Next to them, interpreters took up residence, who acted as go-betweens in trade and diplomatic relations. This was reflected in the names of several by-streets, for example Bolshoi (Big) Tolmachevsky Pereulok *(tolmach* being the Russian for interpreter).

On the street of Bolshaya Ordynka there is an architectural monument: the *Church of All The Pious.* Its belfry was erected in the 1780's (architect—Vasily Bazhenov), and the church proper (architect—Osip Bove),

---

1) *Zamoskvorechye*—an old district of Moscow located on the right bank of the Moskva River, opposite the Kremlin.

St. Kliment's Church

later, in 1828-1833. The beautiful rotunda, with its columns and figured cast-iron floor, leaves a lasting impression.

Bolshaya Ordynka is a very pleasant street. Even in sweltering weather it is cool under the dense foliage of the Dutch lindens that were planted at the turn of the century. And with time it will become still more beautiful: considerably widened, straightened and lined with tall well-proportioned buildings. Only monuments of Russian architecture and several large old buldings will be reminiscent of the past.

This street will become part of a long thoroughfare that will cut across the city from north to south: from Ostankino to Warsaw Highway. Work on this major reconstruction job has already been completed in places.

A small, narrow lane connects Bolshaya Ordynka and Lavrushinsky Pereulok. At the end of it, at the corner of Bolshoi Tolmachevsky and Lavrushinsky, there stands a large apartment house that was built in the 1930's. It belongs to the Union of Soviet Writers. Anton Makarenko, Vsevolod Vishnevsky and Mikhail Prishvin used to live there. For ten years the prominent German poet and anti-fascist Johannes Bechler also lived there.

On the opposite side of Lavrushinsky Pereulok there is a low red and white brick building with a glass roof. It is the famous Tretyakov Art Gallery.

In 1856, Pavel Tretyakov acquired two pictures, one being *Seduction* by Nikolai Shilder. That was how he began building up this famous art collection, which occupied him for nearly 40 years, right up to his death.

In the early 1870's, Pavel Tretyakov together with his brother Sergei built a special gallery for the pictures. Twenty years later he bequeathed it to Moscow as a gift, as he wrote, "wishing to help organize useful institutions in the city so dear to me, to further the flourishing of art in Russia, and, at the same time, to preserve for all time the collection I have built up..."

The building was refaced at the beginning of the present century. This gave it the appearance of a Russian *terem* (tower) with a coloured-tile peaked roof. The facing of the main peak is embellished with the old emblem of Moscow: Georgy Pobedonosets (St. George) slaying a reptile with a lance. The façade was reconstructed and decorated according to sketches drawn by Victor Vasnetsov, the eminent Russian painter.

In 1918, Lenin signed a decree which transformed the Tretyakov Art Gallery from a city institution into a national gallery. In 1925, the pictures in the former Rumyantsev Museum and those in several private collections—paintings dating back to the 11th-17th centuries—were turned over to the gallery. Year after year the museum's collection has been replenished with items of Soviet fine art. During the Great Patriotic War (1941-1945), the gallery's art treasures were evacuated deep into the rear, but in the unforgettable days of victory in May 1945 the doors of the Tretyakov Art Gallery were once again thrown wide open to the public.

The first halls of the museum contain works of ancient Russian art. There is an unusually decorative mosaic here called *Dmitry Solunsky*. It comes from a Kiev monastery and denotes the high level of the pictorial art of Kievan Rus in the 11th and 12th centuries. Here, too, is the *Trinity* by Andrei Rublyov (15th century), a picture whose silhouetting and colour, completeness, harmony, and amazing perfection overwhelm you. Dionisy is another outstanding Moscow painter, who carried on the tradition of Rublyov (15th and early 16th century).

Then come examples of the art of Novgorod, Pskov and Moscow Rus. Here one is bound to pause before *The Miraculous Image of the Saviour* by Simon Ushakov, a distinguished painter of the second half of the 17th century.

In the section devoted to Russian art of the 18th century, we find that religious works have given way to paintings on non-ecclesiastical themes. The host of portraits is the distinctive feature here. And that is not accidental: portraiture was the principal genre in Russian painting in that period. Among the exhibits are canvases by Alexei Antropov (portraits of Peter III and Izmailova), Fyodor Rokotov *(Unknown Woman in Pink)*, Dmitry Levitsky *(Portrait of the Painter's Father,* and *Demidov)*, Fedot Shubin (sculptured portraits

Outside the Tretyakov Gallery

of Golitsin and Pavel I), and Vladimir Borovikovsky (portraits of Lopukhin and Kurakin).

The section on painting of the first half of the 19th century includes portraits by Orest Kiprensky. Also on display are masterpieces by Karl Bryullov—the portraits of Kryiov and Kukolnik, *The Horsewoman*, and a *Self-portrait*.

Alexander Ivanov dedicated over 20 years, nearly the whole of his creative life, to painting the canvas *Christ Appears Before the People*. There are always many art lovers around it.

Pavel Fedotov's creative life was cut short, but he left a great imprint on Russian art with his profoundly realistic genre painting. "My work in the studio is only a fraction, a tenth of my creative activity," the artist wrote about himself. "Most of it occurs in the streets and in other people's homes. Life is my teacher. I work with both eyes open, my subjects are scattered all over the city and I must find them myself." That is how his canvases *The Major's Match-Making, An Aristocrat's Breakfast, A New Cavalier, Encore, Encore!* and *The Pretty Young Widow*, among others, came into being.

The year 1871 saw the opening of the first exhibition organized by the Association of Mobile Art Shows. The painters belonging to this association were called *Peredvizhniki* (from the Russian word for Mobile Art Shows). Ivan Kramskoi and Vasily Serov headed the *Peredvizhniki*. The *Peredvizhniki* were united by progressive democratic ideas; they expressed the thoughts and feelings of the people and championed realistic national art. Ivan Kramskoi called art divorced from the interests of the people "an empty pastime, the amusement to empty people and parasites." The association of *Peredvizhniki* functioned for half a century.

The pictures of the Peredvizhniki are the museum's most precious possession, which most vividly express the national singularity of Russian painting, the force of its profound realism.

We'll mention a few of the canvases, although it is exceedingly difficult to single out any particular ones from this valuable collection.

Vasily Perov's canvas *At the Last Pub* is

in keeping with the verses of the great Russian poet Nikolai Nekrasov (1821-1877), full of pity for downtrodden, ragged Russia of that time. Other pictures by the painter, too, arouse wrath and protest against a society based on exploitation, poverty and suffering. A lasting impression is left by his *Troika*—three exhausted children dragging uphill a sled with a large ice-covered barrel—, his *Drowned Woman* and *Funeral of a Peasant.*

Ilya Repin was a shining light in Russian painting. He meant to Russian fine arts what Lev Tolstoi meant to literature, and Pyotr Tchaikovsky, to music. His *Barge Haulers on the Volga, Zaporozhye Cossacks, Sending Off a Recruit, Refusal to Confess, Arrest of a Propagandist, Not Expected, Religious Procession in Kursk Province* are all precious pages in the book of Russian fine art. A staggering canvas is *Ivan the Terrible and His Son Ivan, November 16, 1581,* painted by Repin on a historical theme but bound up with the realities of his time. Created under the profound impression left by the assassination of Alexander II by the *narodovoltsy,* [1] the showing of this picture was forbidden "by imperial decree." He also created a wonderful gallery of portraits, among them pictures of Modest Moussorgsky, Nikolai Pirogov, Vladimir Stasov, and Lev Tolstoi.

The museum's exhibits include canvases by Vasily Surikov, a master of historical painting. His works breathe of the heroic, the monumental and the tragic. He created epic pictures of profound content. Among them are his *Morning of the Execution of the Streltsy, Boyarynya Morozova* and *Menchikov in Beryozovo.*

"Serov's art is like a rare gem," said Ilya Repin about the work of his pupil. "The more intently you examine it, the more you feel the depths of its charm." Valentin Serov created marvellous landscapes, genre and historical pictures, and book illustrations. But he was first and foremost a portrait painter. His *Girl With Peaches, Lass in the Sunlight,* and portraits of Maria Yermolova, Fyodor Shalyapin, Maxim Gorky, Anton Che-

"Girls on the Volga" by Petrov-Vodkin, Tretyakov Gallery ▶

---

1) *Narodovoltsy*—Members of "Narodnaya Volya" (People's Will) secret revolutionary organization.

216

khov, Alexander Glazunov, Isaac Levitan and others amaze art lovers to this day.

Russian nature is reflected in the inimitable landscapes of Ivan Shishkin, Alexei Savrasov, Arkhip Kuindji, Ivan Aivazovsky and other painters. A special place among them is occupied by Isaac Levitan, that subtle poet of the brush, who had an original way of conveying the lyrical charm of nature in central Russia.

The Tretyakov Art Gallery also has on display many of the finest works by Soviet painters.

It also has on display works by Russian and Soviet sculptors: Vladimir Beklemishev, Ivan Martos, Sergei Volnukhin, Anna Golubkina, Mark Antokolsky, Nikolai Andreyev, Sergei Merkurov, Matvei Manizer, Vera Mukhina, Sergei Konenkov, Stepan Erzi and others.

When Pavel Tretyakov bequeathed his gallery to Moscow, there were 1,200 pictures and 500 drawings in it; some 8,000 persons visited it during the first year after it was opened. From 1927-1935 an annex with 16 more halls (architect—Alexei Shchusev) was added to the original building, which almost doubled the exhibition space. Today the Tretyakov Art Gallery has over 5,000 canvases, more than 3,000 works of ancient Russian art, 900 sculptures, and upwards of 30,000 drawings and engravings. In 1931, it was visited by 400,000 persons, and in 1965, by 1,340,000.

Interest in this treasure-house of Russian culture is mounting from year to year and the present premises cannot handle the growing stream of art lovers. The Soviet Government has therefore decided to provide more spacious premises for this precious collection. The new home of the Tretyakov Art Gallery is now going up on the Krymskaya Embankment opposite the main entrance to Gorky Central Recreation Park.

In the Tretyakov Art Gallery

EXCURSION **9** STARTING POINT:
DZERZHINSKAYA
METRO STATION

DZERZHINSKY SQUARE

YOU step out of the subway station into
a square of the same name. It is very
easy to recognize from the statue that
stands in the centre, a 12-metre bronze monument (sculptor—Yevgeny Vuchetich; architect—Grigory Zakharov), unveiled in 1958, to
Felix Dzerzhinsky, one of Lenin's closest
comrades-in-arms and head of the All-
Russia Extraordinary Commission for Re-
pression of the Counter-Revolution and
Sabotage. Established for the purpose of
protecting the state security of the young
Soviet Republic, this Commission was also
made responsible for looking after the home-
less children who had lost their parents
during the October Socialist Revolution and
the subsequent Civil War. Special schools
were opened for these children, where they
received an education and developed work
habits. All received a start in life: some
became industrial experts in various fields

Monument to the
heroes of Plevna

220

221

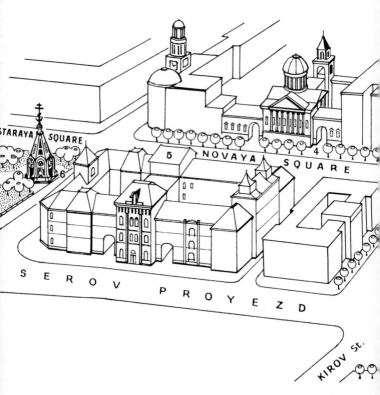

STARAYA SQUARE

6

5 NOVAYA SQUARE 4

S E R O V P R O Y E Z D

KIROV St.

DZERZHINSKY AND NOVAYA SQUARES

222

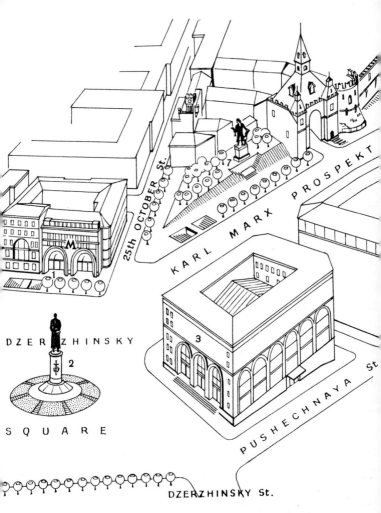

1. "Dzerzhinskaya" Metro Station; 2. Memorial to Felix Dzerzhinsky; 3. "Children's World" Department Store; 4. Museum of the History and Reconstruction of Moscow; 5. Politechnical Museum; 6. Monument to Grenadiers who fell in battle at Plevna; 7. Memorial to Ivan Fyodorov.

and went to work in factories and plants; others became prominent scientists, actors, military men, and so forth. In the last years of his life (he died in 1926), Felix Dzerzhinsky did much to build the young Soviet industry.

Nine streets diverge from the square, making a complicated traffic problem. Cars have to go around the traffic circle with the statue in the centre.

Many outstanding events in Russian history are bound up with Dzerzhinsky Square *(Ploshchad Dzerzhinskogo)*. In the year 1612, for instance, there was fierce fighting in the vicinity of 25th of October Street between invading forces of the Polish *szlachta* (nobility) and the people's volunteer corps led by Kuzma Minin and Dmitry Pozharsky, to whom there is a monument on Red Square.

In the 17th century a settlement of the *streltsy* with wooden huts and small yards occupied the site of the present square. The wooden Church of Feodosy stood on the northern side. In 1662, what was then referred to as "a provocative letter" was hung out on its fence. This was a proclamation exposing the abuses committed by persons in attendance on Tsar Alexei (father of Peter I). High food prices and intensified speculation with copper coins roused the resentment of the poor people of Moscow. After the proclamation was read to a public gathering, the throng set off for the village of Kolomenskoye, where the tsar was staying at the time. That was how the "copper riot" began, which was savagely repressed by Tsar Alexei, described at the time as "a most quiet person." The leaders of the riot were executed at the Church of Feodosy.

Meetings were held on this square in the October days of 1905, the year of the first Russian Revolution, and on October 20, an impressive, 200,000-strong procession, a real political demonstration, filed through, following the coffin of Nikolai Bauman, a prominent revolutionary, who was killed by agents of the tsarist police. The square was the scene of fighting in October 1917 and was the place from which revolutionary detachments launched an attack on the Kremlin through Nikolskaya Street (now 25th of

October Street) and Tatralny Proyezd (today Karl Marx Prospekt).

Start your stroll around the square at the subway station; it was opened in 1935, when trains began to run on the first line, between Sokolniki and Gorky Park. To the left, Karl Marx Prospekt descends to Sverdlov Square. At the beginning of this avenue there is a huge new building (architect—Alexei Dushkin). This is *Detsky Mir* (Children's World), the largest department store exclusively for tiny tots, and the younger generation in general, here or anywhere in the world for that matter. The store caters to a quarter of a million customers a day.

In bygone days (in the 15th-18th centuries), the place where the Detsky Mir now stands was the site of the Moscow *Pushechny Dvor* (Cannon Works), a state factory where cannon and bells were manufactured. It was here that Alexei Chokhov in the 1580's cast the bronze Tsar Cannon now on display in the Kremlin. Pushechnaya Street, on the northern side of Detsky Mir, was named after this factory.

By following Dzerzhinsky Street, and then its continuations—Sretenka and Prospekt Mira (Peace Avenue), you can get to Riga Railway Terminal, the National Economic Achievements Exhibition, the Ostankino Palace-Museum of Serf Art, and the Botanical Gardens of the USSR Academy of Sciences.

A large edifice that was erected at the end of the last century stands on the corner of Dzerzhinsky Street and Dzerzhinsky Square, directly opposite the subway station. That is where the *All-Russia Extraordinary Commission* headed by Felix Dzerzhinsky functioned in the first years of Soviet government. An annex was added on the right side some twenty years ago, which can easily be distinguished from the original structure. This new wing faces the already mapped route of a new avenue that will join the centre of town with Komsomol Square. Meanwhile, narrow winding Kirov Street leads to this square with three railway terminals - the Leningrad, Yaroslavl and Kazan stations. On the right side of Kirov Street, a few steps from Dzerzhinsky Square, you will find one

"Detsky Mir" department store ▶

of Moscow's biggest book stores, and the *Main Post Office* is further up the road.

To the right of Kirov Street there is a street called Proyezd Serova, named in memory of a Soviet flyer, a Hero of the Soviet Union. In the second house on the left (No.3) Vladimir Mayakovsky had his study from 1919 through 1930. That is where the famous Soviet poet wrote *Khorosho* (Good), *Vladimir Ilyich Lenin* and other works. Now, you have made the round of Dzerzhinsky Square and the streets running off it. To the south of Dzerzhinsky Square (i.e., to the right of the subway station as you stand facing the square) there is Novaya Square. The best place to take it all in at a glance is the upper floors of Detsky Mir. From here you get a good view of its strictly rectangular contours. And in the distance, a light-coloured monumental edifice towers around the surroundings. This is a tall apartment house on the Kotelnicheskaya Embankment, which stands at the confluence of the Yauza and Moskva Rivers.

And now let us have a closer look at Novaya Square.

A two-story red building with white columns and a cupola attracts your attention on the right side. This used to be the Church of "Ioann Bogoslov Who Lived under the Elms." The name indicates that several centuries ago there was a dense wood in the place where the Novaya (New) and Staraya (old) Squares are situated. A museum of the city's municipal economy was opened in this building in 1896, and in 1940 the *Museum of History and Reconstruction of Moscow* was opened there. Objects of material culture, pictures, sculptures, photographs, scale-models, diagrams, plans and other exhibits tell the visitor about the most important stages in the history of the Soviet capital, about its reconstruction and the prospects for further development.

The opposite side of the square is almost entirely taken up by the building of the *Polytechnic Museum*. In the central section (architect—Ippolite Moniguetti; erected in 1877) and the right-hand section (architect—Shokhin; erected in 1896), extensive use was made of motifs of New Byzantine and ancient Russian architecture, Russian embroidery and wood carving to decorate the façades; the left-hand section (architects—Voeikov and Yeramezhantsev; erected in 1907) is in modern style. The Polytechnic Museum was founded after the Polytechnic Exhibition of 1872. It is interesting to note that Pyotr Tchaikovsky specially wrote a cantata for the beginning of the exhibition glorifying the titanic and heroic labour of the Russian people.

Many of the exhibits trace the development of Russian and Soviet engineering and technology from the first steam engine of Ivan Polsunov to the most complex modern machines and assemblies. Many displays can be seen in operation. The museum acquaints the visitor with the latest machinery and the fundamentals of modern production, and promotes the introduction of advanced methods into industry.

It will shortly be possible to descend directly from the museum's mining section into a pit, where the visitor will see a coal and ore face, modern automatic equipment in use and become familiar with the working conditions of miners.

Meetings and gatherings were held in the museum's auditoriums during the first years of Soviet government. Still earlier, on October 25 (November 7), 1917, a meeting of the Soviets of Workers' and Soldiers' Deputies held in this building elected the Moscow Military Revolutionary Committee— the military body for directing the armed insurrection in the city.

On March 12, 1918, the second day after the Soviet Government moved from Petrograd to Moscow, at the meeting of the Moscow Soviet in the museum's large auditorium Vladimir Lenin made his first public address to the capital's working people after the revolution. Subsequently, Lenin made three more speeches in the building.

The building is also the headquarters of the *All-Union Znaniye* (Knowledge) *Society* with its large and small lecture halls and a demonstration hall. As a matter of fact, the museum is run by this society, which disseminates political and scientific knowledge throughout the country.

The *Central Polytechnic Library* is also

Dzerzhinsky Square

housed in this building. A treasure house of technical knowledge, founded a hundred years ago by Dmitry Mendeleyev, Dmitry Anuchin and other distinguished scientists, it possesses three million volumes in 22 different languages. An average of 1,500 persons visit it daily.

Here, too, you will find the *All-Union Technical Patent Library* and the *Young Technicians Club.*

If you walk ahead to the far end of this building, where the Znaniye Publishing House has its premises, a wide, old boulevard opens up before you, beginning with a stone monument in the form of a chapel decorated with zinc bas-reliefs. It was erected in 1887 (designer—Vladimir Sherwood) to commemorate the heroic deeds of the Russian grenadiers who fell in battle near Plevna during the Russian-Turkish War of 1877-1878, which liberated Bulgaria from the Turkish yoke. The funds for the monument were contributed by fellow-soldiers of those who lost their lives.

Near the boulevard, on the corner of Proyezd Serova (where it runs behind the Polytechnic Museum) and Bogdan Khmelnitsky [1] Street there is the building of the *Central Committee of the All-Union Leninist Young Communist League.*

A long and narrow square descends to the right of the boulevard, parallel to it. This is Staraya (Old) Square. Several large buildings, erected at the beginning of the present century, are noticeable on the right side. They house the *Central Committee of the Communist Party of the Soviet Union* and the *Moscow Regional* and *Moscow City Committees of the CPSU.* A red flag is always flying above one of them.

---

1) Bogdan Khmelnitsky was a Ukrainian hetman who headed the struggle for the liberation of the Ukraine from Polish rule and its reunification with Russia in 1654.

MANEGE SQUARE

T HIS station has two exits: the one leading
to Sverdlov Square and Pushkin Street
and the other under the *Moskva Hotel*
to Gorky Street and Karl Marx Prospekt,
which is immediately to the right as you
leave the subway. It is a wide avenue lined
with full-grown linden trees, which stretches
from Dzerzhinsky Square to Frunze Street.
The section between Sverdlov Square and
Manège Square *(Manezhnaya Ploshchad)*
was called *Okhotny Ryad* (Hunter's Row)
not so long ago. The name comes from the
old days, when there used to be rows of
wooden stalls doing a lively business in game
and other food. Later buildings were erected
there with shops, trading in meat, fish,
greens, eggs, live and butchered fowl on the
first floors and taverns, tea-rooms, and beer-
parlors on the second floors.

Alexandrovsky Gardens

The only thing that has remained here from Old Moscow is the present *Dom Soyuzov* (Trade Union House), one of the most outstanding examples of 18th century Russian architecture (architect—Matvei Kazakov). Trade Union House is famous for its *Hall of Columns* with a colonnade of artificial white marble. A gallery runs around the entire auditorium and there are huge sparkling cutglass chandeliers hanging between each pair of columns.

Before the revolution, the building belonged to the Noblemen's Club. The Hall of Columns was then the scene of social gatherings, receptions, charity soirées, concerts and balls. In 1919, the building was turned over to the country's trade unions. Vladimir Lenin made more than 40 speeches in this building from 1918 to 1922.

Endless streams of working people converged on the Trade Union House in those mournful days of January 1924. It was bitter cold. Bonfires were burning on the streets and squares. Day and night, hundreds of thousands of Muscovites and delegates from all parts of the Soviet Union and abroad filed past Lenin's body lying in state in the Hall of Columns to pay their last respects to this great man.

The Hall of Columns is used today for congresses, conferences and meetings of trade unions and other public organizations. It is also a fine concert hall. During the winter college and school vacations, students and schoolchildren take over the hall for New Year balls and parties, which have become a tradition.

The rest of the block, from the Trade Union House to Gorky Street, is occupied by a large building faced with light-coloured stone. This is the building of the *USSR Council of Ministers* (architect—Abram Langman). Across the street there is the Moskva Hotel (architects—Alexei Shchusev and others). Both these buildings were erected three decades ago, when the master plan for the reconstruction of Moscow began.

Karl Marx Prospekt links up with *Manège Square.* The building on the corner of the square and Gorky Street is the *National Hotel.*

Karl Marx Prospekt Manège Square

1. "Prospekt Marksa" Metro Station; 2. Trade Union House; 3. Building of the USSR Council of Ministers; 4. "Moskva" Hotel; 5. "National" Hotel; 6. Intourist Office; 7. Moscow State University, Old Building (architect —Matvei Kazakov); 8. Moscow State University, Old building (Konstantin Bykovsky); 9. Mikhail Lomonosov Monument; 10. Central Exhibition Hall; 11. Reception Room of the Presidium of the USSR Supreme Soviet and the Presidium of the RSFR Supreme Soviet; 12. Obelisk to Revolutionary Thinkers; 13. Mikhail Glinka Museum of Music.

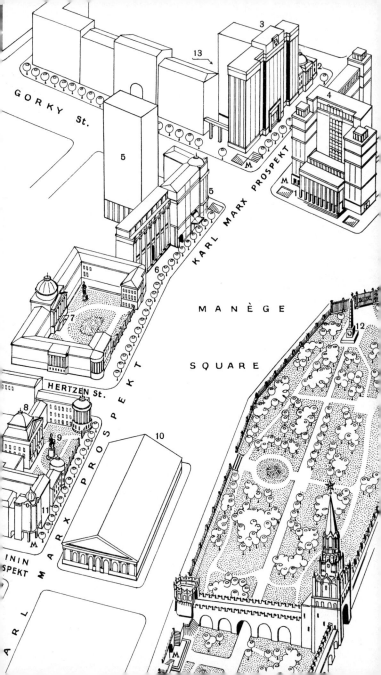

GORKY St.

13

3

2

4

5

KARL MARX PROSPEKT

M

5

6

1

M

MANÈGE

7

SQUARE

12

HERTZEN St.

8

9

KARL MARX PROSPEKT

10

11

M

ININ
SPEKT

RL M A R X

Lenin lived for several weeks in suite 107 after the Soviet Government moved from Petrograd to Moscow on March 11, 1918.

Anatole France, Herbert Wells, John Reed, Henri Barbusse, Martin Andersen-Nexö and other eminent writers abroad stopped at the hotel when visiting Moscow.

The *National Hotel* directly faces the Manège Square.

Manège Square is one of the most recent of the city's central squares, and is also one of the most beautiful. The removal of the drab, congested buildings opened up to view the wonderful group of early 19th-century Russian classical style structures and the radically reconstructed and renovated thoroughfares in the centre of town.

And now let us have a closer look at Manège Square.

Next to *National Hotel* there is a large yellow building, erected in 1934 (architect—Ivan Zheltovsky). The edifice has been executed in Italian Renaissance style: there is an ornate façade with columns crowned by huge capitals of the Corinthian order. It was reconstructed several years ago and now houses the Foreign Tourism Department under the USSR Council of Ministers and the Soviet Travel Agency *Intourist*.

A bit farther down the street you come to the old home of *Moscow State University*, which was built at the end of the 18th century (architect—Matvei Kazakov). All the floors, the assembly hall and the adjacent library and museum were destroyed by the fire of 1812, when Napoleon's troops entered Moscow. In 1819 Domenico Gilardi restored the building, making several modifications in the process.

The university was opened in the spring of 1755. At the outset, it occupied a small two-story building that stood on the site of the present Historical Museum. This first Russian university was founded by the brilliant Russian scientist Mikhail Lomonosov. In Soviet times the university was rightly named after its great founder. Alexander Pushkin said of Mikhail Lomonosov: "He established our first university. To put it better, he himself was our first university." These words by the Russian poet emphasize the extraordinary, unusual abilities of Mikhail Lomonosov, his amazing versatility: he made a great contribution to physics and chemistry, mathematics and astronomy, geology and geography.

On the university grounds, near the wings of the main building, there are statues of two eminent writers and active fighters against tsarism, Alexander Hertzen and Nikolai Ogarev, which were unveiled in 1922 (sculptor—Andreyev).

A second university building (house number 20), built in the second half of the last century stands on the opposite side of Hertzen Street *(Ulitsa Gertsena)* which runs off from Manège Square to the right. The colonnade of a semi-circular rotunda that terminates the protruding corner of this building combines the university and the former Manège, as it were, into a single harmonious architectural group.

Four hundred years ago, the Palace of Ivan the Terrible *(Oprichny Dvor)* was located on the site of the present building N⁰ 20. It consisted of wooden structures surrounded by a high stone wall with solid gates. The courtyard was covered with more than 8 inches of white sand, brought from Vorobyevy (now Lenin) Hills. This sand provided the clue to the exact location of the palace during construction work on the first line of the Metro in 1934. Six years after the palace was erected, it was burned down by the Crimean Tatars, but soon after was rebuilt from the bottom up.

The university building was damaged by a bomb in 1941 (during a Nazi air raid) but two years later was restored. A new, bronze statue of Mikhail Lomonosov (sculptor—Iosif Kozlovsky) was erected in front of the Moscow University building in 1957 to replace the one smashed by the bomb.

After the revolution, the university expanded to a point where it became too crowded, and a huge university complex consisting of many buildings was erected on Lenin Hills. Only the humanities departments temporarily remained in the old premises.

If you walk up Hertzen Street some 300 yards you will come to a building on the left side with an attractive portico. This is the *Moscow State Conservatoire* named after

Pyotr Tchaikovsky. The monument in front to the great Russian composer was erected in 1954 (architects—Vera Mukhina and others). Around it rustle the leaves of birch trees—the symbol of Russian nature, which the composer glorified so lovingly in his works.

Pyotr Tchaikovsky's name is bound up inseparably with the Moscow Conservatoire founded a hundred years ago. He was invited to teach there by its founder, Nikolai Rubinstein, brother of Anton Rubinstein, the eminent pianist and composer. Tchaikovsky was a professor at the Conservatoire for 12 years. It was here that he began his creative work and displayed his talent to the full. His Symphony No.4 and his opera *Eugene Onegin,* which were written in Moscow, were performed for the first time by Conservatoire students.

The Conservatoire's Grand Hall is one of the capital's finest concert halls. Symphony and chamber music concerts featuring the finest Soviet and foreign orchestras and soloists are held there.

The Moscow Conservatoire is the principal Soviet music educational centre. Its five departments train composers, specialists in the history and theory of music, teachers, conductors, vocalists, pianists and performers on instruments. Its gold medalists include Antonin Nezhdanova, Sergei Taneyev, Sergei Rakhmaninov, Alexander Scriabin, Reinhold Gliere, Konstantin Igumnov, Alexander Gedike, Alexander Goldenweiser and many other splendid musicians whose names are engraved in gold on honorary marble tablets at the entrance to the Conservatoire's Small Hall.

A large yellow building with 80 massive white columns faces Manège Square. This is the *Central Exhibition Hall,* the largest hall of its kind in the Soviet capital, formerly the Manège (Riding Academy). It was built in the first quarter of the 19th century (architect—Augustin Betancourt; decor—Osip Bove) as an architectural monument to commemorate Russia's victory over Napoleon's troops in the Patriotic War of 1812. A unique structural feature of the Manège are the 147-foot wall-to-wall wooden girders that hold up the roof without intermediate supports.

Guard of honour at the Tomb of the Unknown Soldier in the Alexandrovsky Gardens

The hall is nearly 500 feet long. Contemporaries maintained that "there was nothing in Europe to equal the Manège in size, architecture and construction of the roof."

More than 100 years ago a big concert was held in the Manège. It featured Hector Berlioz, the famous French composer, conducting an orchestra and choir of 700. They were enthusiastically applauded by an audience of 12,000. "I simply didn't know what to do with myself," Berlioz wrote from Moscow. "It is the biggest impression I have ever made in all my life." The celebrated French musician maintained his ties with Russia after his first trip to Moscow up to his very death.

The Manège was restored and fundamentally re-equipped in the summer and autumn of 1957. Its unique wooden girders, holding up the ceiling, were thoroughly repaired: resting on metal supports, which had been installed previously, they were then finished off with a special material. On November 5, 1957, this remarkable piece of architecture began a new period in its life with an All-Union Art Show.

In between exhibitions, the premises of the former Manège are used for youth balls, dances and concerts. Manège Square is especially lively on holidays. Improvised stages are erected for performances by orchestras, choirs, musical ensembles, soloists and elocutionists, and films are shown. At such times, the square is full of people, young people for the most part, full of life, dancing and singing. And on weekdays too, there are always young people on the square from morning until evening, some going to the Lenin Library, others to the university, and still others to the Conservatoire, the Exhibition Hall, the Kremlin with its museums, the theatre...

On the corner of Karl Marx and Kalinin Prospekts opposite the Central Exhibition Hall, in building n" 22/4, there are the reception rooms of the Presidium of the USSR Supreme Soviet and the Presidium of the Supreme Soviet of the RSFSR.

A narrow thoroughfare runs along the other side of Exhibition Hall, and beyond it, at the foot of the Kremlin wall, there is the *Alexandrovsky Gardens,* or more exactly three gardens: the Upper, Middle and Lower, landscaped more than 146 years ago by Osip Bove. Before that, the Neglinka River flowed there (it was enclosed in a subterranean conduit).

When the first line of the Moscow Metro was being built in the 1930's, the old channel of the Neglinka was discovered on the territory of the Alexandrovsky Gardens. It was found that the original river bed lay 36 feet below the present surface. Such is the development of a big city radically changing the surrounding landscape.

An obelisk in the shape of a tall tetrahedron of light-grey stone has been erected in the Alexandrovsky Gardens, close to the main entrance on the spot where a monument commemorating the 300th anniversary of the House of Romanov (1613-1913) used to be.

In 1918 this monument was reconstructed and a long list of names was engraved on the side of the obelisk facing Revolution Square: Marx, Engels, Liebknecht, Lassalle, Bebel, Campanella, Mélier, Winstanley, Moore, Saint-Simon, Fourier, Jaurès, Proudhon, Bakunin, Chervshevsky, Lavrov, Mikhailovsky and Plekhanov.

That was the first monument of the victorious revolution to great revolutionaries and thinkers. Vladimir Lenin personally drew up the list of names.

The Monument to an Unknown Soldier has been erected not far from here, by the Arsenal Tower, to immortalize the nameless heroes of World War II. In early December 1966 (at the time of the 25th anniversary of the rout of the Nazi Armies near Moscow) the remains of an unknown soldier killed in the Battle of Moscow were buried on the spot, close by the Kremlin Wall.

The Alexandrovsky Gardens with a canopy of branching age-old lime trees, the smooth emerald green lawns, the aroma of the flower beds, which repeatedly change their array from early spring until late autumn, the coolness and quiet so unusual right next to the city's busiest thoroughfares—all this and, of course, the close proximity to the Kremlin, makes the Alexandrovsky Gardens an attractive spot for Muscovites and tourists at any time of the year and day.

Van Cliburn in the Great Hall of Moscow Conservatoire ▶

Hotel "Moskva"

KALININ PROSPEKT, ARBATSKAYA SQUARE

THIS is a major Metro hub at the *Lenin Library*, the country's largest library. It is the point of junction of two subway lines—one running from Sokolniki to the South-West, and the other from Shchelkovskaya to the Kiev Railway Terminal. It is also the starting point of another line—the one to Kuntsevo. Three stations—*Kalininskaya*, *Arbatskaya* and *Biblioteka Lenina*—converge here.

As you step out of the Karl Marx Prospekt exit of the *Biblioteka Lenina* Metro Station, to your right you will see one of the finest

*Reading-room of
the Lenin Library*

KARL MARX PROSPEKT
KALININ PROSPEKT

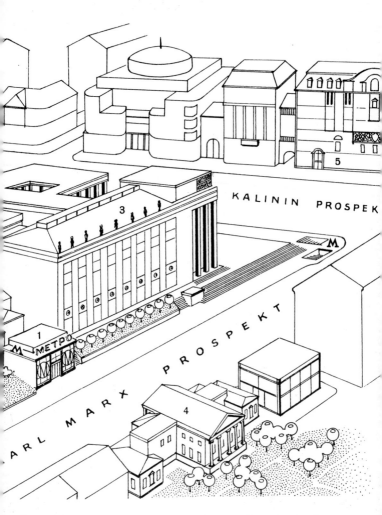

1. "Biblioteka Lenina" Metro Station; 2. V.I. Lenin Library, former "Pashkov House"; 3. V.I. Lenin Library, new building; 4. M.I. Kalinin Museum; 5. House where Maxim Gorky lived; 6. Union of Soviet Societies for Friendship and Cultural Relations with Foreign Countries; 7. House of Friendship with the Peoples of Foreign Countries; 8. Alexei Shchusev Museum of Architecture.

examples of Russian 18th century architecture—the former Pashkov's Mansion.

This edifice, erected in 1784-1786 (architect—Vasily Bazhenov), consists of a three-story central structure connected by galleries with two wings. Resting on a high basis, the central structure is adorned with columns, statues, vases, and stucco mouldings in the shape of wreaths and garlands. It is crowned by a rotunda with a circular colonnade, which is visible from many parts of the city. The Moscow Public Rumyantsev Museum was founded there in 1862, with many valuable exhibits such as manuscripts, paintings, and archaeological and mineralogical collections, among others. There was a library attached to it with a reading room which Lenin used in 1893 and 1897. Many distinguished writers, scientists and artists used the library too, among them Lev Tolstoi, Fyodor Dostoyevsky, Anton Chekhov, Dmitri Mendeleyev, Climenty Timiryazev and the historian Vasily Klyuchevsky.

In 1924, the library began to be called the Lenin Russian Public Library, and the following year received the present name.

To the left of the subway exit from which you have emerged there is a light-grey building with tall black-marble-faced columns. Statues of great scientists, writers and thinkers stand in niches in the walls, including Archimedes, Nicolaus Copernicus, Galileo Galilei, Isaac Newton, Mikhail Lomonosov, Charles Darwin, Ivan Pavlov, Alexander Pushkin, Nikolai Gogol, Ivan Turgenev, Maxim Gorky, and Vladimir Mayakovsky. Engraved over the main entrance in large letters of gold is the inscription: "Lenin State Library of the USSR." This is the library's new home (architects—Vladimir Shchuko and Vladimir Gelfreikh), with reading rooms and service premises.

A tall building can be seen towering up behind it. This is the library's book depository, where the air is kept at the required temperature and humidity. An automotic electrified book carrier has been installed under the library building and there are special vertical carriers. The library has more than 210 miles of book shelves, containing over 24 million volumes. There you will find a complete collection of Russian books, beginning with manuscripts of ancient Rus. There are also many unique editions in the extensive foreign literature department. The manuscript department possesses priceless monuments in Russian, Slavic, West European and Oriental languages. The library's stocks include works in 160 different languages. As many as 10,000 persons use its 22 well-equipped reading rooms daily.

Lenin Library's interlibrary loan service caters to some five thousand libraries in the country. It also participates actively in international book exchanges.

On the other side of the street, opposite the subway station from which you emerged, you will see a one-story building with columns. This is the *Kalinin Museum*. Its 14 halls contain numerous photographs, paintings, manuscripts, books, newspapers, pamphlets, statues, personal belongings and other exhibits concerning the life and work of the "nation's elder," Mikhail Ivanovich Kalinin, who held the country's top post of Chairman of the All-Russia Central Executive Committee, and then Chairman of the Presidium of the Supreme Soviet of the USSR for nearly 30 years.

More than ten years have elapsed since the museum was opened, and to this day those who knew him—workers, farmers and old Bolsheviks—continue to send in their reminiscences of Mikhail Kalinin and documents and photographs connected with his life and work.

Kalinin's name has been given to the thoroughfare that begins at the Central Exhibition Hall and the new building of the Lenin Library.

In 1905, Maxim Gorky lived in the first house on the right-hand side of Kalinin Prospekt. At that time, he came out in support of the Bolsheviks, secured appreciable funds for Party work, took a hand in organizing a publishing house for the diffusion of Marxist books and pamphlets, wrote proclamations and arranged for printing equipment. His apartment was a hiding place for weapons and revolutionary literature; and people engaged in underground

The Lenin Library ▶

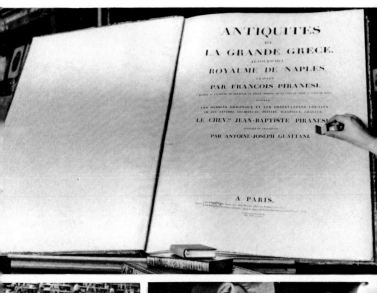

activity came there to obtain important informations.

In the next house on the same side of the avenue, Konstantin Stanislavsky directed the productions of the Society of Art and Literature in the 1890's. Following the foundation of the Moscow Art Theatre, rehearsals were held there for a while. It was at one of these rehearsals that Anton Chekhov met the company for the first time.

The first street to the right of the avenue is named Granovsky Street, after Timofei Granovsky (1813-1855), a professor of general history at Moscow University.

Continuing your stroll down the right-hand side of Kalinin Prospekt, just past Granovsky Street, you come to one of the capital's big department stores (erected in 1913).

Then, on the third block, hidden by a small garden with a fountain, there is a house that most visitors from abroad like to visit. It is the premises of the *Union of Soviet Societies for Friendship and Cultural Relations with Foreign Countries*, established in February 1958. It unites dozens of societies, associations and institutes of friendship and cultural relations with individual countries and groups of countries—more than 120 countries all in all. Thousands of enterprises, offices, collective and state farms, scientific organizations and educational establishments are collective members of these friendship societies and associations.

Further up the block, closer to Arbatskaya Square *(Arbatskaya Ploshchad)* the building at No. 16 Kalinin Prospekt is quite different in architecture from any of its surroundings. It was built at the end of the last century for manufacturer Morozov by architect Mazyrin, who drew on the Moorish and Spanish styles of architecture and decoration.

The *House of Friendship with the Peoples of Foreign Countries,* associated with the Union of Soviet Societies for Friendship and Cultural Relations with Foreign Countries was opened here in the spring of 1959. In connection with the 10th anniversary of the world peace movement, the World Peace Council awarded the personnel of Friendship House a diploma for its "outstanding con-

The old building of the Lenin library (Pashkov's House)

tribution to the cause of strengthening peace and friendship among peoples."

And indeed, in just five years of activity, Friendship House played host to more than 850,000 Muscovites, who took part in gala affairs and meetings commemorating jubilees and other important dates in the life of peoples of various countries. Peoples in arts and sciences, cultural workers, people of good will, fighters for peace, participants in "friendship trains," rank-and-file tourists —all receive a cordial welcome within the walls of Friendship House.

The building at 5 Kalinin Prospekt is also noteworthy. Originally conceived as a two-story structure (architect—Matvei Kazakov) when it was erected in the 1780's, a super-structure was added a century later. Following extensive restorations, which returned the edifice to its former appearance both outside and inside, it was turned over to the *Alexei Shchusev State Architectural Research Museum*. This museum reflects the development of Russian architecture from the 11th century right up to the present. A special hall is devoted to the work of Shchusev.

One of the buildings nearby this museum on the left-hand side of the avenue is occupied by the *Committee of the USSR Council of Ministers for Cultural Relations with Foreign Countries*.

A little farther on there is Arbatskaya Square

The House of Friendship with the Peoples of Foreign Countries

ARBAT

THERE are two subway stations on *Arbatskaya Square (Arbatskaya Ploshchad).*
The one, with a surface foyer in the
shape of a five-pointed star, was built 30
years ago. It is on the Kalininskaya—Molodyozhnaya Line. The other, set back farther
from the road, was built more than ten years
ago to service the Shchelkovskaya-Kievs-
kaya Line. Arbatskaya is one of the oldest
squares in Moscow. The word *arbad* means
suburb in Arabic. In the 15th century what
is now Arbat Street, the adjacent by-streets
and square of the same name, was a suburb
(the city proper was called the Kremlin).
The name probably came from the merchants
of the area who traded with Persia and
Arabia.

In 1439 the Tatars of Khan Mehmet tried
to force their way into the centre of the
city through the Arbat Gates (which stood
on a fortified earthen rampart). But a blind
boyar by the name of Vladimir Khovrin who
lived nearby captained the defence of the
gates, routed the enemy, and rescued the
women and children taken prisoner.

Moscow lights

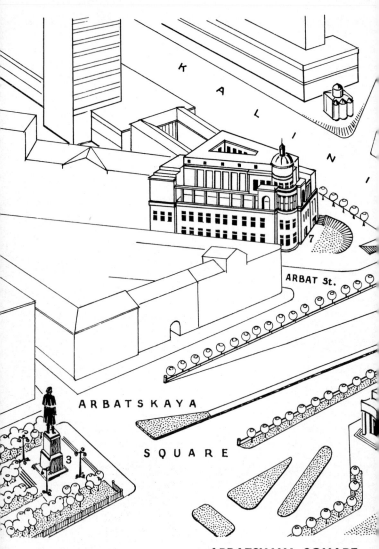

K A L I N I

7

ARBAT St.

A R B A T S K A Y A

S Q U A R E

3

ARBATSKAYA SQUARE

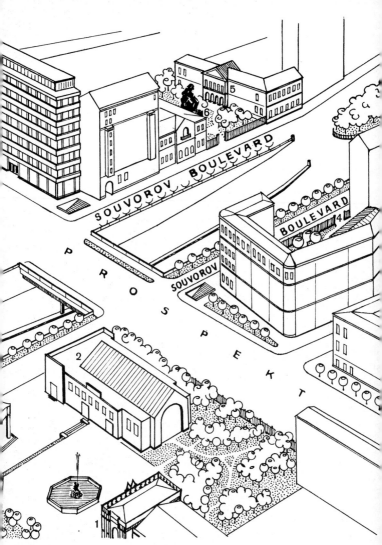

1. "Arbatskaya" Metro Station; 2. "Khudozhestvenny" Cinema; 3. Nikolai Gogol Memorial; 4. Central Journalists' Club; 5. House where Nikolai Gogol lived; 6. Nikolai Gogol Memorial (sculptor—Nikolai Andreyev); 7. "Praga" Restaurant.

In 1572 the warriors of Ivan the Terrible returned to Moscow through the Arbat Gates from a distant campaign against Novgorod. Near these gates Muscovites in 1611 gave battle to a detachment of the Maltese Knight Novodvorsky, hurrying to the aid of the Polish gentry, who had dug in in the Kremlin. The Knight was gravely wounded and his host, after hand-to-hand fighting, took to flight.

To the right of the subway station there is the *Khudozhestvenny* (Art) Motion Picture Theatre, the theatre that showed the first Soviet sound film—*A Start in Life*—in March 1930.

A street that runs off the square to the left is named after Frunze, the renowned Soviet military leader. In 1870, writer Fyodor Dostoyevsky rented a furnished apartment on that street, (house No.9) and, closer to the square, there is house No.14 where Pyotr Tchaikovsky and Nikolai Rubinstein, a prominent figure in the music world, lived a year earlier. Henri Wieniawsky, Alexander Borodin and other prominent musicians and composers visited them in this house.

Arbatskaya Square is situated on a semi-circle of famous boulevards—the so-called *Bulvarnoye Koltso* (Boulevard Ring); *Gogol Boulevard* runs off to the left. It used to be a favourite haunt of Nikolai Gogol, the great Russian writer, who frequently took walks there. In 1952 a new monument was erected to him on this boulevard (sculptor—Nikolai Tomsky) to replace the old pre-revolutionary monument that stood there.

The square has been radically reconstructed during the past few years. A 1,115-foot underpass handles the traffic along the Boulevard Ring. There are also two tunnels for pedestrians.

The transport tunnel begins at *Gogol Boulevard* and ends at *Suvorov Boulevard*, named after the great Russian army leader Alexander Suvorov, who, during the last twenty-five years of his life lived in a house that stood nearby.

On the right side of Suvorov Boulevard, very close to where it starts, there is the *Central Journalists' Club*. Alexander Pushkin read his poem *Poltava* in this building in the 1820's. In March 1920, the premises were taken over by the Press Club where Vladimir Mayakovsky used to read his new verses and take part in public debates; Sergei Yesenin and Alexander Block were frequent visitors there.

The house on the opposite side of the street (No.7a) is associated with Nikolai Gogol, who lived and worked there from 1848 through 1852. That was where he read his immortal The *Inspector General* to an audience of writers and actors. (Among the men of letters at the gathering was Ivan Turgenev, who later wrote: "That was a real treat and an exciting occasion for me.") A few years ago, a statue of the great Russian writer (sculptor—Nikolai Andreyev) was set up in the yard of this house. Up until 1952, it stood at the end of Gogol Boulevard where it joints Arbatskaya Square. Afterwards it was transferred to the grounds of the former Donskoi Monastery to make way for a new monument, and then to the yard on Suvorov Boulevard in 1959. Bas-reliefs covering the pedestal depict Taras Bulba, Gorodnichy, Chichikov, Korobochka, Khlestakov and other unforgettable characters from Gogol's works.

Two old streets, Arbat and Vorovsky (until 1924 called *Povarskaya*, from the Russian word *povar*—meaning cook) diverge from the square. Settlements of craftsmen and "his majesty's out-buildings" were located in the vicinity back in the 16th and 17th centuries. The names of the by-streets are reminiscent of those times: *Kalashny* (a kind of fancy bread), *Kislovsky* (sour), *Khlebny* (bread), *Skatertny* (table cloth), *Stolovy* (dining-room), *Plotnikov* (carpenter), *Serebryany* (silversmith), *Starokonyushenny* (old stable), and so forth. In the second half of the 18th century representatives of the nobility began to settle in this locality. The Moscow aristocracy built many mansions there at that time and in the 19th century.

Many embassies are located today on the quiet shady blocks in this part of the city. The Soviet Government turned the mansions of the aristocracy over to the children, museums, institutes and public organizations.

Between Arbat and Vorovsky Streets, a new stretch of Kalinin Prospekt known as Novy (New) Arbat runs from reconstructed

Gogol Boulevard ▶

Arbatskaya Square to the Sadovoye Koltso. For many years the old, twisting Arbat Street, barely more than 6.5 feet wide, had been unable to cope with the heavy traffic, since the bulk of motor transport heading for Kiev Railroad Terminal, the big new Fili-Mazilovo housing development, Kutuzovsky Prospekt and Moscow-Minsk Highway went through there.

Then, in the spring of 1962, work began on a new thoroughfare, and on November 7 of the following year Muscovites passed down this 260-foot-wide and about two-thirds of a mile long avenue on their way to the popular procession through Red Square. This stretch of Kalinin Prospekt was laid through several old streets and by-streets.

Four twenty-six-storey buildings are under construction on the left side. The first and second floors will consist of large department and specialized stores, a restaurant, café, dining rooms, kindergartens and nurseries.

Six 14- to 16-storey buildings are being erected on the right side. These will have premises for a moving picture theatre seating 2,300 and a book store with rooms where readers can have get-togethers with writers and composers.

A three-story restaurant, the *Praga,* with a summer roof garden, stands on the corner of Arbat Street and Kalinin Prospekt. It was fundamentally remodelled some time ago with the help of Soviet and Czechoslovak architects and artists. The walls are covered with murals based on Czech motifs.

Not far from Arbatskaya Square, quiet *Malaya Molchanovka Street* branches off to the left from Kalinin Prospekt, near the first pedestrian underpass. The most notable structure there is a small house with an attic (No.2). A polished red porphyry tablet mounted on the façade bears the inscription: "The great Russian poet Mikhail Yuryevich Lermontov lived here 1830-1832."

In this small house, the poet wrote his poem *Demon* and his drama *A Strange Person,* and more than a hundred verses.

MOSKVA SWIMMING POOL AND VICINITY

THIS is an interesting district for tourists. Side by side with quiet, secluded blocks characteristic of old Moscow, there are busy thoroughfares, which have been fundamentally modernized and built up during Soviet times. One of the attractions here is the huge open-air *Moskva Swimming Pool*, opened to the public in the summer of 1960 and functioning all year round (the water is heated). It lies in a deep depression right opposite the *Kropotkinskaya* Metro Station, one of the most beautiful in the Moscow subway system.

Built in 1935, the station has simple but expressive lines. Widely spaced metal columns faced with white marble and shaped to resemble torches, are used as supports. Subdued indirect lights lend lightness to the pillars. The whole design of this magnificent underground station prepares

The "Moskva" swimming-pool

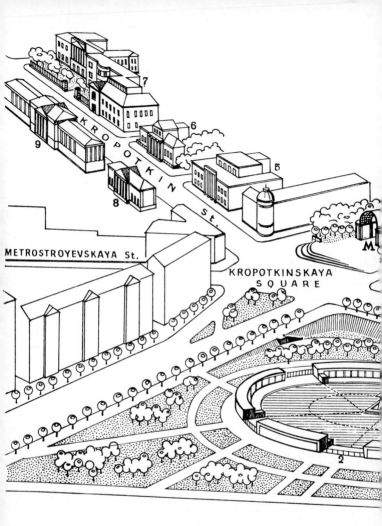

**KROPOTKINSKAYA SQUARE
AND VICINITY**

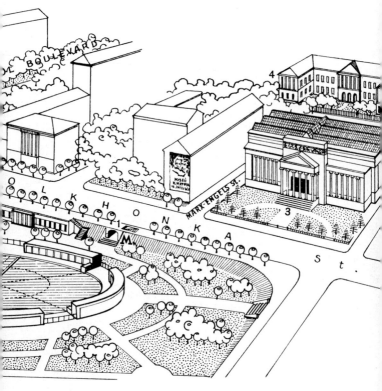

1. "Kropotkinskaya" Metro Station; 2. "Moskva" Swimming Pool; 3. Pushkin Fine Arts Museum; 4. Karl Marx and Friedrich Engels Museum; 5. Soviet Peace Committee; 6. Alexander Pushkin Museum; 7. Scientists' Club; 8. Lev Tolstoi Museum; 9. USSR Academy of Arts.

The Pushkin Fine Arts Museum

you, as it were, for the delightful panorama of the pool that spreads out in all its beauty after you step out of the station.

The pool is located right next to the Moskva River. If you walk to Kropotkinskaya Embankment and turn right, you will come to a two-story building (No.29). Its architecture is in ancient Russian style. There are two memorial plaques mounted on the façade. One of them mentions that this building housed the French Military Mission during the Second World War. French airmen of the Normandie-Niemen Regiment fought side-by-side with Soviet soldiers, and the names of the heroes who fell in battle are engraved on the other plaque.

Volkhonka Street runs off to the left of the observation platform on an eminence overlooking the pool opposite the subway station. A short walk down the street will bring you to a building (No.12) with a tall marble colonnade and green lawns behind an open-work wrought iron fence. This is one of the finest museum premises in the country.

Designed in ancient Greek style (architect —Roman Klein), the building was erected in 1898-1912 as the new premises for the museum called The Fine Arts Study founded in the last third of the 19th century on the initiative of professor Tsvetayev of Moscow. Now known as the *Pushkin Fine Arts Museum* (since 1937), it has one of the world's best collections of art of the Ancient East, antiquity and Western Europe and in the Soviet Union is second to the Hermitage collection in Leningrad.

The collection has been substantially supplemented in Soviet times. The additions include many valuable works of art acquired from other Soviet museums and private collections, and also interesting new exhibits discovered during archaeological expeditions sponsored by the museum.

A much-prized possession of the museum is its original collection of antiquities of Ancient Egypt, one of the largest of its kind in the world. It includes papyri, articles of worship, objects of applied art, reliefs, painted sarcophagi decorated with designs, and other priceless relics.

In addition to replicas of all the most

famous pieces of sculpture of Ancient Greece and Rome and replicas of Pompeian frescos and paintings in catacombs, exhibits in the antique art department also include original ancient Greek and Etruscan terracottas and vases, and ancient sculptures.

The pride of the museum is its very rich collection of Byzantine, Italo-Cretan and Italian icons.

There is also an extensive picture gallery. On display are outstanding works by Italian masters of the Renaissance (Sandro Botticelli, Pietro Perugino, and Paolo Veronese, among others) and valuable paintings by artists of the Dutch school (15th-16th centuries), the German, English, and Spanish schools (15th-19th centuries), and the Flemish school (17th century). There is an especially big collection of works by French painters of the 17th-20th centuries, among them Nicolas Poussin, Jean Baptiste Chardin, François Lemoyne, Ferdinand Victor Eugène Delacroix, Jean Baptiste Camille Corot, Gustave Courbet, Paul Cézanne, and Pablo Picasso. The French landscape painters of the 19th century belonging to Barbizon school, and also the impressionists (Pierre Auguste Renoir, Claude Monet, Camille Pissarro and Hilaire Germain Edgar Degas among others) are brilliantly represented.

The museum periodically arranges exhibitions on the art of various countries and the work of individual outstanding painters of the past and present. It does extensive scientific work to study world art heritage and has scientific ties with many of the world's finest museums.

A narrow street runs off Volkhonka Street to the left of the Pushkin Fine Arts Museum. It is called Marx-Engels Street. If you walk down it about 500 feet, you will come to the *Karl Marx and Friedrich Engels Museum,* a graceful-looking two-story mansion set deep in a garden with busts of the founders of scientific communism on low pedestals out in front. The exhibits deal with their revolutionary activity against the broad background of the international labour and communist movements. They include a rich collection of the original manuscripts of works by Karl Marx and Friedrich Engels, first editions of their works and editions that came out during their lifetimes, collections of photographs of Marx, Engels and their comrades-in-arms, a unique collection of the personal belongings of Marx and Engels, and also works of art related to their life and activity.

This museum can be considered an international undertaking. Communist and Workers' Parties of various countries co-operated in establishing it.

Retracing your steps along Marx-Engels Street, you will notice a commemorative plaque on one of the houses to the right with a bas-relief and an inscription telling you that the great Russian painter Vasily Surikov lived and worked there in 1910.

Now you are back on Volkhonka Street, walking towards the Metro. When you reach the corner opposite the subway station you will see a three-story building (No. 16) with a small signboard. This is the home of the *Russian Language Institute of the USSR Academy of Sciences*. Before the revolution, it was the secondary school where playwright Alexander Ostrovsky once studied.

Beyond the entrance to the *Kropotkinskaya* Metro Station there is a shady boulevard running towards Arbatskaya Square. This is Gogol Boulevard, the first section of the incomplete Boulevard Ring that embraces the centre of the city in its horseshoe-shaped belt of greenery. The Central Chess Club occupies an old two-story mansion (No. 14) on the right side, closer to Arbatskaya Square. There enthusiasts of this intriguing game can come to meet over the chess table Soviet champions.

At the *Kropotkinskaya* Metro Station two streets can be seen running off to the right: Kropotkin and Metrostroyevskaya. The first is especially interesting. It leads to a district of old Moscow where the city's aristocracy, after the fire of 1812, built estates and mansions, many of which are still standing. But a stroll through the quiet, secluded little streets and side streets of this district is not merely an excursion into the past, enabling you to see interesting examples of 19th-century civil architecture. Many of the streets and houses here are bound up with the names of great Russian people.

At first Kropotkin Street is slightly uphill. On this upgrade, to the right there is a two-storey building (No. 10) which houses the boards of several national public organizations: the *Soviet Peace Committee,* the *Soviet Afro-Asian Solidarity Committee* and the *Soviet War Veterans' Committee,* among others.

Next to it there is an old estate with a former manor-house, now preserved by the state as an interesting monument of 19th-century Russian architecture. It was built in 1814 (architect—Afanasy Grigoryev). One façade with six columns faces Kropotkin Street; the other, with four rows of graceful columns, the side street. Since 1961, this building, which embodies the finest features of Russian architecture of the first third of the 19th century, has been the premises of the *Pushkin Museum.*

The museum's exhibits include manuscripts, works of art and personal belongings reflecting various aspects of the life and creative work of Russia's "foremost poet." There is a concert hall in the building where visitors can hear live recitals or tape recordings of his works by prominent elocutionists, singers and musicians or see films based on his life and work.

Opposite the museum, on the left side of the street, there is a three-storey building (No.7) with a commemorative plaque on the façade. A bas-relief on the plaque depicts Red Guards and soldiers in action in October 1917 as they attacked and seized the White Guard Headquarters of the Moscow Military Area, which was quartered in this house at the time.

Farther up the right side of the street there is a building (No.16) set deep in a yard behind gates topped by two stone lions. This is the *Moscow Scientists' Club* with a membership of some 4,000. It has a concert hall which is very popular among Muscovites.

On the left side of the street, opposite the Scientists' Club, you can see a one-storey building with a six-column portico on a white stone basis. A wooden structure with an imitation stone finish, it was built in 1822 by the same architect who designed the Pushkin Museum—Afanasy Grigoryev. Today it houses the *Lev Tolstoi Museum.*

This museum began as a small exhibition

organized in 1911 on the first anniversary of the great Russian writer's death. In 1939, the Soviet Government decided to make it the focal point of all the materials connected with his life and work Today it possesses more than 160,000 manuscript pages of the writer and about 10,000 of his letters. Among the exhibits are many works of art—painted and sculptured portraits of Lev Tolstoi made during his lifetime by Ilya Repin, Ivan Kramskoi, Nikolai Ghe and other prominent artists. There are recordings of Tolstoi's voice, and also moving pictures made of him. Scientific workers on the museum staff are engaged in making a further study of his literary heritage.

Two other interesting architectural monuments on the street are a building on the left side (No. 17), in which Denis Davydov, poet, guerilla fighter, hero of the Patriotic War of 1812, lived in 1835 and a building on the right side (No. 22, opposite Davydov's former estate), which was built at the end of the 18th century (architect—Matvei Kazakov).

Still another building worth seeing is the one occupied by the *USSR Academy of Arts* (No. 21, on the left side of the street), with exhibition facilities which are usually used for jubilee or personal shows of paintings, sculptures and drawings by Soviet artists.

At this point we end our stroll down Kropotkin Street, the street named after Pyotr Kropotkin, an eminent Russian geographer and traveller and a theorist of anarchy, who was born in 1842 in 26 Kropotkin Lane. Writing about the district you have just visited, Pyotr Kropotkin once said: "This is where the old Moscow nobility lived and slowly passed into extinction... In those days 'ideas' were not in vogue yet; the time had not yet come when a struggle was to begin in each of these homes between "fathers and children"—a srtuggle that would end either in a family drama or in a nocturnal visit by policemen."

A century has passed since then. Not a trace has remained of the nobility. New people are living in the secluded side streets running off Kropotkin Street, and with them have come new ideas and a new life.

GORKY RECREATION PARK

THERE are two subway stations called *Park Kultury:* one on the Circle Line and the other on the Sokolniki—Yugo-Zapad Line. They are interconnected by passenger tunnels. Their two entrance and exit foyers are on *Krymskaya Square*, not far from the Moskva River, to the south-west of the Moskva Swimming Pool. This is not a typical Moscow square. It is quite small in comparison with the others.

An overpass 1,310 feet long and 50 feet wide spans the square at this point on a single row of well-proportioned reinforced concrete piers. It was erected in 1950 when work was drawing to a close on a new high-speed traffic artery linking the centre with new residential districts in the south-western

Swings in Gorky Park

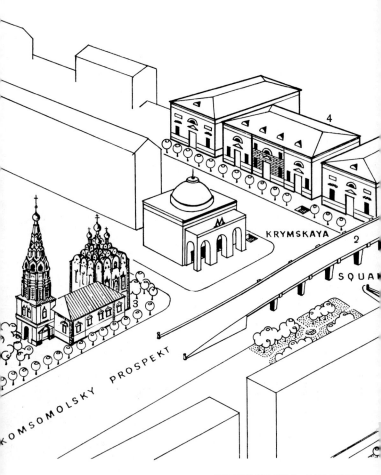

KRYMSKAYA
SQUA
KOMSOMOLSKY PROSPEKT

KRYMSKAYA SQUARE

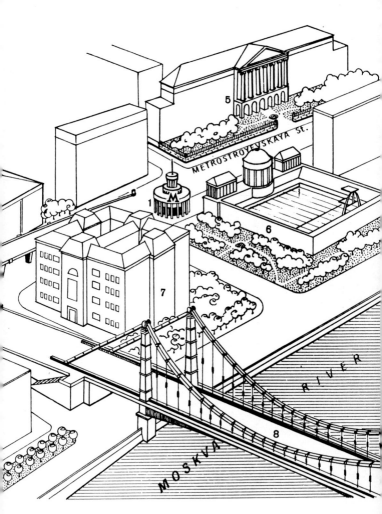

1. "Park Cultury" Metro Station; 2. Viaduct; 3. St. Nicholas Church in Khamovniki; 4. Food Depôts; 5. Moscow Pedagogical Institute of Foreign Languages; 6. "Chaika" Swimming Pool; 7. Institute of Foreign Relations; 8. Krymsky Bridge.

In Gorky Park

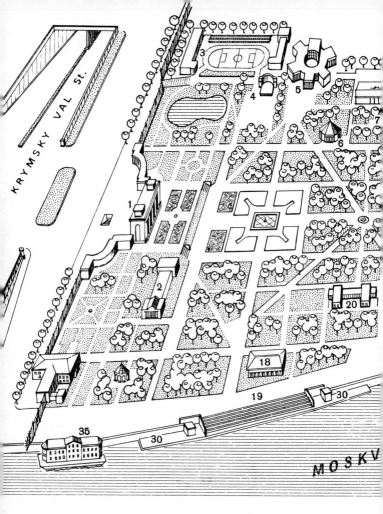

GORKY RECREATION PARK

1. Main Entrance; 2. Exhibition Pavilion; 3. Sports Area; 4. Small Variety Stage; 5. Dance Hall; 6. "Ring of Fun"; 7. "Path of Fun"; 8. Summer Theatre; 9. Chess Club; 10. Large Ferris Wheel; 11. "Caucasus" Restaurant; 12. Central Variety Stage; 13. Table Games Area; 14. Small Ferris Wheel; 15. Children's Merry-Go-Round; 16. Cafe-Express; 17. Swings; 18. "Plzen"

Restaurant; 19. Granite Stands; 20. Exhibition Pavilion; 21. Youth
Club; 22. Large Variety Stage; 23. Summer-Houses designed by
Matvei Kazakov; 24. "Arctica" Ice-cream Café; 25. Golitsinsky
Pond; 26. "Lastochka" Restaurant; 27. "Rendez-vous" Restau-
rant; 28. Rosarium; 29. Labour Protection Museum of the All-
Union Central Council of Trade Unions; 30. Boating Station; 31.
River Tram pier; 32. Green Theatre; 33. Neskuchny Gerden;
34. Way to the reading hall and Young Pioneers' and School-
children's Area; 35. Restaurants on the water.

part of the city. *Komsomolsky Prospekt,* the name of the thoroughfare, has become one of the most beautiful avenues in town. It was given the name because the builders were young Muscovites, mostly members of the Komsomol (Young Communist League). The route was laid in a record time of 11 months on land previously covered by a mass of old wooden dwellings—all that remained of pre-revolutionary *Khamovniki* [1].

Komsomolsky Prospekt became the main transport artery of a huge district that stretched for a distance of 1.25 miles along the Moskva River. Large apartment houses faced with light-coloured ceramic tiles and provided with modern amenities line both sides of the new thoroughfare and form whole well-planned, landscaped blocks along the adjoining side streets. More than a thousand lindens and hundreds of other trees have been planted there.

This avenue is the shortest route from the centre to the sports complex in Luzhniki and the traffic has all it can bear on days scheduled for soccer games and other interesting sports meets. The only sight of historical interest on this avenue is the small *Church of St. Nicholas,* which was preserved during reconstruction of the district by narrowing the roadway at one point.

There are two other old structures on this avenue: the so-called *Shefsky Dom* (Chief's House), a three-storey building with a four-column portico erected at the end of the 18th century, and the long monotonous buildings of the Khamovniki Barracks, built at the beginning of the 19th century (architect—M. Kazakov, son of the famous Russian architect Matvei Kazakov). Neither of these buildings is of special interest architecturally. But the Chief's House (13 Komsomolsky Prospekt) played a prominent role in the history of Russia. In 1817 officiers of the Guard's Corps, quartered in the Khamovniki Barracks, gathered there in the apartment of Colonel Artamon Muravyev. Among them were Sergei and Matvei Muravyev-Apostol, Ivan Yakushkin and others, who were to become the future Decembrists, the first revolutionaries in Russia to take part in

---

1) Khamovniki was an old Russian settlement for weavers, who once used to live in this district.

an armed uprising against the tsar in 1825 on Senate Square in St. Petersburg.

The other end of the overpass runs flush with Metrostroyevskaya Street, which has still to be reconstructed.

Several light, shapely structures can be seen on the right side where this street starts. They are the premises of the *Chaika* open-air swimming pool, finished in time for the opening of the 6th World Youth and Student Festival in 1957 in Moscow.

And on the opposite side, one of the most interesting monuments of early 19th-century Russian architecture—the *Proviantskiye Sklady* (food depots)—stands on the corner of Metrostroyevskaya Street and the Sadovoye Koltso. There are three large buildings, which were erected in 1832-1835 (architects—Vasily Stasov and Fyodor Shestakov) and form together an architectural ensemble.

Two commemorative plaques are mounted on a wall of the food depots; one with the name of the architects and the date of construction; the other noting that fierce fighting took place here in October 1917 as Red Guards and revolutionary soldiers stormed the Proviantskiye Sklady, where counter-revolutionary officers and cadets had entrenched themselves.

Farther down the same side of Metrostroyevskaya Street beyond the *Proviantskiye Sklady*, there is a three-story building with a six-column portico set back in the depths of a small flower garden. Once the birthplace of Sergei Solovyev (1820), a distinguished Russian historian and author of the monumental research *History of Russia from Ancient Times*, and later the School of Commerce where Ivan Goncharov, the Russian writer and author of the well-known novels *Oblomov*, *The Precipice* and *A Common Story*, studied in 1822-1830.

During the difficult days of the Second World War, when the German fascist troops were close to Moscow, the entire population rose up in defence of their capital. Muscovites joined people's volunteer corps. One of these corps was formed in this house.

Today the building houses the *Moscow Pedagogical Institute of Foreign Languages*, named after Maurice Thorez. Incidentally,

A café in Gorky Park ▶

most of the guides and interpreters of *Intourist,* who help visitors from abroad to get to know Moscow, received their training at this institute.

Beyond the overpass and perpendicular to it, a bridge can be seen spanning the Moskva River. This is the *Krymsky Bridge.* It is suspended on giant chains and joins the two banks with a single span. Notwithstanding its immense weight (10,000 tons), the bridge seems amazingly light. Four tall pylons hold up the silvery chains formed of metallic plates from which the beautiful bridge is suspended with the help of steel cables. The bridge is more than 131.2 feet wide. It was erected in 1938 in the exceptionally short time of 56 days (designing engineer—Konstantinov, and architect—Alexander Vlasov).

Near the park you will see a large construction site on your left. The new premises of the USSR Art Gallery are to be located here. There will be more than five times the exhibition space now available at the Tretyakov Art Gallery. The finest paintings, sculptures, drawings and works of applied art by Soviet masters will be on display in its 150 halls.

At the point where the Krymsky Bridge ends, you come to the main entrance of the *Gorky Park.* The gates in the open-work fence are always flung wide open: there is no admission fee (except on days when there are carnivals or masquerades). A domain of bright flowers, quaint flower-beds, rosariums, shady lanes, and endless velvety lawns begins on the other side of the fence. There are more than three hundred kinds of trees and shrubs in the park grounds, which cover an area of some 300 acres. There are oak, birch, elm, lime, blue Siberian fir, spruce, southern chestnut, Ukrainian poplar, and taiga larch, and also apple, pear and other fruit trees. But you will find more flowers there than anywhere else: over two million are planted every year.

This beautiful park was laid out on land that lay idle or was used as vegetable gardens 45 years ago. In 1923, the first Soviet All-Russia Agricultural Exhibition was opened there. Then the exhibition grounds were relandscaped and made into a recreation park, which was opened in 1928.

A wide central lane begins at *Fountain Square,* immediately beyond the terrace of the main entrance. It leads to the picturesque *Golitsynsky Pond,* with numerous row boats rippling its glassy surface. An amusement zone with a lot of attractions, including a huge Ferris wheel, lies to the left of the central alley. On the right side, you will find a number of large exhibition pavilions somewhat closer to the river embankment. Foreign organizations and commercial firms and companies hold exhibitions there. In this section of the park too, there is a large new dance hall and the *Pilzen Restaurant* serving Czech beer and dishes.

Beyond the Golitsynsky Pond, the *Neskuchny Garden* begins, which can also be reached from the main entrance by walking along the river embankment (incidentally, the latter runs along the edge of the park for nearly two miles). This is a huge stretch of greenery with age-old trees, picturesque ascents and descents, deep ravines, and rolling slopes, hidden by the dense tops of trees and shrubs. Here it is always cool and quiet. People come to rest and "commune with nature." There are no amusements or stages, and the sound of music does not reach you, except, of course, from the open-air *Green Theatre* with a seating capacity of 10,000. This theatre is located right at the river embankment, not far from the wharf where busy little "river trams," as the Muscovites call the diesel passenger boats plying the Moskva River, moor every now and then.

Folk choirs, song and dance groups, and circus troupes perform in the Green Theatre; films are shown there and variety programmes are staged. This is the largest concert stage in the park. There is also a summer theatre, a large motion picture theatre, several concert stages, bandstands, and arbours where young people gather to sing their favourite songs to guitar accompaniment.

This park is a pleasant place to spend the day or evening in summer, and in winter too, when all its alleys are flooded and some 120,000 square yards of ice are at the disposal of Moscow's skating enthusiasts.

On the lake in Gorky Park

Gorky Park

EXCURSION **15**

SOKOLNIKI

OF all the Moscow parks, *Sokolniki* is probably the favourite. The huge tract of woodland, which covers 1,500 acres, is a splendid reservoir of fresh pure air, so essential to life in a big city. The pride of the park is its rosarium. Pinkish-white, crimson, orange and yellow roses adorn many of its alleys.

Unlike in other parks, the landscapers have striven to preserve the natural greenery, the original Sokolniki woods, and not to mar the picturesque surroundings with superfluous structures, paved alleys and lanes. Muscovites come there for family outings, often for the entire day. The park has many cafés, restaurants and snack bars, and there are plenty of picturesque secluded spots where one can spend a quiet, restful time.

Moscow's first Metro line was laid to the Sokolniki district in 1935 to provide the central, densely populated parts of the city with rapid, modern transport to the city's favourite recreation grounds. And the subway station there is called Sokolniki. A wide, straight boulevard lined with trees and

Autumn in Sokolniki

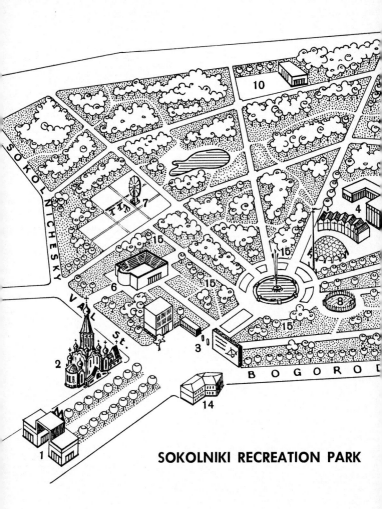

SOKOLNIKI RECREATION PARK

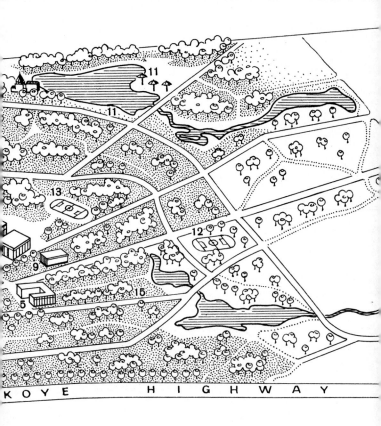

KOYE   HIGHWAY

1. "Sokolniki" Metro Station; 2. Church of the Resurrection of Christ; 3. Main Entrance; 4. Exhibition Pavilions; 5. Libraries and reading rooms; 6. Summer Skating Ring; 7. Children's Town; 8. Dance Pavilion; 9. "Quiet" zone, chess and draughts area; 10. Riding School; 11. Beach; 12. "Spartak" Stadium; 13. Central Arm Club Stadium; 14. Bicycle station and skiing base; 15. Restaurants and cafés.

Today the Fire tower in Sokolniki commands a view of new housing estates under construction

bordered by flower-beds leads to the main entrance of the park.

As you approach the park, you will see a nine-dome church to the left. This is the *Church of the Resurrection of Christ.* There are several glass-covered icons mounted on its outside walls.

The entrance to the park is simple in design, devoid of superfluous, attention-catching advertisements. To the left is a large slab with the name of the park and a decorative schematic lay-out of the main alleys. A few steps farther on you find yourself in a greenery kingdom. The main lane leads you to a large waterspout 82 feet high surrounded by a wide flower-bed.

Extensive exhibition grounds stretch out beyond the huge golden cupola of the former American pavilion. They are used by different countries for organizing industrial, scientific and technological exhibitions that are very popular with Muscovites. During the past few years, exhibitions from Great Britain, Czechoslovakia, Japan, Italy, France and Bulgaria have been a great success.

Two large pavilions were added to the exhibition space in 1961. They were designed by Soviet architects, and built in less than a year.

To the left of the park's main entrance you will find the amusement zone, with swings, a merry-go-round, distorting mirrors, and many other attractions. Here too, on open-air dance floors people go in for round dancing to band music. In other, quieter spots, there are reading rooms and places to play table-games.

The park has an open-air theatre seating 4,500, an indoor summer theatre seating 1,100, several bandstands and platforms for variety-stage performances, a large dance hall called *Vesna* (Spring), and a summer iceskating rink. In winter, the park alleys and lanes are flooded and turned into a huge rink for numerous Moscow's skating enthusiasts. And on New Year's eve a huge decorated fir-tree flashes up with merry twinkling lights and the traditional *Ded-Moroz* (Grandfather Frost) cheerily hands out New Year's gifts to young visitors.

Sokolniki only became a recreation park in 1931, but it has a long, interesting past.

Forests grew there three hundred to four hundred years ago. In the 17th century they became the favourite *sokoliny* (falconry) grounds of the Russian tsars. The settlement located not far from the present main entrance to the park was used by the tsar's huntsmen and falconers. Thirty hunting birds were maintained there for Tsar Alexei Mikhailovich.

Peter I was the first, it seems, to start celebrating the May "spring holiday" in Sokolniki (as the place began to be called owing to the falconry practised there). And from the beginning of the 18th century Sokolniki groves became the scene of traditional popular festivities. In the difficult days of 1812, when Napoleon occupied Moscow, quite a number of people took refuge in the dense thickets of Sokolniki.

Beginning with the 1890's workers and Marxist groups would gather there in secret from the tsarist authorities, and in 1905 workers belonging to fighting groups were trained there to handle revolvers. The frightened authorities ordered the police to cut down the densest shrubs and trim the lower branches of the trees to a man's height to make it easier to keep an eye on "suspicious elements."

A great deal of landscaping has been done in Sokolniki since 1931 in order to beautify and improve the maintenance of this huge park.

THE SQUARE WITH THREE RAILWAY TERMINALS

MUSCOVITES call this district the "railway gates of the city." Dozens of trains depart daily for the north, east and south from the three railway terminals there. The square is called *Komsomol Square (Komsomolskaya Ploshchad)*. It is also the site of two *Komsomolskaya* Moscow Metro Stations: the one, on the Sokolniki—Yugo-Zapad Line, was erected in 1935 (architect—D. Chechulin), and the other, on the Koltsevaya Line (Circular Line), in 1954 (architect—Alexei Shchusev).

The size and decorative finish of the circular line station is striking. The underground vestibule is 30 feet high, and the station itself with the boarding platform is 40 feet wide. Two rows of massive columns support its vaulted ceiling. Mosaic panels

Komsomol Square at night

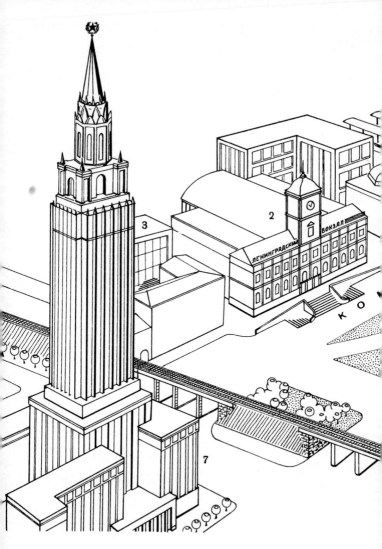

KOMSOMOL SQUARE

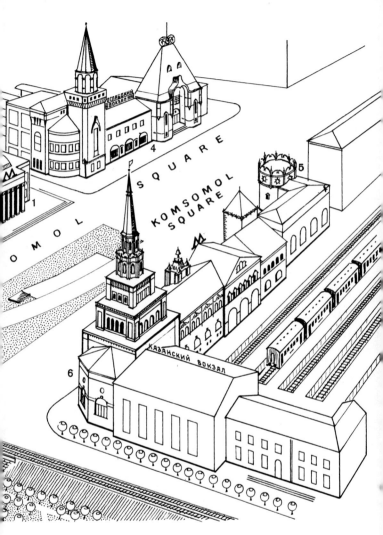

1. "Komsomolskaya" Metro Station; 2. Leningrad Railway Terminal; 3. International Post Office; 4. Yaroslavl Railway Terminal; 5. Central Railwaymen's Club; 6. Kazan Railway Terminal; 7. "Leningradskaya" Hotel.

(artist—Pavel Korin) depict landmarks in the many centuries of struggle of the Russian people for national independence.

Both stations are interconnected by passenger tunnels. The surface vestibule is in the form of a massive pavilion with two six-column portals, crowned by a cupola with a star-topped spire. It is situated between the *Leningrad* and the *Yaroslavl* Terminals. The radial line station can also be entered from the *Kazan Railway Terminal,* which faces the Leningrad station with the broad expanse of Komsomol Square in between. The pedestrian underpass, built in 1962, has considerably improved the organization of the constant flow of heavy traffic.

The first railroad in Russia, linking Moscow and St. Petersburg, was built in 1851. That same year the capital's *Leningrad Terminal* (architect—Konstantin Ton), was built with a clock tower to match the one on the Moscow Terminal in Leningrad. Express trains leaving Moscow cover the distance to Leningrad (400 miles) in less than five hours. From Leningrad there are railway connections to Tallinn and other cities in the north-western part of the country, and also to Helsinki, the capital of Finland. On March 11, 1918, the train from Petrograd bringing the first Soviet Government, headed by Lenin, to the new capital of revolutionary Russia, pulled into this station.

The *Yaroslavl Terminal,* on the other side of the Metro station, was built in 1906 (architect—Franz Shekhtel). This structure is in the style of an ancient Russian fairyland manor with a graceful tower and a steeply sloping roof over the main entrance. It is the terminal of a line more than 6,000 miles long linking the Soviet capital with cities in Siberia and the Far East. It takes six days by train to cover the 5,300 miles from Moscow to Khabarovsk, which a TU-114 airliner reaches in 8 hours, 20 minutes.

In 1964, the Yaroslavl Terminal was partially reconstructed: an annex was added, the boarding platforms were widened, and a huge vestibule and passage were built below to link it with the Metro.

On the opposite side of the square stands the *Central Railwaymen's Club* which provides railwaymen and their families with facilities

Morning in the train

Trains, trains...

for participating in technical, amateur art, sports and hobby groups. Before the revolution this was the site of a store trading in goods needed by workers. In December 1905 it served as the main strong point of the railwaymen who rose up in armed struggle against tsarism.

Commemorative plaques on the walls of the club and the Kazan Terminal recall this heroic struggle waged by the railwaymen against tsarism.

The *Kazan Terminal* (architect—Alexei Shchusev) stretches from the club to the other corner of the block. It took a long time going up: begun back in 1913, the job was completed only in 1926. The traditions and forms of ancient Russian architecture were creatively used in this attractive complex, which is one of the finest architectural monuments of the Soviet capital.

A three-story tower with a narrow steeple and spire 240 feet high, reminiscent of the famous Suyumbeki Tower of Kazan Kremlin, is the compositional centre of the edifice. The architect used the resemblance to denote that from there the trains were bound for Kazan.

The façade of the terminal, built of red brick, is beautifully finished with carved white-stone columns and decorative touches duplicating the finest examples of ancient Russian architecture. It is embellished with a huge clock with a black dial and gilded images of the signs of the Zodiac instead of numerals. The interior of this huge terminal is also lavishly decorated with sculptured elements and large painted panels.

On the western side of the square, beyond the Circular Railway, a tall well-proportioned building can be seen. Its 25-story central section with a 78-foot spire towers high above the square. This is the *Leningradskaya Hotel*, built in 1953, with 350 modern suites. It has become the architectural centre of Komsomol Square, its "visiting card," so to say, for its shapely silhouette blends well into the ensemble of this square.

LENINGRADSKY PROSPEKT

THIS subway station is on *Leningradsky Prospekt,* a continuation of Gorky Street. The thoroughfare starts at the Byelorussion Railway Terminal and extends beyond the *Sokol* Metro Station, where it forks into two highways, one linking the Soviet capital with Leningrad 450 miles away.

There are always endless streams of cars speeding along all the lanes of Leningradsky Prospekt, even though it is 328 feet wide. But this thoroughfare is not simply an important traffic artery. It is one of Moscow's most modern, beautiful, verdant streets. Some compare it with the Champs Elysées in Paris: Both have several features in common, especially from a bird's eye view: they are equally wide, have equally heavy traffic, and two strips of green boulevard running along the avenue. But Leningradsky Prospekt does not have the big Champs Elysées

Aeroflot Hotel in Leningradsky Prospekt

312

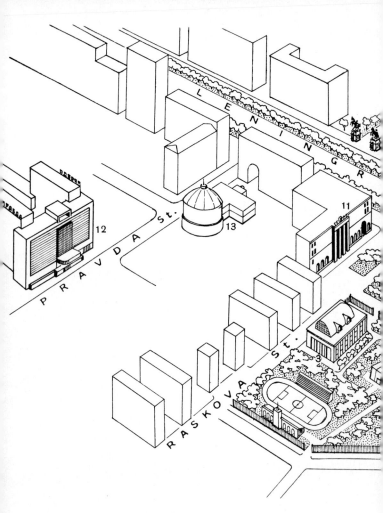

DYNAMO STADIUM AND VICINITY

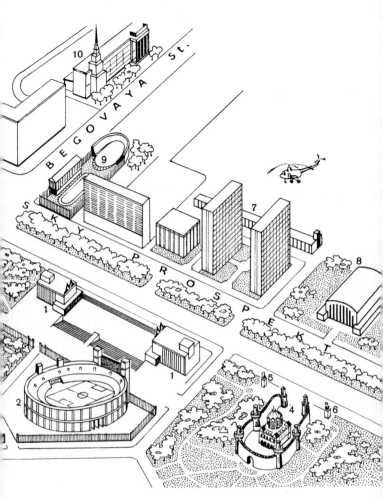

1. "Dynamo" Metro Station; 2. Dynamo Stadium; 3. Swimming Pool; 4. Petrovsky Palace; 5. Nikolai Zhukovsky Memorial; 6. Konstantin Tsiolkovsky Memorial; 7. Moscow Air Terminal; 8. Sports Palace of the Central Sports Club of the Soviet Army; 9. Young Pioneers' Stadium; 10. Hippodrome; 11. "Sovietskaya" Hotel; 12. "Pravda" Printing House; 13. Gymnasium of the "Krylya Sovyetov" Sports Club.

Hippodrome

stores and the Champs Elysées does not have Leningradsky Prospekt's many sports facilities, so popular among Muscovites.

The largest of these facilities is the *Dynamo Sports Complex*, belonging to one of the most popular sports clubs in the country. You can see the big stadium as soon as you step out of either of the subway station's two identical ground vestibules.

A high wrought-iron fence skirts the extensive sports grounds, with the stadium's numerous fields, courts and other facilities. On days when there isn't a big soccer game, the whole complex is open to all sports enthusiasts. The big sports arena (built in 1934), with grandstands seating 60,000, is Moscow's second largest stadium (next to the one in Luzhniki). To the right, you can see the large, dome-shaped roof of an indoor swimming pool (built in 1957). Other sports facilities include tennis, volleyball and basketball courts, soccer training fields, and gymnasiums where people go in for weight-lifting and gymnastics.

Moscow engineers are now designing a roof over the big arena to convert it into a winter stadium. Though the arena is 885 feet long and 557 feet wide, the roof will not have any intermediate supports.

A noteworthy 18th-century architectural group stands to the left of the stadium on Leningradsky Prospekt. It is the *Petrovsky Palace*, erected in 1775-1778 (architect—Matvei Kazakov). Built of red brick with white-stone decorative details, the palace and its front yard are surrounded by a wall with small towers. This picturesque ensemble is reminiscent of an ancient Russian fortress—although more a retreat than a military stronghold. That impression is heightened by the romantic character of the palace architecture and features of 16th-17th century Moscow architecture creatively incorporated by Matvei Kazakov.

The Petrovsky Palace was a temporary residence of the tsars—a place where the royal family used to rest en route from Petersburg to Moscow. A frightened Napoleon, who abandoned the Kremlin during the big Moscow fire, spent several days there in 1812.

Fundamentally restored in 1958, the palace

is now used by the *Air Force Engineering Academy.* Two monuments to Russian scientists who played an outstanding role in the foundation and development of Russian aviation and astronautics stand in front of the main entrance.

One is a bust of Nikolai Zhukovsky (sculptor—G. Neroda), whom Vladimir Lenin called the "father of Russian aviation," the other, a bust of Konstantin Tsiolkovsky (sculptor—Sergei Merkurov), the founder of the theory of rocket engineering and space flight.

On the left side of Leningradsky Prospekt, opposite the Petrovsky Palace, you can see the city air terminal with its helicopter station. It is used only as a transfer point for transit passengers; airliners flying regular routes do not land there. The three Moscow airports—*Sheremetyevo, Vnukovo* and *Domodedovo*—are linked with the air terminal by helicopter. Two blue buildings of glass and reinforced concrete can be seen above the terminal. They are quite recent additions to the Moscow skyline (1964). One of them houses the *Aeroflot Hotel* for transit passengers, and the other the various services of the USSR Ministry of Civil Aviation.

The landing field beyond the air terminal building was laid out on empty lots called the *Khodynskoye Field* before 1917. On May 18, 1896, a tragic event took place there. Throngs of people, attracted by widely publicized promises of presents on the occasion of the coronation of Tsar Nikolai II, were innocent victims of carelessness on the part of the authorities and lack of elementary concern for the safety of people. The wooden scaffolding collapsed and there were 2,690 victims in the ensuing crush. Of these, 1,384 perished. This event aroused a wave of indignation against tsarist rule. The word "Khodynka" became a byword. The vivid description of the tragedy is found in Maxim Gorky's novel *The Life of Klim Samgin.*

Farther up the avenue, on the same side of the thoroughfare as the air terminal, you come to another sports complex—the *Sports Palace* and *Swimming Pool* belonging to the *Central Sports Club of the Soviet Army.*

And there is a third sports centre in the neighbourhood beyond the air terminal. This

Rugby

is the *Young Pioneers' Sports Complex,* which occupies an entire block almost opposite the Dynamo Swimming Pool. Here children wishing to go in for sports can use the indoor facilities for gymnastics, weight-lifting, boxing and other events; tennis, basketball, and volleyball courts; an indoor skating rink; a soccer field with grandstands seating 7,000, and a velodrome where 10,000 fans can watch exciting bicycle and motorcycle races. The sports school affiliated to the stadium is attended by over 2,000 children.

As you walk along Leningradsky Prospekt towards the centre of town, you will notice an archway on the right with sculptured compositions. The latter are bronze replicas of the famous man-and-horse statues cast at the end of the 19th century by Klodt (the grandson) and Sergei Volnukhin. From here, a shady alley, called *Skakovaya* (Racecourse) *Alley,* extends far into the block. It leads to the *Moscow Hippodrome,* whose imposing main entrance faces *Begovaya Street.* Here, there is a huge portal with 12 tall columns and a three-story tower adorned with the statues of prancing steeds designed in 1955 by a group of Moscow architects working under the supervision of Ivan Zholtovsky. The hippodrome itself is older. It was opened in 1883, and since then, its grandstands have always been filled with horse-racing fans. There is a "pari mutuel" (totalizator) at the hippodrome.

On the other side of Leningradsky Prospekt, facing the Skakovaya Alley, you will see an attractive building on the corner. This is *Sovietskaya Hotel,* one of the finest in the capital. It was built in 1950 (architects—N. Loveiko and others). The building has a concert hall with an entrance on the side facing the avenue, where artists, and sometimes Moscow theatre companies, give performances. The hotel restaurant, with its huge mirrored hall that always attracts many Muscovites in the evenings, is well known for its excellent cuisine.

The stretch of Leningradsky Prospekt running from the hotel towards the centre of town is the most beautiful part of the thoroughfare. It has been completely reconstructed in Soviet times. Today beautiful big apartment houses line the avenue, and the

Leningradsky Prospekt—the Moscow Champs Elysées

two green belts of boulevards which divide it into three thoroughfares, gives it a very pleasant appearance.

Approximately in the middle of this stretch a street runs off to the left leading to the Pravda Printing and Publishing House, one of the biggest in the country. That is where the newspaper *Pravda,* founded by Vladimir Lenin in 1912, and many other popular newspapers and magazines are printed in millions of copies. The gray seven-story building with outside walls almost completely of glass was erected in 1936 (architect—Panteleimon Golosov). The street was named accordingly. Pravda Street is now being built up with big new apartment houses.

Still another major sports structure, the fourth in the area, is set far back, near the corner of Leningradsky Prospekt and Pravda Street. This is the *Palace of Physical Culture* (24 Leningradsky Prospekt) belonging to the *Krylya Sovetov* (Wings of the Soviets) *Sports Club,* which was built in 1934. It has splendidly equipped gyms with facilities for training and holding meets in gymnastics, wrestling, boxing, fencing, and weight-lifting. Several times a year the large gymnasium is converted into premises for fashion shows, at which Soviet and foreign stylists demonstrate the latest modes.

To get back to the subway from here you can either retrace your steps to the Dynamo Metro Station or else keep walking ahead towards the centre of town and across the overpass above the railway line to another subway station—*Byelorusskaya* (Byelorussian).

KRASNAYA PRESNYA

I F you take a good look at the bas-reliefs as you go up the escalator you will get some idea of the history of the district and why it means so much to Muscovites.

One of the bas-reliefs depicts a memorable event in which two young women textile-workers, Maria Kozyreva and Anyuta Pchelka, were the heroines.

On December 10, 1905, a 10-thousand-strong demonstration of workers filled Bolshaya Presnya Street. Some were carrying streamers with the slogans "Down with the Tsarist Government" and "Long Live the Popular Uprising!" Two women headed the column carrying a red banner with the words "Soldiers, Don't Fire at Us!" Mounted Cossacks blocked the path of the demonstrators. Just as their officer cried "Let'm have it!" the young women dashed forward and took up a stand face to face with the row of Cossacks, shouting: "You can crush us! But we won't give up the banner alive!" And the Cossacks did not dare to open fire, to heed the officer's command.

Here in Presnya, Moscow workers rose arms in hand against Tsardom

324

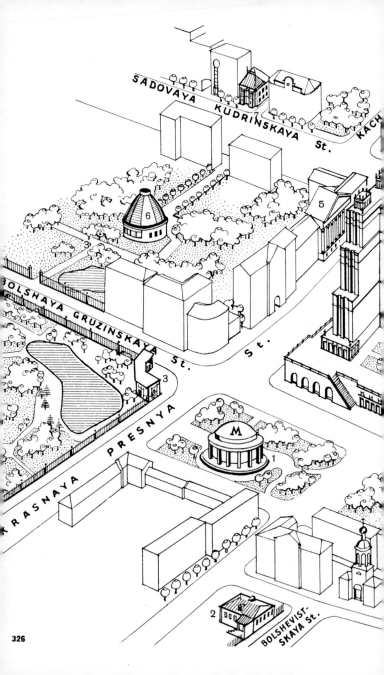

SADOVAYA KUDRINSKAYA St.

KACH

6

5

BOLSHAYA GRUZINSKAYA St.

St.

3

KRASNAYA

PRESNYA

M

1

2

BOLSHEVIST-
SKAYA St.

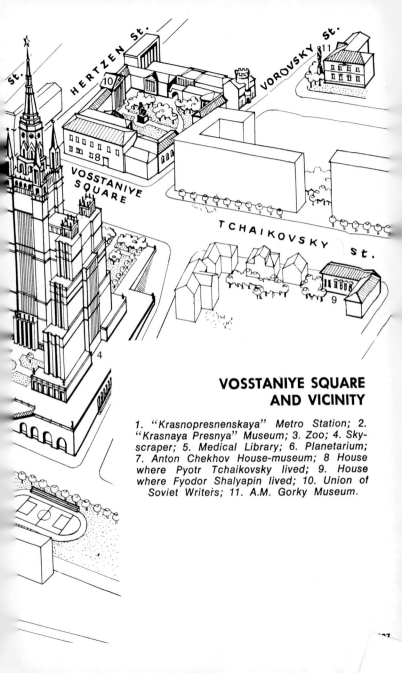

VOSSTANIYE SQUARE
AND VICINITY

1. "Krasnopresnenskaya" Metro Station; 2. "Krasnaya Presnya" Museum; 3. Zoo; 4. Skyscraper; 5. Medical Library; 6. Planetarium; 7. Anton Chekhov House-museum; 8 House where Pyotr Tchaikovsky lived; 9. House where Fyodor Shalyapin lived; 10. Union of Soviet Writers; 11. A.M. Gorky Museum.

Krasnaya Presnya is an industrial district. It has major engineering enterprises, metal-working plants, textile mills and shoe factories.

The workers of this district played a heroic role in the armed insurrection in December 1905. At the call of the Moscow Soviet of Workers' Deputies, on December 7, 1905, Krasnaya Presnya blew the first factory whistle heralding the beginning of the open struggle of the proletariat of Moscow against the tsarist autocracy. Some 100,000 workers poured out into the city's streets and erected barricades from which they fought the tsarist troops and police. The squads of armed workers from Krasnaya Presnya were especially daring in the armed struggle.

For ten days, men and women workers of this district heroically fought the tsarist soldiers. There were nine barricades just on Bolshaya Presnya (now Krasnaya Presnya) Street. The shooting and shelling caused great destruction. Fires started. Many of the inhabitants were killed, among them women, old folk and children. But the squads of armed workers defending Krasnaya Presnya did not waver. They abandoned the barricades in an organized fashion only after the decision of the Moscow Soviet to discontinue the armed struggle.

The enraged tsarist butchers committed many outrages in Krasnaya Presnya. They beat up, arrested and shot workers without trial. All in all, more than one thousand persons were killed in Moscow, including 137 women and 86 children. The courage and fortitude of the Krasnaya Presnya workers was a model for the entire Russian proletariat.

Lenin highly appraised the results and significance of these events.

The station's circular surface vestibule with its tall marble columns was built in 1955 (architect—Karo Alabyan). There is a commemorative plaque mounted on the façade with the inscription: "Krasnaya Presnya was the main stronghold of the insurrection, its centre. The finest squads of armed workers, led by the Bolsheviks, were concentrated here." A monument stands in front of the entrance: the statue of a young armed worker (sculptor—A. Zelensky).

Krasnaya Presnya District lies to the left of the subway station. It is now being reconstructed: old dwellings are giving way to light-coloured, tall apartment houses, streets are being widened and lined with trees; new stores, cafés, children's institutions and schools are going up. There are still quite a few old dwellings in the district. But their days are numbered. The one at 3 Bolshevistskaya Street, however, will be preserved. It was the headquarters of the Krasnaya Presnya District Military-Revolutionary Committee that guided operations there during the October Revolution of 1917. Today it is the *Krasnaya Presnya Museum of the History of the Revolution.*

Opposite the subway station, a high openwork wrought-iron fence can be seen extending for half the block. It is the *Moscow Zoo.* Founded over 100 years ago (in 1864), today it has 3,000 animals from various parts of the world.

If you turn right along Krasnaya Presnya Street after stepping out of the Metro, a two or three-minute walk will bring you to Vosstaniye Square (*Ploshchad Vosstaniya),* which lies on the Sadovoye Koltso.

This square, which has still not been fully reconstructed, is dominated by an impressive 22-story apartment house erected in 1954 (architects—M. Posokhin and A. Mndoyants), with a 98-foot spire topped by a large five-pointed star. Its first floor is given over to one of the city's biggest food stores, and its ground floor to a moving picture theatre— the *Plamya* (Flame).

The street that begins to the left of Vosstaniye Square (if you stand facing it, with your back to the tall apartment house) is called *Sadovo-Kudrinskaya.* On the near corner you will see a building with a colonnade. Erected at the end of the 18th century, it was severely damaged during the big Moscow fire in 1812, and later restored by architect Domenico Gilargi. Today it houses the medical library of the USSR Ministry of Public Health, one of the biggest of its kind in the world. In 1874-1877, the well-known Russian writer Alexander Kuprin lived there with his mother. Before the revolution, this was a Widows' Home—an asylum for officers' widows and children.

In the Zoo ▶

Beyond this building lies another section of the Zoo (which Muscovites call the new grounds). And a little farther on, the silvery cupola of the *Moscow Planetarium* can be seen set back off the same side of the street. It was erected in 1928 (architects—M. Barshch and M. Sinyavsky).

On the right side of Sadovo-Kudrinskaya (almost opposite the entrance to the Zoo), there is a plain little two-story house that could easily be passed by unnoticed. This dwelling, "resembling an old-fashioned chest of drawers," as its former tenant put it, was the home of the great Russian writer, Anton Chekhov, during 1886-1890. Those were the years when his talent reached maturity. There, he wrote his wonderful novels *Steppeland* and *Boring Story*, and his plays *Ivanov*, *The Bear*, and *The Wood-Goblin*.

Today the house has been made into an *Anton Chekhov Museum*. The writer's study and bed-room look exactly as they did during his lifetime. But the other rooms have been turned into exhibition premises with displays denoting his life and work.

On the opposite side of Vosstaniye Square, across the street from the tall apartment house, there is a plain little building (house No. 46) bound up with the history of Russian culture. A commemorative plaque mounted on the façade (at second-floor level) denotes that Pyotr Tchaikovsky lived there in 1872.

The street running off to the right from the tall apartment house as part of the Sadovoye Koltso has been named Tchaikovsky Street, in honour of the great Russian composer. It might well be called a "musical" street. Muscovites cherish 25 Tchaikovsky Street (on the right side) as a precious monument of Russian culture, the home of the great singer Fyodor Shalyapin from 1910-1922. Among his many guests in those years were Maxim Gorky, Alexander Kuprin, Sergei Rakhmaninov and other "greats" in the field of culture. A marble bust of the singer stands in a niche in the house.

Two more streets start at Vosstaniye Square. They run to the centre of town almost perpendicular to Sadovoye Koltso. The one to the right is called *Vorovsky Street*. This is a very pleasant, quiet street on which you will find several small mansions housing foreign embassies.

One of the old mansions, at 25 Vorovsky Street, which was built back at the beginning of the 19th century (architect—Domenico Gilardi) is now a *Maxim Gorky Museum.* A monument to the writer, to the "stormy harbinger of the revolution" (sculptor—Vera Mukhina), stands in front of the entrance.

The thoroughfare to the left of Vorovsky Street has been named after Alexander Hertzen, a revolutionary democrat, philosopher and writer. On the right side of the street, not far from the corner where it starts, you will find the *Central Writers' House*—the club of Moscow's writers. It occupies a new building and an old mansion with a garden, whose gates open onto Vorovsky Street. They say that this was the mansion so warmly described by Lev Tolstoi in his novel *War and Peace* as the house of the Rostovs, where the charming Natasha spent her childhood and adolescence. Today the Board of the Union of Soviet Writers has its offices there.

Hertzen Street *(Ulitsa Gertsena)* is much like Vorovsky Street: here, too, you will find many mansions housing embassies, and traffic is not heavy. Most of the houses were erected long ago and are not large. Following the fire of 1812, the Moscow aristocracy built comfortable mansions there, surrounded by green gardens and quiet. Alexander Pushkin frequently came there to visit the Goncharovs, whose mansion, at the beginning of the 19th century, was located on the site of the present houses No. 48 and No. 50.

Farther down the street, you will come to the former Church of the Great Ascension, built at the end of the 18th century (architects—Matvei Kazakov and Vasily Bazhenov), where Alexander Pushkin was married to Natalya Goncharova.

Not far from the church (6 Kachalov Street), there is a mansion, built in 1906 (architect—Frants Shekhtel), which is a fine example of Russian modern architecture of the early 20th century. Maxim Gorky lived there from 1931 through 1936.

A view of Krasnaya Presnya ▶

FROM THE KIEV RAILWAY TERMINAL TO THE UKRAINA HOTEL

THERE are three subway stations called *Kievskaya.* They are interconnected underground by passageways that enable passengers to transfer from the Circular Line to the Kievskaya-Centre-Shchelkovskaya Line or the Kalininskaya-Molodyezhnaya Line.

The hall of the Circular Line station, which was designed by Ukrainian architects and built in 1952-1953, is decorated with 18 mosaic panels depicting episodes from the

Near Kalininsky Bridge

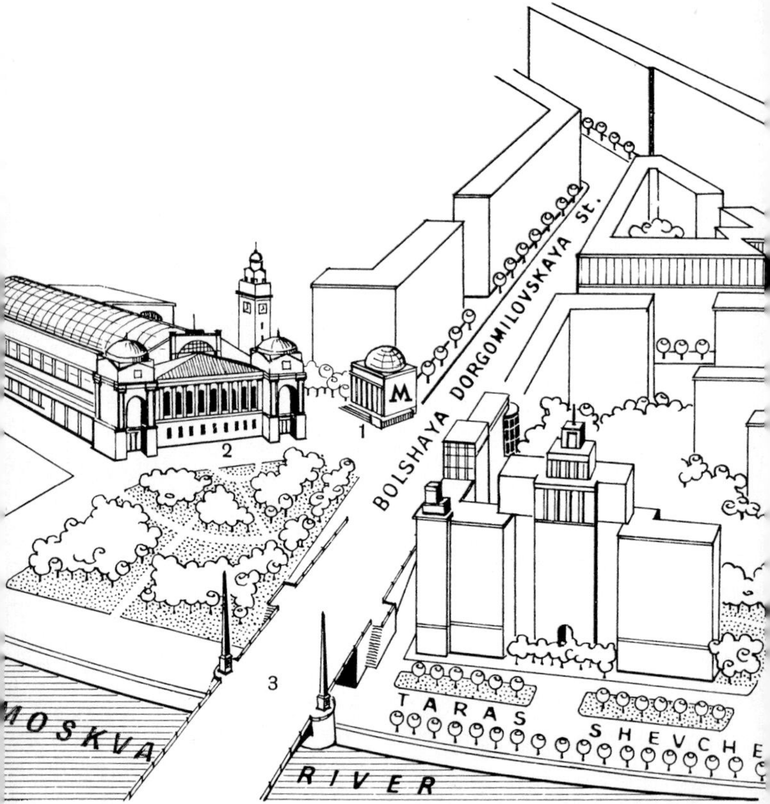
BOLSHAYA DORGOMILOVSKAYA St.
M
1
2
3
MOSKVA
RIVER
TARAS
SHEVCHE

KIEV RAILWAY TERMINAL AND VICINITY

1. "Kievskaya" Metro Station; 2. Kiev Railway Terminal; 3. Borodinsky Bridge; 4. Kalininsky Bridge; 5. "Ukraina" Hotel; 6. Taras Shevchenko Monument; 7. All-Union Association "Vneshposyltorg".

View from Kiev Railway Terminal

glorious many-century-old history of the Ukrainian people, denoting their friendship with the Russian people.

Two surface halls open onto the square in front of Kiev Railway Terminal. One of them is some 65 feet away; the other is built right into the terminal.

The Kiev Railway Terminal was erected in 1913-1917 (designing engineer—Ivan Rerberg). A huge hangar-like glass roof covers the platforms. The façade of the building facing the Moskva River is topped by a tall decorative tower with a clock. Trains depart daily from this station for the south: Kiev, the capital of the Ukraine, a run of 540 miles and Odessa, a major port on the Black Sea, a run of 950 miles. Trains also go to Prague, Budapest, Bucharest and Sofia.

The broad square between the Kiev Railway Terminal and the Moskva River was formed by tearing down the little old houses that had remained from pre-revolutionary times and completely reconstructing the area.

The workers' families who once lived in these blocks received modern new apartments in houses built by the state on Kutuzovsky Prospekt, not far from the Kiev Railway Terminal.

In the postwar period, a public garden was laid out on the square near the Moskva River and the Borodinsky Bridge. A monument is to be erected in the centre in memory of an historical event—the reunification of the Ukraine with Russia in 1653. Steps lead down from the Moskva River embankment beyond the square to a wharf where you can board a passenger motor vessel [1] for the Kremlin.

The *Borodinsky Bridge* across the Moskva River, about 500 feet wide here, was erected in 1912 (architect—Roman Klein; engineer—N. Oskolkov) on the occasion of the centenary of the Patriotic War of 1812. It was conceived as a triumphal monument reflecting the victory of the Russian army.

---

1) Dubbed by Muscovites *rechnoi tramvai* ("river tram").

*Monument to Taras
Shevchenko facing
Ukraina Hotel*

A group of buildings under construction for the Council of Mutual Economic Aid

At the immediate approach to the bridge there are two obelisks, one on each side, with the names of the famous leaders of the Russian army who drove Napoleon out of Russia: Mikhail Kutuzov, Pyotr Bagration and Mikhail Barclay de Tolly, and also the names of guerilla captains and heroes who especially distinguished themselves. Two commemorative slabs bear the inscriptions: "In memory of the heroic exploit of the Russian people and the glorious Russian army, which upheld the independence of our Homeland in the Patriotic War of 1812." They were set up in 1954, when the bridge was reconstructed to double its former width. Now it is 144 feet wide. The other end of the bridge is decorated on both sides with semi-circular granite colonnades crowned by bronze laurel wreaths.

The Borodinsky Bridge leads you to *Smolenskaya Square*, where the tall 26-storey building of the *USSR Ministry of Foreign Affairs* and the *USSR Ministry of Foreign Trade,* erected in 1947-1951, is located.

A wide street runs along the river embankment to the left of the Borodinsky Bridge. This riverside road has been named after Taras Shevchenko, the great Ukrainian poet and revolutionary.

The roadway along the embankment is separated from the houses lining the street by a belt of lawn planted with trees and shrubs. This is one of Moscow's modern residential quarters, occupying the area between the Borodinsky and Kalininsky Bridges. And between them there is an elegant single-span subway bridge, erected in 1936.

A few words about the *Kalininsky Bridge,* built in 1957. This is a unique structure 140 feet wide and, together with its elevated approaches, about 1,640 feet long. Traffic can move over it in twelve lanes.

Still another tall building, the *Ukraina Hotel,* can be seen to the left of the bridge. There are 29 stories with more than a thousand suites in the central part of the edifice.

The hotel was opened in 1957 and in 1964 a monument to Taras Shevchenko was unveiled on the public square in front. The six-metre bronze statue of the inspired bard of freedom stands on a granite pedestal built of blocks brought from the Ukraine.

On the opposite bank of the Moskva River, an office building and hotel are going up to the left of the Kalininsky Bridge. Intended for CMEA (Council for Mutual Economic Aid) the job is being financed by all the members of the Council and socialist countries who are coordinating the development of their national economies in the interests of their peoples.

A wide thoroughfare called *Kutuzovsky Prospekt* begins at Kalininsky Bridge. It is faced on both sides by tall, light-coloured apartment houses of modern architectural design, which lends it a gay, festive appearance. This is one of Moscow's most modern and beautiful avenues. It has many fine stores, among them *Dom Igrushki* (Toy House), the city's largest specialized store of this kind, on the right side, and across the way a big jewelry store and craft shop, where you can buy delightful souvenirs in the way of highly artistic handicrafts. Just before you get to the craft shop there is a twelve-story building on the left side of the avenue where you can buy Soviet goods with foreign currency. *V/O Vneshposyltorg*, the organization that handles such matters, has display rooms on the first floor.

The point where Kutuzovsky Prospekt meets Bolshaya Dorogomilovskaya Street was once known as *Dorogomilovskaya Zastava* (check-point gate) which marked the city limits. Today Moscow has pushed out far to the West. Kutuzovsky Prospekt runs on for several more miles, leading to places dear to the heart of every Muscovite, of every Russian. But these will be dealt with elsewhere, in the excursion around the area in the vicinity of Kutuzovskaya Metro Station.

From this fork in the road, it is best to turn left and return by Bolshaya Dorogomilovskaya Street to the already familiar place —the Kiev Railway Terminal.

To the right of the Kiev Railway Terminal, there is another hotel—*Kievskaya*. It also caters to tourists from abroad.

KUTUZOVSKY PROSPEKT

THIS is not a subway station in the strict sense of the word, for it was built on the surface, like the greater part of the Kalininskaya-Molodyezhnaya Line, running from the centre of town to a west residential district. The station was assembled from prefabricated reinforced concrete elements in a simple convenient layout. The platforms are situated under the viaduct that takes Kutuzovsky Prospekt over the Okruzhnaya (Circular) Railway Line.

Kutuzovsky Prospekt, as you already know, begins at Kalininsky Bridge. Beyond the bridge (on the right bank of the Moskva River), Novodorogomilovskaya Street, laid out fairly recently, joined the former Mozhaisk Highway. It was followed by Kutuzov Settlement Street and Moscow-Minsk Highway. At the end of 1957, this whole chain of streets was named Kutuzovsky Prospekt.

But it was not merely a matter of renaming already existing streets. The new name was given to an entirely new traffic artery of a completely reconstructed district.

Near the entrance to the Battle of Borodino Panorama Museum

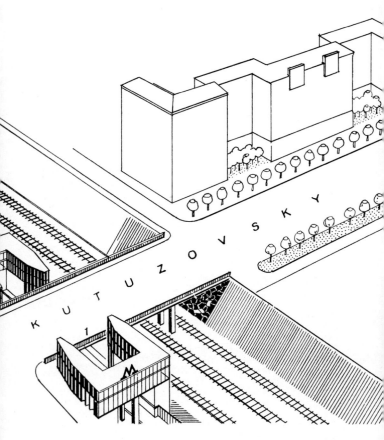

KUTUZOVSKY PROSPEKT

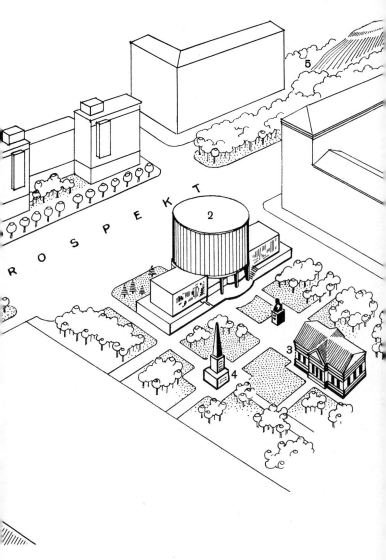

1. "*Kutuzovskaya*" Metro Station; 2. *Battle of Borodino Panorama Museum;* 3. *Kutuzov Hut;* 4. *Obelisk over the common grave of warriors killed in the Battle of Borodino;* 5. *Site where Victory Monument is to be erected.*

Hairdressers in Kutuzovsky Prospekt   353

Before the revolution the locality through which Kutuzovsky Prospekt was laid had been a wretched city suburb, with small, mostly wooden houses.

Today a paved roadway 260 feet wide runs through the place. Both sides of it are faced for miles by tall modern apartment houses. schools, libraries, laundries, drugstores, and moving picture theatres. There are wide sidewalks lined by shady trees, underpasses for pedestrians and good connections with other parts of the city (motorbus, trolley-bus, and subway). The Moskva River flowing nearby has been turned into a clean, deep waterway between gray granite embankments—the site of the busy Western River Port.

Not far from the viaduct, a unique structure on a spacious square is bound to attract your attention. Executed in the shape of a huge cylinder of glistening glass and aluminum about 135 feet in diameter, and 80 feet high. The *Battle of Borodino Panorama Museum* was opened in this building and adjacent wings (architects—Alexander Korabelnikov, Alexander Kuzmin and Sergei Kuchanov; designing-engineer—Yury Avrutin) in October 1962 on the 150th anniversary of the Patriotic War of 1812.

The famous Panorama of the Battle of Borodino by Academician Franz Rubo (also famous for his Defence of Sebastopol Panorama), is on display here. It was exhibited for the first time on Chistoprudny Boulevard (opposite the present *Kolizei* Moving Picture Theatre) in 1912, on the occasion of the 100th anniversary of the Battle of Borodino. After being on view for only two years, the canvas, 380 feet long and 50 feet high, was seriously damaged during a fire and lay rolled up for many years. Part of the panorama —a section 30 feet long and 16 feet high— was lost, the part depicting the episode in the battle where the mortally wounded Russian General Pyotr Bagration was carried off the battlefield. And only a few bits of the "sky" remained.

To restore the panorama to its original appearance, the painting had to be cleaned, the paint had to be renewed where it had crumbled off, and the missing episode reconstructed. Ernst Thaelmann Factory in Leningrad wove a canvas 400 feet long and 35 feet wide. Then the "sky" was painted onto it right inside the new building and joined with the "earth," with the part of the gigantic painting by Franz Rubo which had survived. To bolster up the old canvas, it was attached to the new one. The finally completed panorama together with its supporting frame now weighs more than seven tons.

Besides, the whole foreground had to be recreated, that is, the 40-foot distance from the viewing platform to the canvas had to be filled up with tridimensional figures. Here there are practically full-size reproductions of the streets of the village of Semyonovskaya, the Semyonovsky ravines, the positions of Russian troops, the figures of the soldiers, big and small guns, dead horses, breast-works, sacks of earth, trees and many other objects.

After much painstaking and arduous work, a team of artists and other specialists restored the Battle of Borodino Panorama, and the hot noon of August 26, 1812, blazed up again on the canvas.

On that day a "battle of giants"—the Army of Napoleon and the Russian Army under Mikhail Kutuzov—was fought to the west of the city of Mozhaisk, 75 miles from Moscow. It involved a quarter of a million soldiers and officers, locked in fierce combat, and 1,200 guns.

In creating his amazing canvas, Franz Rubo scrutinized historical documents and literature devoted to the Battle of Borodino. And the panorama very faithfully conveys the crucial moment of the battle. Standing on the viewing platform in the centre of the cylindrical building, you become a witness, as it were, of what is taking place before you. The whole scene is tremendously impressive: you seem to hear the commands of the officers, the thunder of the bursting shells, the neighing and snorting of the horses, the groaning and moaning of the wounded, the rolling of the drums, and the clanking of the sabers; you seem to sense the smell of gunpowder and burning straw...

Alongside the Battle of Borodino Panorama Museum there stands another memorial of the war of 1812—the "*Kutuzov Hut*" *Military History Museum.*

In the "Souvenir" shop

It was in this peasant hut in the village of Fili that Fieldmarshal Kutuzov, on September 1, several days after the battle of Borodino, summoned the Military Council of the Russian Army that had retreated to Moscow. It was here that he made his historical decision: "The loss of Moscow does not mean the loss of Russia. For the good of our Homeland, I order you to retreat!"

The hut, which belonged to a peasant by the name of Frolov, burned down in 1868, but 20 years later it was rebuilt and restored to its original appearance. And today it accommodates this unique museum, which recreates, as it were, the great events of 1812.

On the way from the panorama to the hut-museum, you will notice a large dark-gray stone obelisk to the right. This monument was originally erected at the Dorogomilovsky Cemetery in 1940 over the common grave of 300 soldiers who had fought in the Battle of Borodino. In 1953 the obelisk, together with the remains of the soldiers, was transferred to its present site.

Somewhat closer to the peasant hut there is a tall pedestal surmounted by a bust of Mikhail Kutuzov.

In the Kiev District, where the Battle of Borodino Panorama Museum and the "Kutuzov Hut" Museum are located, the names of many of the streets commemorate the heroes of the war of 1812; Generals Pyotr Bagration, Mikhail Barclay de Tolly, and Alexei Yermolov; Denis Davydov, the poet and guerilla-fighter, and Vasilisa Kozhina and Gerasim Kurin, simple peasants who organized guerilla detachments.

Several of these streets run into Kutuzovsky Prospekt; others are some distance away.

One of the streets that became part of Kutuzovsky Prospekt—the former Mozhaisk Highway—witnessed many events throughout its history. The Smolensk Road which passed along it and continued west, was used in the 15th-17th centuries by ambassadors of West European states to get to Moscow and Russian ambassadors travelled along it to the West. It was the road taken by the Polish szlachta (gentry) when they invaded Russia in 1606-1612 and then hurriedly fled the country after tasting the bitterness of defeat at the hands of Russian warriors led by Minin and Pozharsky. And there are places along it bound up with the history of Napoleon's invasion.

Beyond General Yermolov Street, which runs off Kutuzovsky Prospekt to the right, this thoroughfare continues as the Moscow-Minsk Highway, which shortly brings you to *Poklonnaya Gora* (The Hill You Bow To), to the left of the highway. This hill got its name from an old custom: people arriving in the ancient Russian capital would bow to it (poklonitsya means to bow before someone or something).

If you climb to the summit of Poklonnaya Gora and face the centre of the city, you will clearly see before you three tall buildings—the apartment-house on Vosstaniye Square, *Ukraina Hotel* and the apartment-house on Kotelnicheskaya Embankment; the TV tower; the arrow-shaped flagstaff on the Palace of Young Pioneers; the ski jump on Lenin Hills, and the huge edifice of Moscow University, which seems to be just a stone's throw away.

In the other direction, residential districts amidst green fields and woods meet your eye on both sides of the Moscow-Minsk Highway. They stretch out before you to the very horizon. Cranes, cranes and more cranes protrude from this never-ending sea of housing developments.

Many saplings and shrubs have been planted around Poklonnaya Gora. Here, on the loftiest spot amidst the young trees, three roughly hewn rocks are laid one on top of the other. On the polished side, there is the following inscription: "On this site a monument is to be erected to commemorate the victory of the Soviet people in the Great Patriotic War of 1941-1945." To be erected in the recently laid out 250-acre Victory Park, it will commemorate the biggest battles and denote the army units and guerilla detachments which glorified the Soviet Army, the enterprises and collective farms which made a significant contribution to the country's defence, and the names of valiant heroes in the war against Hitler's Germany.

A CRUISE ALONG THE MOSKVA RIVER

BEFORE going on an excursion outside the city limits, let us make another trip inside the city, this time a boat ride on the Moskva River.

On the right bank of the Moskva River near Kiev Railway Terminal, there is a motor ship landing-embarkation wharf called *Kievsky Bokzal.* We'll begin our excursion there on a small motor-vessel, or "river tram," as the Muscovites call it.

To the left of the wharf you can see the triple-span *Borodinsky Bridge,* erected as a unique monument in memory of the war of 1812.

Moscow Kremlin

We board a "river tram" sailing down stream. The first thing you notice on the left bank is a fortress wall with the graceful and shapely belfry of the *Novodevichy Convent* towering above it. "The Bell-Tower of Ivan the Great is worth seeing," wrote Vasily Bazhenov, a great Russian architect of the 18th century, "but the belfry at the Devichy Convent by architect Pyotr Potapov is still more fascinating for a person with taste." The convent was built in the first quarter of the 16th century, and the belfry in 1690.

The grounds to the left of the monastery were formerly called *Devichye Polye* (Maidens' Field). Up until the end of the last century, it was the site of folk celebrations with shows, swings, merry-go-rounds, and the like.

Now we are sailing under the open-work *Krasnoluzhsky Bridge*, erected in 1908. The Okruzhnaya (Circular) Railway Line crosses it onto a high embankment running to the other side of a big bend in the Moskva River, where the Andreyevsky Railway Bridge, the duplicate of this one, carries the line over the river again.

Just beyond the Krasnoluzhsky Bridge, the *Luzhniki sports centre* begins on the left and, on the right, the steep green slopes of *Lenin Hills* descend to the river bank.

Next we come to the two-level *Metro Bridge* and the *Andreyevsky Bridge*. The latter got its name from a monastery whose structures are still visible amidst the green hills. Founded in the 17th century, the monastery was closed in the middle of the 18th century. More than 300 years ago, one of the first Moscow schools was opened there and instruction was given in ecclesiastical and secular sciences, including grammar and philosophy.

Between the Andreyevsky Bridge and the Krymsky Bridge, visible in the distance, *Gorky Central Recreation Park* can be seen stretching along the right bank, and the 1.25-mile long Frunze Embankment, completely built up with modern apartment houses, along the left bank.

You can't mistake *Krymsky Bridge*. It is the only suspension-bridge. Its striking design enhances the view of the river. It is about 2,500 feet long.

This and 16 other bridges were erected in the 1930's over the Moskva and Yauza Rivers and the Drainage Canal in the space of just two years. Nearly all of them replaced old bridges which, by that time, had become traffic bottlenecks.

The 1930's was also a time of intensive construction of granite embankments on the rivers and canal, which by 1939 stretched for approximately 30 miles. Today the overall figure has been boosted by another 15 miles. By way of comparison only 2.5 miles of rock embankments were erected over the many centuries before the revolution.

Farther on, the high diving tower for the large open-air *Moskva Swimming Pool* comes into view. Then, at the *Bolshoi Kamenny Bridge,* you will see to your left an old building with six columns. At the beginning of the 19th century, this house belonged to Alyabyev, the father of the well-known composer who wrote the popular romance *The Nightingale.*

Today the *All-Union Book Chamber,* founded more than 47 years ago, occupies these premises. This is a scientific institution that collects and stores copies of all books, newspapers, pamphlets, placards, sheet music, maps—in other words, everything that is printed in the country. More than 30 million books, magazines and other publications have been stored here. The chamber registers, systematizes and describes all Soviet publications.

Somewhat below the stretch where the *USSR Picture Gallery* is going up, the Drainage Canal branches off to the right. This canal was constructed in 1786 along the old channel of the Moskva River. The aquatic sports station and grandstands belonging to the *Trud Sports Club* are located at the point where the canal and river meet.

On the right bank, below the junction of the river and the canal, there is a rare architectural monument: the sole surviving 17th-century *boyar* urban estate, the so-called chambers of Averky Kirillov, a town council official. All that has remained is the church and the dwelling, which was partially reconstructed at the beginning of the 18th century and now has been completely restored. The Institute of Museology is housed in the church premises.

Nearby, a tall dark-grey apartment house can be seen stretching along the bank, a building Muscovites call *Government House*. It would probably be hard to find another building in Moscow with so many memorial plaques mounted on it. These denote that Alexander Serafimovich, the distinguished Soviet writer, lived there (his name has been given to the street where the building stands); it was also the home of Grigory Petrovsky and Pavel Postyshev, eminent Communist Party functionaries and Soviet statesmen; Nikolai Podvoisky, Chairman of the Military Revolutionary Committee in Petrograd in October 1917 and an outstanding organizer of the Red Army; and Mikhail Tukhachevsky, a Soviet military leader.

To the right of "Government House" you can see the smokestacks of the *Krasny Oktyabr Confectionery Factory*. This factory, whose products are very popular throughout the country, was awarded a Grand Prix at the World's Fair in Brussels.

There is a spacious square with a public garden to the left of "Government House." Long ago there was a bog here, and this was remembered in the name of the square —Bolotnaya *(boloto* is the Russian for bog). Its present name is Repin Square. In 1775, Yemelyan Pugachev, the leader of the peasant insurrection, and several of his comrades-in-arms were executed on this spot.

Here we pass under a bridge that spans the river from "Government House" to the Kremlin with a 345-foot steel arch. It is called *Bolshoi Kamenny Bridge* (Big Stone Bridge) to commemorate the first stone *(kamen* is the Russian for stone) arched bridge, which was built at the end of the 18th century by a Russian craftsman named Filaret. The bridge has a total length of nearly 1,650 feet.

The former Stone Bridge, the predecessor of the present one, spanned the river a little higher upstream and had a total length of some 330 feet. It was replaced by the new bridge just before the Second World War.

Beyond the Bolshoi Kamenny Bridge, the Kremlin can be seen in all its splendour on a high hill, on the left bank. You will never forget this admirable view of the Kremlin from the Moskva River, its walls, towers, cathedrals, palaces, the Bell-Tower of Ivan the Great, the emerald green of the hill, and the ruby stars against the background of the lofty, light-blue Russian sky—all of which looks different, still more colourful, like a delightful picture that keeps changing every few feet of our downstream cruise.

The river embankment opposite the Kremlin has been named after the late Maurice Thorez, a French Communist Party leader. Here the British Flag can be seen fluttering over one of the buildings. This is the *British Embassy*. Nearby there is a graceful, shapely belfry, built in the second half of the 19th century (architect—Kozlovsky). Decorative elements of both Gothic and Moscow styles (a steeple-shaped top and *kokosniks* [1]) have been combined in its architectural design.

Next to the belfry, there is a group of buildings that were erected at the end of the last century and once belonged to a millionaire merchant Kokorev. They included warehouse facilities and a hotel visited by many prominent people, among them painters Ivan Kramskoi, Ilya Repin, Vasily Vereshchagin and Appolinary Vasnetsov, composers Pyotr Tchaikovsky and Anton Arensky, and Emile Verhaeren, the Belgian poet. Herbert Wells lived in one of the houses on this embankment in 1920.

Now we are passing under *Moskvoretsky Bridge,* one of the city's biggest reinforced concrete overpasses, which was opened to traffic in November 1937. Faced with pink granite, monumental and at the same time light, both imposing and simple, it blends well with the Kremlin.

Right after the bridge, you can see *Bukharest Hotel* on the right bank, then Moscow State Power Station with its many smokestacks. A section of the city called Zaryadye begins on the opposite bank. The *Rossiya,* the biggest hotel in the Soviet Union and in Europe, is there.

---

1) A *kokoshnik was a kind of woman's head-dress* in old Russia. Here it is a decorative element on building façades (in the form of a semi-circular shield, reminiscent of such a head-dress), motif widely used in Russian architecture of the 16th and 17th centuries.

Today many narrow side streets and lanes run right up to the hotel. But not a trace of them will remain. The entire adjacent territory is to be replanned, relandscaped and modernized, making it one of the finest spots in the Soviet capital.

After the hotel, the entire stretch from *Kitaisky Proyezd* practically up to the Bolshoi Ustinsky Bridge is taken up by the former Foundling Hospital, built in the 1760's. The central section (consisting of three parts), which protrudes towards the embankment and is crowned by a cupola, projects from the huge structure with a façade stretching about 1,250 feet. The eastern wing was completed in Soviet times (in the 1930's).

The next bridge we pass under is the *Bolshoi Ustinsky*. It was given that name because the Yauza, the second largest Moscow river, empties into the Moskva River nearby *(ustye* is the Russian for river mouth). Navigable since old times, Peter I launched a yawl on it, the "grandfather" of the Russian navy. In the past, the green groves on the banks were hacked down to make room for factories, which polluted the water with waste.

An extensive river reconstruction programme was tackled in 1937 to improve the Yauza. The river channel was nearly doubled in width and the dilapidated banks strewn with rubbish and refuse were replaced by new granite embankments. Two hydraulic installations were erected on the Yauza, which noticeably raised the river's level, making a considerable stretch of it navigable.

The Bolshoi Ustinsky Bridge was erected nearly thirty years ago. It is the lightest in design of the capital's arch bridges. That is why it blends well with the light-coloured, tall apartment house that rises to a height of 500 feet nearby on the left bank, forming a harmonious unit with the edifice.

Beyond the bridge, the *Kotelnicheskaya* and *Goncharnaya Embankments* run along the river to your left, and, to your right, *Maxim Gorky Embankment* built up with tall new apartment houses behind a wide green belt, very much resembling the *Frunzenskaya Embankment* you have already seen on the left bank.

After the Bolshoi Ustinsky Bridge comes the *Bolshoi Krasnokholmsky*, erected in 1938, with an overall length of 2,380 feet including the approaches. This is the largest of the Moscow bridges, except for the Metro overpass. It enables you to get a good view of the bends of the Moskva River with its clear-cut granite embankments (erected in the first years of reconstruction of the Soviet capital, before the Second World War), tugs hauling trains of barges, self-propelled barges, motor boats and racing boats.

The river began its present vigorous life in 1937, when it was swelled by channelling water into it from the Volga, 80 miles away.

Farther down stream we come to triple-span *Novospassky Bridge*, and nearby you can see the walls, towers and belfry of a monastery of the same name. The bridge was erected in 1911 and, twenty-seven years later, was reconstructed. The monastery is a major monument of 17th-century architecture.

The wharf near the Novospassky Bridge is the last stop on the river cruise. However, you will find it more convenient to ride back on the same boat and get off at the stop near the Krasnokholmsky Bridge, which is only a short walk to the *Taganskaya* Metro Station (to the left of the bridge) or the Paveletskaya Metro Station (to the right).

A CRUISE ALONG THE MOSCOW CANAL

TWO years ago, it took an hour to travel from the centre of town to the *Northern River Port Passenger Terminal*. Now you can cover the 9 miles by Metro in less than 20 minutes.

Rechnoi Bokzal (River Terminal) Metro Station is one of Moscow's newest subway stations, the last on this line. As you step out of the modern, austere and well-proportioned surface hall, the first thing that strikes your eye is a young, attractively landscaped park behind a beautifully wrought iron fence.

A graceful building with arcades and galleries can be seen towering high above the tops of the trees. The central section is in the shape of a tower with a spire of stainless steel topped by a five-pointed star 280 feet above the ground. From afar it resembles a two-deck river passenger ship standing at the quay. This is the Soviet capital's North-

The river station at Khimki

Cruising and motor-boating

ern River Port Passenger Terminal (architect—Alexei Rukhlyadev). It stands on the bank of the Khimki Reservoir on the Moscow Canal. The park, the terminal and the reservoir are all 30 years old.

The first floor of the terminal building is skirted with stately white stone columns. Five tall doors open into a vaulted hall and a two-tone marble-faced waiting-room with an electrified schematic diagram of the canal. A broad granite staircase leads from the waiting-room to the central quay.

A long quay with moorings for suburban motor and diesel river vessels runs off to the left of the central section; and the big Northern Cargo Port, to the right.

There is a restaurant called the *Volga* in the terminal building and a roof garden café on the second floor with a splendid view of the expansive reservoir.

On the opposite side of Leningrad Highway, facing the grounds of the Northern River Port Passenger Terminal, there is the *Friendship Park* laid out in August 1957 by delegates from other countries to the Sixth World Youth and Student Festival. Here a mighty oak surrounded by five luxuriant lindens, symbolizing the friendship and unity of the youth of all five continents, is seen raising its lofty crown on high above the greenery in the central circular parterre from which a host of alleys, lanes and paths diverge like rays.

Several years ago the Northern River Port seemed somewhat isolated from the busy capital. To get to it you had to pass sprawling warehouse grounds, summer cottage areas and straggly rows of one-time villages.

Today tall modern apartment houses have sprung up all along the Leningrad Highway inside the city limits.

Practically all the water in the huge reservoir of the Northern River Port, the copious Moscow River, the water supply for the city's many fountains and the water pouring out of the faucets in the homes, institutes, hotels, etc.—practically all of it comes from the Volga River. Back in 1937 the city would have used every drop of water in the Moskva River, for it was consuming 155 million gallons a day, exactly as much as the river could supply.

By then a canal linked the Volga to the Moscow River by a system of locks, eleven altogether. It has an average width of some 280 feet, a depth of no less than 18 feet, and an overall length of nearly 80 miles. About a sixth of the canal passes through man-made reservoirs, of which there are seven along the route.

Volga water is forced to Moscow by powerful pumping stations, each with a rated transfer capacity of 21,000 gallons a second, which is five to six times greater than the average summer expenditure of the Moskva before. The water transferred from the Volga in a year would fill a train of railway tank cars stretching from the Earth to the Moon.

Moscow Canal made the Soviet capital first a port of three seas—the White, Baltic and Caspian, and then, following the construction of the Volga-Don Shipping Canal, of two more—the Black Sea and Sea of Azov. It has ensured the population and industry of the Soviet capital an adequate, steady supply of water and turned the Moskva River into a deep navigable waterway within the city limits, where it had become shallow.

There is plenty to be seen along the canal with its 240 different structures, including reinforced concrete and earthen dams, locks, hydroelectric stations, bridges, tunnels and pumping stations. Engineering skill and architectural fancy have combined to produce a uniform complex—severe lines, well-proportioned and expressive.

Still more attractive are the fascinating places through which the canal passes, possessing the inimitable nature of Central Russia. Man-made reservoirs with numerous coves and creeks; woods, hills and fields; beaches, boating stations, and fishing grounds; vacation hotels, sanatoriums and Young Pioneer camps drift by before your eyes, long to be remembered.

There are places near this man-made waterway which are bound up with the life and work of several distinguished Russians: *Pushkino* is associated with Vladimir Mayakovsky, the great Soviet poet, and with Konstantin Stanislavsky and Vladimir Nemirovich-Danchenko, the founders and directors of the Moscow Art Theatre; *Vitenevo,* with Mikhail

Saltykov-Shchedrin, the eminent Russian writer; *Rozhdestveno-Suvorovo*, with Alexander Suvorov, the gifted Russian military leader; and *Dmitrov*, with Pyotr Kropotkin, the eminent geographer and traveller and one of the principal advocates and theoreticians of anarchism.

Dmitrov, like Moscow, was founded by Yury Dolgoruky. Peter I visited this ancient town. Three of the interesting sights are the Dmitrovsky Cathedral, a monument of 16th-century Russian architecture; a fortress, and an earthen rampart.

The canal also passes near the village of *Fedoskino*—centre of a Russian school of lacquered miniature painting which enjoys world renown. There is a small museum of miniature paintings in the village and a school providing training in this art.

Comfortable two- and three-deck motor and diesel-electric river liners depart regularly from the Northern River Port during the summer navigation season on voyages down the Moscow Canal and also farther, down the Volga.

Cruises can be made all the way down the canal and back on special excursion vessels.

Motor ships depart regularly from the Northern River Port during the summer navigation season to ply the canal and its reservoirs. These skimming *Rockets* and *Meteors*, developments of the Krasnoye Sormovo Shipbuilding Yards in the city of Gorky, make several dozen trips a day.

If you do not have much time, you can get an idea of what the canal is like by taking in part of it, the stretch between the terminal and, say, the *Khvoiny Bor* (Pine Woods), *Lesnoye* (Forest), *Solnechnaya Polyana* (Sunny Glade) or *Beryozovaya Roshcha* (Birch Grove) wharves.

And for those whose time is very limited, just a few hours, there is another suggestion: you can take a pleasure motor ship in the evening as far as the *Klyazma Reservoir*, make a short stop at the Gorky or Troitskoye wharves, and then return.

Guests of the Soviet capital call the Moscow Canal, which has been travelled by over 100 million persons in the past twenty-five years, the "Moscow souvenir."

Beside the Moscow Canal

THE MOSCOW METRO

ON our sightseeing trips around Moscow, we frequently travelled by *Metro,* using the subway stations as reference and starting points for our excursion. Now let us return to the Metro and get a good idea of what it is like.

The Moscow Metro, which has been named in honour of Vladimir Lenin, rounded out 30 years of public service in 1965. On May 15, 1935, regular traffic began on the first 5.6-mile line from Sokolniki to Gorky Park. This line was laid in record time—three-and-a-half years. By now the length of track has multiplied many times and become a ramified subway system.

There are large wall-mounted schematic diagrams of the Metro system in the surface vestibules of many of the stations. They show, in distinctive individual colours, the various *radial lines* converging towards the centre and merging there; the *circular line* intersecting and linking them all; and three branch lines running off from it which do not as yet have continuations running towards the centre. Were we to superimpose such a diagram on a map of Moscow, we would find that it takes in both the centre and the outskirts of the city. The lines of the underground railway system duplicate, in the main, the radial-ring layout of the city.

In 1957, the first radial line, linking the centre of town with Sokolniki and the Gorky Recreation Park, was extended from the park to the Lenin Central Stadium in Luzhniki and two more stations were built—*Frunzenskaya* and *Sportivnaya.*

Further extension of this line, in the direction of the South-Western District of the Soviet capital, was tackled at both ends of the new stretch simultaneously. As a result, this track, running from the Lenin Central Stadium (*Sportivnaya* Station) across a two-level bridge over the Moskva River to a residential district beyond the tall Moscow University building, was built in a very short time, by the end of 1958. Here, too, two new stations were built—*Leninskiye Gory* (Lenin Hills) (located on the bridge itself) with two exits—one to Luzhniki and the other to Lenin Hills, and *Universitet* (University).

At the end of 1963, the line was further extended for another three miles and two more stations were opened: *Prospekt Vernadskogo* and *Yugo-Zapadnaya* (South-Western), and just a short while ago the other end of the line was extended from Sokolniki to Preobrazhenskaya Square. This line, stretching more than 12.5 miles, provides speedy service between the capital's north-eastern part and its rapidly growing South-Western District.

It seems strange that the *Yugo-Zapadnaya* Stations is not in the actual city, but some distance from it. The residental quarters of the expanding city have dropped far behind, and there are only villages, vast empty lots, and isolated small buildings here and there.

Previously, it was thought that the subway system should follow the expanding city. Now the policy has been completely reversed, and the city is catching up to the expanding subway system: additional lines are being laid in new development districts before they are built up. This method of expanding the system simplifies the work, cuts construction costs and, what is more important, immediately provides new settlers with the most convenient means of transport.

A bold stride like that made by the subway system not only outstrips housing construction but also brings the city closer to its outskirts, to its suburbs. The *Yugo-Zapadnaya* Station made it possible to improve connections with Vnukovo Airport by motor-bus, with departures every five minutes.

The second radial line of the municipal subway system connected the district around the nationally known Likhachev Automobile Plant with *Sokol*, via the centre, a 9.3-mile route.

At the end of 1964, a 4-mile extension from *Sokol* to Northern River Port went into operation with three new stations: *Voikovskaya, Vodny Station* (Aquatic Sports Stadium) and *Rechnoi Bokzal* (Passenger River Terminal).

The terminal stations on the third radial line are *Shchelkovskaya* and *Kievskaya*. Between them there is a stretch of nearly 12.5 miles partly under ground, partly surfaced and partly elevated. *Arbatskaya* is the most outstanding station on this line, with a 820 -foot-long underground boarding platform, the longest in the Moscow Metro system, stretching from Kalinin Prospekt to Arbatskaya Square. *Izmailovsky Park,* the largest station on this line, has three tracks.

In 1958, a line went into operation consisting of the old Arbatskaya radial line running from the centre (with four stations—*Kalininskaya, Arbatskaya, Smolenskaya* and *Kievskaya),* and its surface continuation, on which two stations were built: *Studencheskaya* and *Kutuzovskaya*. This route crosses the Moskva River by bridge. Later, it was extended farther and farther to the west, and by the middle of 1965 reached Kuntsevo *(Molodyozhnaya* Station). It is now nearly 9.3 miles long, from the centre of town to its western outskirts.

The Moscow subway Circular Line is about 12 miles in circumference. This route, with stations where you can transfer to any of the radial lines, connects with seven of the city's nine railway terminals: the Kazan, Yaroslavl, Leningrad, Byelorussian, Kiev, Paveletsky and Kursk stations.

Besides the Circular Line, the three radial lines running through the centre, and the Arbat-Kuntsevo Line, which begins at the centre, there are three branches, which begin at the Circular Line and run to several new residential districts of the city.

One of these branches is a 3.4-mile line with four stations: *Prospekt Mira, Rizhskaya* (Riga), *Shcherbakovskaya* and *VDNKh* (National Economic Achievements Exhibition).

The second branch runs from *Oktyabrskaya* to *Noviye Cheryomushki*. There are six stations along its over 6-mile route: *Oktyabrskaya, Leninsky Prospekt, Akademicheskaya, Profsoyuznaya, Noviye Cheryomushki* and *Kaluzhskaya,* in the vicinity of what were formerly the villages of Vorontsovo and Semyonovskoye.

The newly built Moscow Metro line links Taganskaya Square and Vykhino, a progressively growing residential area. The eight-mile line has seven stations : *Taganskaya, Proletarskaya, Volgogradsky Prospekt, Tekstilshchiki, Kuzminki, Ryazansky Prospekt* and *Zhdanovskaya.* It was commissioned late in 1966.

The total length of line in the Moscow subway system with its 82 underground and surface stations extends for some 78 miles.

Each station has its own distinctive design, devoted to a definite theme. But diverse as the stations are in design and decoration, they all have one feature in common, which makes it hard to believe you are far below the surface.

"You get the impression that you are in a crystal palace, flooded with sunlight, and not deep down underground," said Alexander Kuprin, the eminent Russian writer, describing the Moscow Metro after returning to his homeland from Paris, where he had lived for many years.

In most of the subway stations passengers go up and down on smoothly-running escalators.

More than 3,500,000 persons use the Metro daily. This is more than 30 per cent of the total passenger traffic handled by the city's public transport facilities. In the 30 years it has been in operation, the Moscow subway system has transported over 20 billion passengers—more than six times the total world population.

As time marches on, the Soviet capital grows and expands. The area and population recently increased considerably when the new limits were fixed. And the city's subway system is expanding accordingly.

Another line, 8 miles long, is to branch off from Taganskaya Square and run along the Highway of Enthusiasts. It has six stations.

A subway is already in operation in Leningrad, Kiev and Tbilisi. A subway line is under construction in Baku, and one in Kharkov is in the offing.

STAR SIGHTS IN THE MOSCOW COUNTRYSIDE

It is hard to tell you about everything in the Moscow countryside, particularly in a tourist guide where space does not permit detailed description. We shall therefore limit ourselves to brief information about some of the notable places, the star sights.

Arkhangelskoye

The *Arkhangelskoye estate,* located at a picturesque spot on the bank of the Moskva River, is an extremely interesting monument of 18th- and 19th-century Russian culture. There are good roads leading to the place, which is only 10 miles from Moscow. The route runs along the Volokolamsk Highway, and then follows the road to Petrovo-Dalneye.

The architectural group of the Arkhangelskoye estate—a palace, park, theatre, and service structures—was built in forty years. The first orchards were laid out back at the beginning of the 17th century. In 1810, the lands passed into the hands of Prince Yusupov, who owned vast stretches of land in many parts of Russia and had thousands of serfs. Yusupov held the post of director of the imperial theatres and the Hermitage.

The most outstanding feature of the estate is the palace, built in classic style. Osip Bove and other eminent Russian architects worked on the design. The real creators of this beautiful architectural group, however, were the gifted craftsmen among Yusupov's serfs, above all the serf architects Vasily Strizhakov and Borunov.

The courtyard on the estate is framed by colonnades lining the sides of the central part of the palace, whose numerous halls are sumptuously decorated with antique sculptures, tapestries and porcelain.

Incrustated furniture, cut-glass chandeliers, numerous mirrors, artistic murals, and parquet floors of different designs add to the rich interior decorations.

A splendid park surrounds the palace, its alleys and lanes decorated with sculptures, colonnades, decorative stairways, pavilions and arbors. The triumphal arch over the gates, which was erected in 1817, leads into the estate, where all of aristocratic Moscow used to gather before the revolution.

Today Arkhangelskoye is a splendid museum possessing valuable works of art. It is the most complete and best-proportioned estate ensemble in the Moscow outskirts. A permanent exhibition "The Serf Theatre in Arkhangelskoye" has been opened in the building of what used to be the theatre, built in 1817.

Borodino

On August 26, 1812, a tremendous battle took place on a field near the *village of Borodino* between the troops of Napoleon and the Russian army under the command of its great military leader Mikhail Kutuzov.

Napoleon hurled 135,000 soldiers and 587 guns against the Russian army, which had 120,000 men and 640 guns on the eve of the battle.

The Battle of Borodino lasted 15 hours. Here for the first time, Napoleon failed to win a decisive battle. This he later acknowledged when he wrote: "The Russians won the right to be called invincible."

The Battle of Borodino marked a turning point in the course of the war in favour of the Russian Army. After Borodino, the French Army was unable to recover, even after invading Moscow.

Borodino is 77 miles from Moscow on the Minsk Highway. Numerous monuments denoting the courage and heroism of the Russian soldiers have been erected on the site of the historic battle. Most of them were put up in 1912 to mark the centenary of the battle with funds contributed by soldiers and officers of Russian Army units that had participated in the battle.

An obelisk, made of gray granite with a bronze eagle on top, stands at a point some 500 feet from the Shevardinsky redoubt, where on August 24, two days before the Battle of Borodino, fierce fighting took place between a forward detachment of the Russian Army and the advancing French regiments. An inscription in French reads: "To the dead of the Great Army." This obelisk was also set up in 1912 with funds raised in France.

At the entrance to a chapel raised as a monument to the soldiers of the 1st and 19th Chasseur Regiments of the Russian Army who were killed in action, there is an inscription in gold letters which reads: "We piedged to die and we kept our vow to be loyal in the Battle of Borodino."

On the Borodino battlefield there is the Borodino State Military History Museum with an interesting collection of documents and various other exhibits concerning events in the Patriotic War of 1812 and one of its most important stages—the Battle of Borodino.

Near the monument to Mikhail Kutuzov there is a common grave of Soviet guardsmen, who fell there in action against the German fascist troops. In the winter of 1941, Borodino was again the site of military operations. The Borodino battlefield was covered with entrenchments, anti-tank ditches, and other defence works. For five days and nights, outnumbered Soviet soldiers battled the enemy. Only two houses in the large village of Borodino remained standing after the fighting was over. But today, Borodino has been rebuilt.

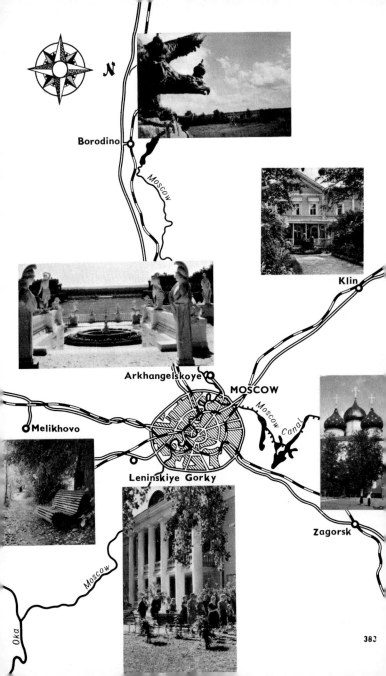

N

Borodino

Moscow

Klin

Arkhangelskoye

MOSCOW

Moscow Canal

Melikhovo

Leninskiye Gorky

Zagorsk

Moscow

Oka

Leninskiye Gorki

22 miles from Moscow on the Kashira Highway there is a country estate called *Gorki*. The mansion stands on a high hill amidst venerable trees in an extensive old park. From September 1918 on, Lenin would frequently go there to relax and from March 1923 to January 1924, spent the last days of his life there.

A *Lenin Memorial Museum* was opened in the Gorki estate on the 25th anniversary of his death. Soviet people revere the memory of Lenin and everything in Gorki has remained just as it was during his lifetime.

The room in which Lenin lived and died is very simply furnished. There is nothing superfluous in it: an upholstered armchair, a small table with an inkwell, paper-knife, eyeglasses and several books on it.

Representatives of the workers and peasants of Soviet Russia, anxiously following the state of Lenin's health, came to see him in Gorki. In November 1923, Lenin was visited by a delegation of textile workers, who brought him a gift of a red calico shirt, made by the best weavers, and 18 cherry saplings. In their letter to him, the workers wrote: "May these cherry trees freshly planted in your garden bring you speedy recovery."

Lenin's visitors included Maxim Gorky, Romain Rolland, Martin Andersen Nexö, and Henri Barbusse.

Zagorsk

A 33-mile ride to the north of Moscow along the Yaroslavl Highway will bring you to the *Zagorsk Historical and Art Museum-Reservation* with a collection of priceless antiquities of Russian 14th-17th century culture.

Here you will find the Troitse-Sergiyev Monastery, one of the oldest in the Moscow countryside, built in the 1340's, which played an important part in the history of Moscow and the Russian state. It was a stronghold which more than once defended the principal city of ancient Russia from foreign invaders. Its stone fortress walls, built in 1540-1580, are up to about 40 feet high. In the years 1608-1610, some three thousand defenders of the monastery heroically withstood a 16-month seige against 15,000 well-armed Polish and Lithuanian invaders.

From the 14th to the 17th centuries, this monastery was a major seat of culture in ancient Russia. Books were written, transcribed and collected there, and master icon-painters, wood carvers, silversmiths and other handicraftsmen worked at their craft. Wonderful art treasures were accumulated in the monastery churches.

A 1920 Government decree made the monastery grounds a national reservation and its architectural complex a museum. Today the Moscow Ecclesiastical Academy and Ecclesiastical Seminary function there.

Some of the finest and most characteristic specimens of ancient Russian architecture and painting have been preserved there. The most important architectural monument is the white-stone *Troitsky Sobor* (Trinity Cathedral), built in 1422-1423, an example of early Moscow architecture. Pilasters and a frieze enriched with sculptures adorn the façade of the cathedral, which is crowned by a massive cupola. The paintings on the iconostasis and the murals, fragments of which have been preserved to this day, are the work of Andrei Rublyov, a distinguished Russian painter of the late 14th early 15th centuries, and other artists of his school. The Dukhovnaya Church, built in 1476-1477, is a striking piece of architecture, with a dome in the shape of a two-storey tower, a belfry in the lower storey and an observation platform in the upper one.

In 1559-1585, the monumental five-dome Uspensky Cathedral was erected in the monastery grounds by order of Ivan the Terrible. Subsequently considered the principal cathedral there, it was patterned after the well-known Uspensky Cathedral in the Moscow Kremlin. Seventeenth-century frescoes and an 18th-century iconostasis with wonderfully gilded carvings and paintings by Russian artists have been preserved inside.

There are also other architectural monuments in the monastery grounds, among them various service structures.

Klin

To the north-west of Moscow, there is an old Russian town called *Klin,* founded in 1318 on the high bank of the Sestra, a small tributary of the Volga. It is a 55-mile drive from Moscow along the Leningrad Highway.

But Klin is known for something else.

The town was for many years the home of *Pyotr Tchaikovsky,* and tens of thousands of tourists wish to go there to see the home of the great Russian composer. Everything in the house, which has been made into a museum, has been kept exactly as it was during his lifetime.

There is a grand piano in the centre of one of the rooms. It was on this instrument that Pyotr Tchaikovsky composed many of his romances, his ballet, *The Sleeping Beauty,* the *Hamlet* overture, and the *Fifth Symphony.* It was here that he worked on his ballet *The Nutcracker.*

A simple table made of birch boards stands in Tchaikovsky's bedroom. It was on this table that he wrote his *Sixth Symphony,* a masterpiece of world classical music.

Composers and musicians who come to the Soviet Union from all over the world make sure they visit Tchaikovsky Museum in Klin. They deeply appreciate the great contribution Tchaikovsky made to the treasurehouse of world music. Twice a year, on the anniversary of the birth and the death of Tchaikovsky, the best Soviet musicians sit down at his piano and play his music. And not only Soviet musicians. In 1958 Van Cliburn, the well-known American pianist who won first prize at the First International Tchaikovsky Piano Competition in Moscow, visited Klin. And he, too, was given the great honour of playing on Tchaikovsky's piano.

This house-museum has an interesting history. After Tchaikovsky's death, A. Sofronov, his servant, purchased the estate from the merchant who owned it in order to keep it intact. And in 1920, the Society of Friends of the Pyotr Tchaikovsky House-Museum was organized.

A terrible ordeal befell this wonderful monument of Russian culture during the

Second World War, when it was devastated by the German fascist troops which seized Klin. But after Klin was liberated (December 15, 1941), the house was restored and on May 7, 1945, the anniversary of Tchaikovsky's birth, the museum reopened its doors to its numerous visitors, to all for whom Tchaikovsky's music is an inexhaustible source of joy and inspiration.

Melikhovo

Melikhovo is the name of a small village in which Anton Chekhov—a great writer and fine man—lived from 1892 through 1899.

Chekhov was very fond of Melikhovo, to the south of Moscow, a 50-mile drive from the Soviet capital along the Moscow-Simferopol Highway.

Anton Chekhov did a great deal of writing in Melikhovo. That was where he produced his famous *The Seagull,* and his stories *Ward No. 6, Person in a Case, Three Years, An Artist's Story,* and *Gooseberries,* among others. Isaac Levitan, the distinguished Russian painter, frequently visited Chekhov at his estate in Melikhovo, which he reproduced in his watercolour called *Derevushka* (The Hamlet).

While living in Melikhovo, Anton Chekhov devoted much of his time to social work. Being a doctor, he gave the local peasants medical assistance, which was especially important during the cholera epidemic. Chekhov painted a truthful picture of the wretched, drab life of the surrounding peasants in his famous story *In the Ravine.* In 1899 failing health forced Chekhov to leave Melikhovo for the Black Sea coast (he was suffering from tuberculosis).

By decision of the Moscow Regional Soviet of Working Peoples' Deputies, the great writer's estate in Melikhovo was turned into a Chekhov Memorial Museum.

USEFUL INFORMATION, ADVICE AND ADDRESSES

Useful Advice

To make certain an Intourist representative meets you on arrival, check up before departure to see if the travel agency has notified *Intourist* of all the pertinent facts: date of arrival, means of travel, and flight or train number. If that has been done, an Intourist representative will be there to help you with the border and customs formalities.

If it happens that you are not met, just ask the first airport or railway station employee or militiaman you meet for Intourist and you will immediately be guided to an Intourist office. There is one at all international airports and railways and seaport stations. The staff will take care of you and make arrangements to get you and your luggage to the hotel. If you have booked a tour, there is no charge for transporting your baggage (up to two pieces per person) from the station or airport to the hotel and back.

Upon arriving at your hotel (at the first point of your itinerary), you must present your passport to the deskman on duty for customary registration formalities. It will be returned as soon as it has been stamped. You are also required to fill in a form giving your name, citizenship, where you are from, length of sojourn, and other information. More often than not the hotel employees themselves will fill it in for you if you tell them what to put down.

Every Soviet hotel frequented by tourists from abroad has a *Service Bureau*. It is there to help the tourist spend his time to the best advantage and make his stay here as pleasant as possible.

Hotel Service Bureaux are open from nine in the morning until late in the evening (usually 10 p.m.) and there are always people on duty who speak several languages.

The Service Bureaux are a big help. They can find out whatever you want to know about your stay in the USSR; make reservations for individual or group sightseeing excursions or for visits to museums, exhibitions, picture galleries, etc.; arrange for tickets to theatres, moving picture houses, the circus, concerts and sports events. The Service Bureaux always have a list of the plays being staged at Moscow theatres for the coming ten days, so you can order the ticket you want well in advance.

Your passport and tour documents are registered at the Service Bureau, and it can help you with any questions pertaining to your visa, or other papers, the itinerary, hotel or restaurant service, and so forth.

Every Hotel Service Bureau has an official who looks after transportation matters. He will reserve your train, plane or ship ticket, order a cab for you, and the like.

You can also find out about store shopping hours, their location, and so forth at the Service Bureau.

Tipping the waiter, chambermaid, taxi driver and other service personnel is not customary in the USSR, as it is in many other countries. It is not expected and is considered somewhat belittling. However, should you wish to thank your guide-interpreter or Intourist bus driver with a personal gesture it would be quite proper to present them with some inexpensive souvenir of your country.

There are no night clubs in the USSR. Most restaurants close at 11 p.m., a few at midnight. The *Metropole* and *National* Hotels have bars which are open until 2 a.m., and some of the restaurants and cafés have dancing to orchestra music.

Evening performances at theatres begin at 6:30 p.m. and usually end between 10 and 11 p.m. Concerts begin at 7 p.m.

In all theatres and concert halls, coats and hats should be checked in the cloak-room. There is no charge for this.

Moving picture houses are open from 9 a.m. until about midnight. Spectators are admitted in the intervals between shows. The programme includes a newsreel or a short and a full-length feature film, and lasts as a rule about two hours. In moving picture theatres, spectators usually do not remove their coats. The seats are numbered.

Dance halls in the parks close at 11 p.m.

The basic Soviet banknote is the rouble. It is equal to 100 kopecks. There are one, two, three, ten, fifteen, twenty, fifty kopeck and one rouble coins in circulation. Paper money consists of one, three, five, ten, twenty-five, fifty and one hundred rouble banknotes. As of January 1, 1966, the official rate of exchange of the USSR State Bank was 90 kopecks for one US dollar.

Currency

You may bring any amount of foreign currency into the country with you but, upon arrival, you must declare it at the customs office, and obtain a certificate to that effect. On leaving the country, you cannot take out more foreign currency than indicated in the customs certificate, that is, more than you brought in.

While touring the country, you may exchange any amount of foreign currency you brought in for Soviet roubles at the rate of exchange of the USSR State Bank. This can be done at any of the currency exchange offices that you will find at all airports and seaport and railway stations, and in most tourist hotels. Each time you are given a certificate stating the exact amount of foreign currency you have exchanged, which you should keep until your departure from the country. It you have not spent all your Soviet roubles during your trip, you may re-exchange them for foreign currency, as long as you produce the certificate showing the total amount of foreign currency you previously exchanged for roubles.

Foreign currency transactions (sale, exchange and so forth) not conducted by foreign currency exchange offices of the USSR State Bank or Intourist agencies are illegal.

Medical Service for Tourists

All medical care in the Soviet Union is free of charge and available to everyone in town and countryside. Foreign tourists who fall ill during their sojourn in the Soviet Union are also given first aid free of charge.

Should you fall ill, notify your Intourist interpreter or hotel service bureau and a doctor will be called immediately. There is no charge for the doctor's visit. The medicines are paid for by the patient at the prices in all Soviet drug stores.

Rules for taking Photographs and Motion Pictures

In Moscow, and everywhere else in the USSR, you are welcome to photograph or film architectural monuments, streets, squares, dwellings, public buildings, theatres, museums, and so forth, and also various landscapes, historical and other sights; you may also make sketches of them.

Just as in all countries, there are definite rules for filming and photographing. By observing them you will help avoid any misunderstandings.

In the first place, you may only take photographs and motion pictures for your own personal (non-commercial) use. Photographs and films taken in the Soviet Union may be shown in moving picture theatres and on television or sold only with the permission of the *Sovexportfilm* Agency (7 *Maly Gnezdnikovsky Pereulok,* Moscow. Tel. 29-32-02).

Naturally, it is prohibited to film or photograph military facilities and equipment, and also seaports, bridges, tunnels, radio stations, and so forth. It is also prohibited to film or photograph from on board aircraft.

Motion pictures and photographs may be taken at factories and plants, on farms and in state institutions with the permission of the management.

If you wish to photograph or film someone or a group of persons, it is best to first ask permission to avoid offence.

Souvenirs

A Soviet camera is a splendid souvenir, and Moscow stores have a wide range of models, including good cameras at reasonable prices.

Moscow watches make another excellent keepsake.

If you are a music lover, you will not go wrong buying records of Russian folk songs or classical music. Both conventional and long-playing records are on sale.

There are many hand-made art objects to choose from for souvenirs; wood carvings, lacquered boxes, ivory figurines, chased, enamelled and filigreed metalware, embroidered goods, and rugs.

Handicrafts by Soviet folk artists have won prizes at international and Soviet exhibitions abroad (the Paris World's Fair in 1937, the New York World's Fair in 1939, and the Brussels World's Fair in 1958).

Many tourists eagerly buy Palekh painted and lacquered art objects made of papier mâché. The work of the craftsmen in Palekh (the name of a village where this art of miniature painting arose) is unusual for its fineness, richness of colour, and ornamentation. There are cigarette cases, powder and jewelry boxes, among other objects.

Then there are the lacquered boxes made in the villages of Mstera and Fedoskino, which very much resemble the Palekh boxes. The miniature paintings on them depict characters from fairy tales, scenes from urban and rural life, and Russian nature.

Articles made of lacquered birch make a fine souvenir. These are both durable and attractive and include cigarette cases and boxes, humidors, desk sets and powder boxes. And they are quite inexpensive.

Wooden art objects painted bright red and gold on a black background invariably attract the attention of all foreign tourists who visit Moscow stores. This is the work of craftsmen from Khokhloma, who have passed down their art from generation to generation for over 300 years. The objects include wooden spoons, bowls, diversely shaped goblets, trays and furniture—all painted in traditional old Russian style with a very attractive design; Khokhloma dishware may even be washed in hot water.

Bone-carvings by craftsmen from the Soviet North, usually on mammoth and walrus tusks, likewise make a suitable souvenir. There are filigree pins and picture frames, paper knives, boxes and figurines to choose from.

You are sure to find foreign tourists crowding around counters where they sell *matryoshki*. These are wooden nests of dolls painted in bright colours and highly polished. Sometimes there are as many as twelve, one inside the other. Made in the town of Khotkovo, near Moscow, they have long since become widely known abroad.

A gift box of Soviet wines including a bottle of *Stolichnaya* or *Petrovskaya vodka* and a jar of the famous Russian caviar are likewise ideal things to take home from the USSR.

If you are pressed for time, the best thing is to do all your souvenir shopping at the kiosk in your hotel or at *GUM*, the State Department Store, on Red Square, *TSUM* (Central Department Store), on Petrovka Street, or the *Magazine Podarkov* (Gifts Store), on Gorky Street.

Several Additional Recommended Specialized Stores

Antiques: 19 Arbat; 31 Sretenka.

Second-hand book shops: 3 Proyezd Khudozhestvennogo Teatra; 10 Arbat; 31 Arbat; 13 Ulitsa Kirova; 24 Ulitsa Gertsena (this store buys and sells books in foreign languages).

Wines: 4 Ulitsa Gorkogo; 7 Stoleshnikov Pereulok.

Records; 17 Ulitsa Kirova; 6/2 Arbat.

Toys: Dom Igrushki (Toy House), 14 Kutuzovsky Prospekt.

Rugs: 9 Ulitsa Gorkogo.

Sheet Music: 14 Neglinnaya Ulitsa; 13 Ulitsa Gertsena; 15 Ulitsa Gorkogo (Soviet Music Store).

Perfumes: 7 Prospekt Marxa; 12 Ulitsa Pushkina; 6 Ulitsa Gorkogo.

Gifts: 12 Ulitsa Gorkogo; 4 Ulitsa Gorkogo; 13/15 Stoleshnikov Pereulok; 10 Ulitsa Petrovka; 24 Kutuzovsky Prospekt; 8 Ulitsa Dvadtsat Pyatogo Oktyabrya (25th of October Street).

Porcelain and earthenware: 5/20 Stoleshnikov Pereulok; 8/2 Ulitsa Kirova; 4 Ulitsa Gorkogo.

Cameras and accessories: 44 Komsomolsky Prospekt; 19/21 Ulitsa Dvadtsat Pyatogo Oktyabrya; 25 Ulitsa Gorkogo; 15 Ulitsa Petrovka; 16 Kutuzovsky Prospekt.

Cut-glass: 15 Ulitsa Gorkovo; 8/2 Ulitsa Kirova.

Art Objects: 12 Ulitsa Petrovka; 15 Ulitsa Gorkogo; 46 Ulitsa Gorkogo; 24 Kutuzovsky Prospekt; 8 Ulitsa Dvadtsat Pyatogo Oktyabrya.

Jewelry: Beryozka (the finest jewelry store in town)—12 Ulitsa Gorkogo; Yantar—13 Stoleshnikov Pereulok (specializes in amber wares); 11 Arbat; 120 Prospekt Mira.

Books in foreign languages: 15 Ulitsa Gorkogo; 18 Kuznetsky Most.

Books in Russian: 8 Ulitsa Gorkogo; 6 Proyezd Khudozhestvennogo Teatra; 4 Arbat; 5/7 Pushkinskaya Ulitsa; Dom Knigi

(Book House) in the grounds of the National Economic Achievements Exhibition (VDNKh); 18 Kuznetsky Most; 6 Ulitsa Kirova.

Seeing Moscow in One, Two or Three Days

You will need at least five days in Moscow to see just the most interesting sights. Here are several suggestions which may prove useful.

Seeing Moscow in Three Days

First Day:

Red Square and Kremlin	Preferably in the morning, before lunch. Three hours. (See Excursions 1 and 2)
Lenin Hills (new Moscow University building, observation platform, a panoramic view of the city)	After lunch. One hour. (See Excursion 6)
Bolshoi Theatre	Performances begin at 6:30 p.m.

Second Day:

National Economic Achievements Exhibition and the Circorama Theatre there	In the morning, before lunch. No less than four hours, including the show. (See Excursion 5)
Sightseeing in the centre of the city, shopping	After lunch (See Excursions 3 and 10)
Bolshoi Theatre performance in the Kremlin Palace of Congresses	Performance begins at 6:30 p.m.

Third Day:

A cruise (in summer) on the Moskva River aboard a river boat	In the morning before lunch. Two hours. (See Excursion 21)
Tretyakov Art Gallery	After lunch. Two hours. (See Excursion 8)
A stroll along Gorky Street, from the Mayakovsky Metro Station to the Karl Marx Prospekt Metro Station	In the evening, before supper. Two hours. (See Excursion 4)

Seeing Moscow in Two Days

First Day:

The Kremlin and Red Square	In the morning, before lunch. Three hours. (See Excursions 1 and 2)
Lenin Hills (new Moscow University building, observation platform, a panoramic view of the city)	After lunch. One hour. (See Excursion 6)
Bolshoi Theatre	Performance begins at 6:30 in the evening.

Second Day:

National Economic Achievements Exhibition and the Circorama Theatre there	In the morning, before lunch. No less than four hours, including the show. (See Excursion 5)
Tretyakov Art Gallery	After lunch. Two hours. (See Excursion 8)
A stroll along Gorky Street, shopping	In the evening, after supper. Two hours. (See Excursion 4)

Seeing Moscow in One Day

We suggest two ways of seeing Moscow in one day

First Way:

The Kremlin and Red Square	Preferably in the morning before lunch. Three hours. (See Excursions 1 and 2)
National Economic Achievements Exhibition	After lunch. Three hours. (See Excursion 5)
A stroll along Gorky Street, shopping	After supper. About one hour. (See Excursion 4)

Second Way:

The Kremlin and Red Square	Preferably in the morning, before lunch. Three hours. (See Excursions 1 and 2)
Moscow State University and the Lenin Sports Complex	After lunch. About three hours. (See Excursions 6 and 7)

A stroll along Karl Marx Prospekt

In the evening, after supper. About one hour. (See Excursions 9 and 10)

Theatres and Concert Halls

Theatres

Kremlin Palace of Congresses, the Kremlin. Tel. 26-79-01
Kremlin Theatre, the Kremlin. Tel. 23-92-81
Bolshoi Opera and Ballet Theatre, 2/7 Ploshchad Sverdlova. Tel. 29-17-51
Moscow Art Theatre, Main stage—3 Proyezd Khudozhestvennogo Teatra. Tel. 29-25-46. Annexe—3 Ulitsa Moskvina. Tel. 29-20-58
Maly Theatre, Main stage—1/6 Ploshchad Sverdlova. Tel. 23-26-21. Annex—69 Bolshaya Ordynka. Tel. 31-37-28
Vakhtangov Theatre, 26 Arbat. Tel. 41-07-28
Mossoviet Drama Theatre, 16 Bolshaya Sadovaya (in the Aquarium Gardens). Tel. 99-20-35
Mayakovsky Theatre, 19 Ulitsa Gertsena. Tel. 29-46-58
Stanislavsky and Nemirovich-Danchenko Musical Theatre, 17 Ulitsa Pushkinskaya. Tel. 29-42-50
Central Soviet Army Theatre, 2 Ploshchad Kommuny. Tel. 81-51-20
Lenin Komsomol Theatre, 6 Ulitsa Chekhova. Tel. 99-19-92
Pushkin Drama Theatre, 23 Tverskoi Boulevard. Tel. 95-44-18
Stanislavsky Drama Theatre, 23 Ulitsa Gorkogo. Tel. 99-72-24
Moscow Drama and Comedy Theatre, 76 Ulitsa Chkalova. Tel. 72-63-00
Yermolova Theatre, 5 Ulitsa Gorkogo. Tel. 29-90-61
Gogol Theatre, 8a Ulitsa Kazakova. Tel. 61-55-28
Light Opera Theatre, 6 Pushkinskaya. Tel. 29-45-02
Theatre of Satire, 18 Bolshaya Sadovaya. Tel. 99-63-05
Central Children's Theatre, 2/7 Ploshchad Sverdlova. Tel. 29-41-59
Central Puppet Theatre, Director S.V. Obrazov, People's Artist of the USSR, 32a Ulitsa Gorkogo. Tel. 51-33-61
Romain Gipsy Theatre, 26 Pushkinskaya. Tel. 29-43-76
Variety Theatre, 20/2 Bersenyevskaya Naberezhnaya. Tel. 31-08-85
Sovremennik Theatre, 1/29 Ploshchad Mayakovskogo. Tel. 51-36-72
Drama Theatre, 2 Malaya Bronnaya. Tel. 21-40-93
Miniature Theatre, 3 Karetny Ryad. Tel. 99-66-01
The Circus, 13 Tsvetnoi Boulevard. Tel. 28-82-31
Open Air Theatre at the National Economic Achievements Exhibition, Prospekt Mira. Tel. 1-81-91-50
Open Air Theatre at the Gorky Central Recreation Park, 9 Krymsky Val. Tel. 32-53-85

Open Air Theatre at the Sokolniki Recreation Park, 62 Russakovskaya Ulitsa. Tel. 68-59-91

Summer Variety Theatre at the Gorky Central Recreation Park, 9 Krymsky Val. Tel. 33-00-14, extension 13

Summer Drama Theatre at the Sokolniki Recreation Park, 62 Russakovskaya Ulitsa. Tel. 68-58-80

Summer Mass Theatre in the Garden of the Frunze Central House of the Soviet Army, 2 Ploshchad Kommuny. Tel. 84-00-00, extension 2-96

Zerkalny Theatre in the Hermitage Gardens, 3 Karetny Ryad. Tel. 99-65-75

Variety Theatre in the Hermitage Gardens, 3 Karetny Ryad. Tel. 99-50-65

Variety Theatre at the National Economic Achievements Exhibition, Prospekt Mira. Tel. 1-81-90-66.

Concert Halls

Tchaikovsky Concert Hall, 31 Ulitsa Gorkogo. Tel. 99-03-78

Large Hall of the Moscow Tchaikovsky Conservatoire, 13 Ulitsa Gertsena. Tel. 29-81-83

Small Hall of the Moscow Tchaikovsky Conservatoire, 13 Ulitsa Gertsena. Tel. 29-99-06, extension 3-47

The Hall of Columns of Trade Union House, 1 Pushkinskaya Ulitsa. Tel. 29-36-12

The October Hall at Trade Union House, 1 Puskhinskaya Ulitsa. Tel. 29-91-81

Concert Hall at Scientists' Club, 16 Kropotkinskaya Ulitsa. Tel. 46-66-84

Concert Hall at Sovietskaya Hotel, 32/2 Leningradsky Prospekt. Tel. 50-73-53

Concert Hall at the Central Railwaymen's Club, 4 Komsomolskaya Ploshchad. Tel. 62-86-04.

Sports Palace, Luzhniki. Tel. 45-87-85.

Motion Picture Theatres

Barrikady (children's theatre), 21 Barrikadnaya Ulitsa

Circorama, at the South Entrance of the VDNKh, Prospekt Mira

Cosmos, 109 Prospekt Mira.

Dynamo (at the Dynamo Stadium), Leningradsky Prospekt

Forum (wide screen), 14 Sadovaya-Sukharevskaya

Gorky Central Recreation Park (summer theatre), 9 Krymsky Val

Hermitage, 3 Karetny Ryad

Khudozhestvenny (wide screen), 14 Arbatskaya Ploshchad

Kiev, 30/32 Kutuzovsky Prospekt

Kolizei, 19a Chistoprudny Boulevard

Leningrad (wide screen), 12 Novopeschanaya Ulitsa

Leto, Izmailovo Recreation Park, 17 Narodny Prospekt

Metropole, 1 Prospekt Marxa
Mir (Panorama), 11 Tsvetnoi Boulevard
Moskva, 2/2 Ploshchad Mayakovskogo
Mossoviet (wide screen), 25 Ulitsa Bakhrushina
Ogonyok, 99 Prospekt Mira
Otdykh, 12 Frunzenskaya Naberezhnaya
Patriot (wide screen), 4 Salyam Adil Boulevard
Pioneer (children's theatre), 25 Kutuzovsky Prospekt
Plamya (wide screen), 1 Ploshchad Vosstaniya
Povtornogo Filma (Revivals), 23/9 Ulitsa Gertsena
Prizyv, 29 Kutuzovsky Prospekt
Progress (wide screen), 17 Lomonosovsky Prospekt
Raketa (wide screen), 12 Ulitsa Grimau
Record (Lenin Sports Complex), Luzhniki
Rossiya (wide screen), Ploshchad Pushkina
Sokol, 71 Leningradsky Prospekt
Sport, 53/55 Bolshaya Pirogovskaya Ulitsa
Start, 56/2 Frunzenskaya Naberezhnaya
Stereokino, 3/3 Ploshchad Sverdlova
Strela, 23/25 Smolensky Boulevard
Udarnik (wide screen), 2 Ulitsa Serafimovicha
Ukraina, 9 Ulitsa Barklaya
VDNKh (summer), in the exhibition grounds, Prospekt Mira;
     there is a large viewing room (widescreen) and a small
     viewing room.
Vstrecha, 5/9 Sadovaya-Chernogryazskaya
Zenit (wide screen), 40/42 Taganskaya Ulitsa

Parks and Gardens

Gorky Central Recreation Park, 9 Krymsky Val
Izmailovo Recreation Park, 17 Narodny Prospekt
Sokolniki Recreation Park, 62 Russakovskaya Ulitsa
Dzerzhinsky Recreation Park, 7 Pervaya Ostankinskaya Ulitsa
The Gardens at the Soviet Army Club, 2 Ploshchad Kommuny
The Hermitage Gardens, 3 Karetny Ryad.

Museums and Exhibitions

History

Central Lenin Museum, 2 Ploshchad Revolyutsii. Tel. 95-48-08
Pavilion-Museum with the Lenin Funeral Train at the Paveletsky
     Railway Terminal, 1 Kozhevnichesky Skver. Tel. 31-73-00
Karl Marx and Friedrich Engels Museum, 5 Ulitsa Marxa-Engelsa.
     Tel. 94-10-43
Museum of the Revolution, 21 Ulitsa Gorkogo. Tel. 99-96-83

Kalinin Museum, 21 Prospekt Marxa. Tel. 23-03-28
Historical Museum, 1/2 Krasnaya Ploshchad. Tel. 28-84-52
Pokrovsky Cathedral Museum (St. Basil's Cathedral), Krasnaya
 Ploshchad. Tel. 21-33-04
Kolomenskoye 16th-17th Century Estate Museum, Kolomenskoye.
 Tel. 34-24-52
Battle of Borodino Panorama Museum, 38 Kutuzovsky Prospekt.
 Tel. 48-19-71
The Kutuzov Peasant Hut, annex of the Battle of Borodino
 Panorama Museum, 38 Kutuzovsky Prospekt. Tel. 48-19-29
Museum of the History and Reconstruction of Moscow, 12
 Novaya Ploshchad. Tel. 94-84-90
Central Soviet Army Museum, 2 Ploshchad Kommuny. Tel.
 84-00-00, extension 1-20
Frunze Central House of Aviation and Cosmonautics, 14 Krasno-
 armeiskaya Ulitsa. Tel. 1-51-56-61.

Science

Polytechnic Museum, 3/4 Novaya Ploshchad. Tel. 23-07-56.
Darwin Museum, 1 Malaya Pirogovskaya Ulitsa. Tel. 1-46-64-70
Moscow State University Museum of Geography, Leninskiye
 Gory. Tel. 1-39-14-15
Main Botanical Gardens of the USSR Academy of Sciences,
 Ostankino, 4 Botanicheskaya Ulitsa. Tel. 1-81-96-35
Planetarium, 5 Sadovaya-Kudrinskaya Ulitsa. Tel. 52-18-23
The Zoo, 1 Bolshaya Gruzinskaya. Tel. 52-34-61.

Art and Architecture

Tretyakov Art Gallery, 10 Lavrushinsky Pereulok. Tel. 31-05-65
Pushkin Fine Arts Museum, 12 Volkhonka. Tel. 21-30-56
Museum of Eastern Cultures, 16 Ulitsa Obukha. Tel. 97-48-00
Shchusev State Architectural Research Museum, 5 Prospekt
 Kalinina. Tel. 23-05-51
Annexe of the Shchusev State Architectural Research Museum,
 1 Donskaya Ploshchad. Tel. 32-02-21
Oruzheinaya Palata, the Kremlin. Tel. 21-47-20
Ostankino Serf Art Museum, Ostankino, 5 Ulitsa Akademika
 Korolyova. Tel. 83-46-45.

Literature

Pushkin Museum, 12/2 Kropotkinskaya Ulitsa. Tel. 46-89-82
Lev Tolstoi Museum, 11 Kropotkinskaya Ulitsa. Tel. 46-92-81
Lev Tolstoi Estate-Museum, 21 Ulitsa Lva Tolstogo. Tel. 46-94-44
Gorky Museum, 25a Ulitsa Vorovskogo. Tel. 94-51-30
Mayakovsky Library and Museum, 15/13 Pereulok Mayakovskogo.
 Tel. 71-01-25
Chekhov Museum, 6 Sadovaya-Kudrinskaya. Tel. 55-02-45
Museum of Literature, 38 Ulitsa Dimitrova. Tel. 31-00-60
Dostoyevski Museum, 2, Ulitsa Dostoyevskogo. Tel. 81-10-85
Nikolai Ostrovsky Museum, 14 Ulitsa Gorkogo. Tel. 29-85-52.

Museums of Theatre and Music

Bakhrushin Theatrical Museum, 31/12 Ulitsa Bakhrushina. Tel. 21-26-23

Glinka Museum of Musical Culture, 4 Georgievsky Pereulok. Tel. 29-72-55

Skriabin Museum, 11 Ulitsa Vakhtangova. Tel. 41-03-02.

Exhibitions

Central Exhibition Hall, 1 Manezhnaya Ploshchad. Tel. 28-93-03

Exhibition Hall of the Union of Soviet Artists, 20 Kuznetsky Most. Tel. 28-18-44

National Economic Achievements Exhibition, Prospekt Mira. Tel. 83-95-61

Building Materials and Construction Section of the National Economic Achievements Exhibition, 30 Frunzenskaya Naberezhnaya. Tel. 42-89-41.

Sports Facilities

Lenin Central Stadium, Luzhniki;

Dynamo Stadium, 36 Leningradsky Prospekt;

Young Pioneer Stadium, 31 Leningradsky Prospekt;

Velodrome, 31 Leningradsky Prospekt;

Dynamo Aquatic Sports Centre, 69 Leningradskoye Shosse Khimkinskoye Vodokhranilishche;

Aquatic Sports Palace, 27 Mironovskaya Ulitsa;

Sports Palace of the Sports Club of the Soviet Army, 39, Leningradsky Prospekt;

Weight Lifting Palace of the Trud (Labour) Sports Club, 11 Tsvetnoi Boulevard;

Hippodrome, 22 Begovaya Ulitsa;

Krylya Sovietov (Wings of the Soviets) *Sports Club*, 24a Leningradsky Prospekt;

Moskva Outdoor Swimming Pool, 37 Kropotkinskaya Naberezhnaya;

Chaika (Sea Gull) *Outdoor Swimming Pool*, 1-3 Turchaninov Pereulok (at the Krymsky Bridge).

Russian Cuisine

Intourist tours generally include meals. These, naturally, depend on the class of tour and are usually provided in the hotel restaurants. Tourists are given a book of meal tickets to pay for their breakfasts, dinners and suppers. Each coupon has a definite value, within which the tourist must keep when ordering himself dishes on the menu.

Tourists travelling in a group have a common menu, as a rule. Exceptions are made for those requiring special diets, which they may receive upon request. Mineral and soda water are served with meals free of charge. There is an extra charge, however, for beer, wines and liquors, which are not included in the menu covered by the meal ticket.

Once you come to Moscow you will be sure to sample Russian cuisine.

Russian *zakuski* (appetizers)—various salads, fish and jellied dishes—are well known. Dishes to be especially recommended are crabmeat salad, cucumber salad with sour cream, herring (Russian style), salmon, sturgeon, and jellied pike, sterlet, tongue and calf's knuckles. There is hardly any need to mention Russian caviar, except to suggest you try it on buttered black bread.

As for the first courses, such favourites as *borshch, shchi,* and *solyanka* are worthy of mention. You should also try *borshch* with mushrooms, Russian noodle soup and *rassolnik rybny* or *frikadelkami* (pickled cucumber soup with fish balls). In the summertime the Russians are particularly fond of cold vegetable or meat *okroshka* (made with *kvass*) and cold *borshch.*

Your impression of the Russian cuisine won't be complete without tasting Siberian *pelmeni* (meat dumplings), or *pelmeni* in bouillon, butter or sour cream, or fried *pelmeni.* You should also try Russian *bliny* (pancakes), *oladyi* (yeast pancakes), and *blinchiki* (fritters) with meat, cottage-cheese or apple.

Russians are very fond of cereals, especially buckwheat and farina.

You should also try *kissel,* a time-honoured jelly-like Russian dessert.

And lastly, mention should be made of tea, which Russians are very fond of, especially with pies or home-made cookies.

You have no doubt heard, of course, of Russian *vodka.* There are different kinds: Stolichnaya, Petrovskaya, Yubileinaya and Kristall are to be especially recommended.

In conclusion, it should be pointed out that Russian cuisine is only part of Soviet cookery, which includes many dishes of all the nationalities inhabiting the country. Soviet cookery is equally enhanced by Russian *pirozhki* (meat pies), Ukrainian *borshch,* Uzbek *pilau,* Georgian *shashlik,* Armenian *tolma,* Azerbaijan *piti* and many other superb dishes and *zakuski* of the various Soviet nationalities.

Restaurants Specializing in the Cuisines of Various Soviet Nationalities

Tourists from abroad will enjoy visiting one or more of Moscow's many restaurants specializing in the cuisines of the various Soviet nationalities, where they will discover many new and unusual dishes.

One of the most popular is the *Aragvi,* which serves some thirty of the best-known dishes in the cuisine of the Georgian Soviet Socialist Republic. These include the famous *shashliks, chicken satsivi,* broiled sturgeon, *sulguni cheese,* and the gem of Georgian cuisine—*spring chicken tabaka.*

Famous white, red and pink Georgian wines are also to be had there. Among them are *Tsinandali* (Georgian Wine No. 1— white), *Mukuzani* (Georgian Wine No. 4—red) and the *Kakhetian* wines from Eastern Georgia (Georgian Wine No. 8 and No. 12— both white, and Georgian Wine No. 5—red).

A gourmet of eastern cuisine will enjoy the *Uzbekistan* and *Baku* restaurants.

The *Uzbekistan* features *tkhum-dulma* (a boiled egg within a fried meat patty), *mastava* (a rice soup with specially prepared meat), and *logman* (a spiced soup with sauce, meat and home-made noodles). But the tastiest dish is probably *maniar*—a sharp broth, ground meat, egg, and bits of rolled-out dough.

There is also a big choice of main courses in Uzbek cuisine. These are prepared from fowl, meat and vegetables. *Shashlik* prepared in Uzbek style, is a tasty dish consisting of small bits of pickled meat broiled over hot coals.

Two fine sweet Uzbek wines are *Aleatiko* and *Uzbekiston.*

The *Baku* is an Azerbaijan restaurant famous for the big variety of *pilau* on its menu—up to twenty different kinds (pilau with chicken or stuffed spring chicken, with lamb or beef, milk or eggs, as well as many sweet *pilaus).*

There are very different first courses too. *Piti,* for example, is a soup which is prepared and served in a clay bowl. Other exotic first courses the restaurant has to offer are *dovta,* a sour milk soup with meat, and a nut soup with chicken. The restaurant is also known for such main courses as *shashlik basturma; golubtsy* (chopped meat and rice cooked in grape leaves); *nar-kurma,* a roast with pomegranates; and broiled spring chicken, to mention a few.

Two excellent red Azerbaijan wines are *Matrassa* and *Shamkhor,* and *Akstafa* is a delicious sweet wine.

A no less diversified menu is also to be found at the *Ararat,* an Armenian restaurant. It features some 40 different Armenian dishes. A number of these are well worth tasting, among them *solyanka,* Armenian style; Yerevan *bozbash;* steamed, fried or broiled trout; *shashlik Ararat;* roast lamb, and *pilau* with raisins. The restaurant is known for its *cheburek* (Armenian meat pies fried in deep fat).

Armenia is famous for its cognacs. The best of these are *Yubileiny, Armenia, Yerevan,* and *Dvin.* Armenian muscats and sherry are also well-known. The latter has a delicate fruit bouquet with a hint of nut flavouring. Of the sweet wines, *Aigeshat* is to be recommended.

Of the other restaurants specializing in the cuisines of the Soviet nationalities, you will undoubtedly find the *Ukraina* very interesting with its famous Ukrainian *borshch* and *galushki.* Be sure to try the fine *Massandra* wines (south coast of the

Crimea), and the sweet wines, especially the pink, white and black muscats and tokay. *Krasny Kamen* (Red Stone) is a world famous Crimean muscat. Its bouquet captures the delicate fragrance of mountain pastures and has a slight hint of citrus. The bouquet of black muscat reminds one of an ox-eye daisy, and the pink muscat, of tea roses.

And if you want to sample the food of other lands you should visit the *Praga, Sofia, Budapest, Varshava, Berlin* and *Pekin* restaurants.

Recommended Restaurants

Aragvi—Georgian cuisine, 6 Ulitsa Gorkogo
Ararat—Armenian cuisine, 4 Neglinnaya Ulitsa
Baku—Azerbaijan cuisine, 24 Ulitsa Gorkogo
Berlin—German cuisine, 6 Pushechnaya Ulitsa
Budapest—Hungarian cuisine, 2/18 Petrovskiye Linii
Kristall—88 Leninsky Prospekt
Metropole—1 Prospekt Marxa
Minsk—Byelorussian cuisine, 22 Ulitsa Gorkogo
Moskva—7 Prospekt Marxa
National—14 Prospekt Marxa
Pekin—Chinese cuisine, 1/7 Bolshaya Sadovaya
Praga—Czech cuisine, 2 Arbat
Sofia—Bulgarian cuisine, 32 Ulitsa Gorkogo
Sovietsky—32 Leningradsky Prospekt
Ukraina—Ukrainian cuisine, 10/9 Kutuzovsky Prospekt
Uzbekistan—Uzbek cuisine, 29 Neglinnaya Ulitsa
Varshava (Warsaw)—Polish cuisine, 2/1 Krymsky Val
Volga—on the shore of the Khimki Reservoir, Northern Moskva
    River Port, 89 Leningradskoye Shosse
Zolotoi Kolos—on the grounds of the National Economic
    Achievements Exhibition, Prospekt Mira.

Cafés

Ararat, 4 Neglinnaya Ulitsa
Artisticheskoye, 6 Proyezd Khudozhestvennogo Teatra
Arfa, 9 Stoleshnikov Pereulok
Aelita, 45 Oruzheiny Pereulok
Cosmos, 4 Ulitsa Gorkogo
Druzhba, 5 Petrovka
Druzhba, 7/9 Kuznetsky Most
Kholodok, 10/34 Strastnoi Boulevard
Khrustalnoye, 17 Kutuzovsky Prospekt
Krasny Mak (Red Poppy), 20 Stoleshnikov Pereulok
Landysh (Lily of the Valley), 29/3 Ulitsa Kirova
Leningradskoye, 38 Arbat
Lira, 17 Ulitsa Gorkogo

Mars, 5/6 Ulitsa Gorkogo
Molodyozhnoye (Youth), 41 Ulitsa Gorkogo
Moskovskoye, 8 Ulitsa Gorkogo
National, 1 Ulitsa Gorkogo
Ogni Moskvy (Lights of Moscow), 7 Marx Prospekt
Otdykh, 6 Ulitsa Gorkogo
Praga, 2 Arbat
Prokhlada (Cool), 3 Marx Prospekt
Raketa (Rocket), 6 Ulitsa Gorkogo
Record, Luzhniki (Lenin Central Stadium)
Riga, 79 Miro Prospekt
Romantiky (Romantics), 40 Komsomolsky Prospekt
Russky Chai (Russian Tea), 13 Ulitsa Kirova
Sardinka (Sardine), 7/5 Pushechnaya Ulitsa
Sever (North), 17 Ulitsa Gorkogo
Snezhinka (Snow Flake), 60/2 Leninsky Prospekt
Sokol (Falcon), 61 Leningradsky Prospekt
Sputnik, 78 Leninsky Prospekt
Timur, 27 Komsomolsky Prospekt
Uyut (Cozy), 34 Leninsky Prospekt
Yunost (Youth), 40 Miro Prospekt

Hotels

Altai, 12 Gostinichnaya Ulitsa
Armenia, 4 Neglinnaya
Berlin, 3 Ulitsa Zhdanova
Budapest, 2/8 Petrovskiye Linii
Bucharest, 1 Ulitsa Balchug
Kievskaya, 16 Vtoroi Bryansky Pereulok
Leningradskaya, 21/40 Kalanchevskaya Ulitsa
Metropole, 2/4 Ploshchad Sverdlova
Minsk, 22 Ulitsa Gorkogo
Moskva, 7 Prospekt Marxa
National, 14 Prospekt Marxa
Ostankino, 29 Botanicheskaya Ulitsa
Pekin, 1/7 Bolshaya Sadovaya
Severnaya (North), 50 Sushchovsky Val
Sovietskaya (Soviet), 32/2 Leningradsky Prospekt
Tourist, 17/2 Selskokhozyaistvennaya Ulitsa
Tsentralnaya (Central), 10 Ulitsa Gorkogo
Ukraina (Ukraine), 10/9 Kutuzovsky Prospekt
Vostok (East), 8 Gostinichny Proyezd
Yaroslavskaya, 4 Vtoraya Yaroslavskaya Ulitsa
Yunost (Youth), 36 Frunzensky Val
Yuzhnaya (Southern), 87 Leninsky Prospekt
Zarya (Dawn), 5 Gostinichny Proyezd
Zolotoi Kolos (Golden Ear), 3 Vtoraya Yaroslavskaya Ulitsa.

Note: The *Berlin*, *Metropole* and *National* are Intourist hotels.

How to Get to the Centre of Town From Your Hotel

The *Metropole, National, Berlin, Moskva, Tsentralnaya* (Central), *Budapest, Armenia, Oktyabrskaya* (October) and *Ural* Hotels are situated in the very centre of the city.

Sovietskaya: Dynamo or Byelorusskaya Metro Stations; trolley buses 1, 12, 20.

Pekin: Mayakovskaya Metro Station; trolley buses 1, 10, 12, 20, 29, B.

Ukraina: Kievskaya Metro Station; motorbuses 69, 70, 89, 107, 116, 139; trolley bus 2.

Kievskaya: Kievskaya Metro Station; trolley buses 7, 34, 36, 46; motorbuses 45, 69, 70, 91, 119, 132, 139, 267.

Leningradskaya: Komsomolskaya Metro Station; trolley buses 14, 22, 41; motorbuses 19, 40, 85, 152.

Bukharest and *Balchug Hotels:* Novokuznetskaya Metro Station; motorbuses 6, 25, 28, 115; trolley bus 25.

Ostankino: VDNKh (National Economic Achievements Exhibition) Metro Station; trolley buses 9, 36; motorbuses 24, 76, 85; streetcars 7, 10.

How to Reach Central Key Points in the City

Arbatskaya Square: Metro; trolley buses 2, 15, 31, 39; motorbuses 39, 89.

Byelorussian Railway Terminal: Metro; trolley buses 1, 12, 18, 20; motorbuses 10, 12, 27, 38, 63, 82, 116, 149, 263; streetcars A, 5, 29.

Dzerzhinsky Square: Metro; trolley buses 2, 9, 19, 25, 41, 42, 45, 48; motorbuses 3, 18, 24, 43, 55, 74, 89, 98, 107.

Gorky Central Recreation Park: Park Kultury in Otdykha or Oktyabrskaya Metro Stations; trolley buses B, 10, 17, 28, 31; motorbuses 8, 108.

Kiev Railway Terminal: Metro; trolley buses 7, 34, 39, 46; motorbuses 45, 69, 70, 91, 119, 132, 139, 267.

Komsomol Square: Metro; trolley buses 14, 22, 41; motorbuses 40, 85, 152; streetcars 7, 32, 37, 50.

Kropotkinskaya Square: Metro; trolley buses 11, 15, 31; motorbus 8.

Kursk Railway Terminal: Metro; trolley buses B, 10; motorbuses 40, 78, 81; streetcars 2, 20, 24.

Kuznetsky Most: Dzerzhinskaya and Prospekt Marxa Metro Stations; trolley buses 2, 9, 13, 23, 42; motorbus 24.

Lenin Hills; Metro; trolley buses 7, 28.

Lenin Library: Metro; trolley buses 1, 2, 4, 8, 11; motorbuses 3, 5, 6.

Manège Square: Metro; trolley buses 1, 2, 5, 8, 11, 12, 20; motorbuses 3, 5, 89, 111.

Mayakovsky Square: Metro; trolley buses B, 1, 10, 12, 20, 29.

National Economic Achievements Exhibition: Metro; trolley buses 9, 13, 14, 36, 48; motorbuses 9, 33, 56, 61, 83, 93, 117, 136, 151, 265; streetcars 5, 10, 11, 25.

Noviye Cheryomushki: Metro; motorbuses 37, 41, 42, 49, 101, 103, 113, 156.

Ostankino: VDNKh (National Economic Achievements Exhibition) Metro Station; trolley buses 9, 13, 36; motorbuses 24, 76, 85; streetcars 7, 10.

Pushkin Square: trolley buses 1, 3, 12, 15, 20, 23, 31; motorbuses 5, 18, 87, 107.

Red Square: Ploshchad Revolutsii and Prospekt Marxa Metro Stations; trolley buses 1, 2, 3, 4, 5, 9, 11, 12, 13, 20, 25; motorbuses 3, 5, 18, 24, 25, 28, 87, 107, 111, 213.

Revolution Square: Metro; trolley buses 1, 2, 3, 5, 9, 11, 12, 13, 20, 23; motorbuses 3, 5, 18, 24, 87, 107, 213.

Smolensk Square: Metro; trolley buses 5, 10, 39; motorbuses 64, 132.

Sokolniki: Metro; trolley buses 14, 32, 41; motorbuses 40, 52, 71, 75, 78, 80, 140, 152, 216; streetcars 4, 7, 10, 13, 45.

Sverdlov Square: see Revolution Square.

Trubnaya Square: trolley buses 13, 15, 31, 42; motorbus 24; streetcars A, 1, 18, 25.

Vosstaniye Square: Krasnopresnenskaya Metro Station; trolley buses B, 5, 8, 10; motorbuses 4, 6, 39, 48, 64, 69, 107, 116.

City Transit Systems

Metro. Traffic begins on all lines at 6 a.m. and stops at 30 minutes past midnight. The fare is 5 kopecks and covers transfers to all lines.

Trolley bus. Traffic begins at 6 a.m. and ends at 30 minutes past midnight. The fare, one way, regardless of distance, is 4 kopecks.

Motorbus. Traffic begins at 6 a.m. and ends at 30 minutes past midnight. The fare, one way, regardless of distance, is 5 kopecks.

Streetcar. Traffic begins at 5:30 a.m. and ends at 30 minutes past midnight. The fare, one way, regardless of distance, is 3 kopecks.

Note: Many trolley buses, motorbuses and streetcars operate without fare-collectors. There are cash boxes for the passenger to drop in his fare and tear off a ticket. You should therefore always try to have small change with you (1, 2, 3 and 5 kopeck coins) that will add up to the correct fare, since the cash boxes do not automatically give change.

Taxi. The municipal taxi system has a large fleet of *Volga* and *Moskvich* cabs in constant service. All cabs can be readily recognized by two distinctive indications: a checkered band on both sides, the back and the front of the engine hood and a green light in the top right hand corner of the windshield. If the green light is on, the taxicab is free and at your service if you wish to hail it in the street. There are some 250 taxi-stands in the city. You can call a cab by phone from your hotel (the most convenient way is to have the Service Bureau do it for you). Your fare is registered on the taximeter. Rates are 10 kopecks per kilometre plus a 10 kopeck service charge. Any waiting time is paid for at the rate of one rouble an hour.

A taxicab can be called by phoning 25-00-00.

Fixed-route taxi. There are fixed-route taxicabs that ply between the larger city squares at intervals of five to ten minutes. These have definite stops along their routes, but, if they are not full, they will stop for you at any point when hailed. The fare, one way, regardless of the distance, is 10 kopecks per person.

Postal, Telegraph and Telephone Services

Postal transactions in the Soviet Union are much the same as accepted procedures in other countries. A letter or post-card may be mailed from Moscow to any part of the world. There is a post office in every hotel.

Postage to Foreign Countries (in kopecks)

	Letter	Postcard
First-class mail	6	4
Airmail	16	14
Registered first-class mail	18	18
Registered airmail	28	26

Telegrams and express-telegrams may be sent to any city in the world. Express telegrams are charged at twice the regular rate.

Telegraph Rates
(charge per word in kopecks for telegrams)

Austria	14	Iraq	54
Belgium	16	Italy	16
Chinese People's Republic	18	Netherlands	15
Czechoslovakia	9	Norway	14
Denmark	12	Poland	9
Finland	11	Sweden	13
France	15	UAR	35
FRG	13	USA	30
GDR	10	USA (New York)	23
Great Britain	16		

Telephone calls may be put through to most cities in Europe and America, and also to Australia and several countries in

Asia and Africa. You can make a call right from your hotel room or from special trunk-call offices.

Long-distance Telephone Rates
(charge for a three-minute conversation in roubles and kopecks)

Austria	3,00	Iran	3.53
Belgium	3.29	Iraq	7.50
Bulgaria	2.01	Italy	3.79
Chinese People's		Israel	9.26
Republic	7.23	Japan	10.58
Czechoslovakia	2.35	Korean People's Demo-	
Denmark	2.88	cratic Republic	8.00
Finland	1.23	Netherlands	2.46
France	4.35	Norway	3.44
FRG	3.32	Poland	1.94
GDR	2.65	Rumania	2.29
Great Britain	4.28	Sweden	2.41
Greece	4.07	Switzerland	2.94
Hungary	2.00	Yugoslavia	2.79
Iceland	7.08	USA	10.80
India	7.50		

Note: There are special reduced rates for the following countries between the hours specified:

Bulgaria from 7 p.m. to 8 a.m.	1.21
Czechoslovakia from 7 p.m. to 8 a.m.	1.41
Poland from 7 p.m. to 8 a.m.	0.97
USA Sundays	8.10

Addresses and Telephones

Central Telegraph Office: 7 Ulitsa Gorkogo. Tel. 95-82-78 and 94-95-26; Open round the clock.

International Telephone Service: 7 Ulitsa Gorkogo (Entrance No. 10 on Ulitsa Ogareva). Tel. 95-92-68; Open round the clock.

Moscow Main Post Office: 26 Ulitsa Kirova. Tel. 28-63-11; Open from 8 a.m. until 10 p.m.

Note: For tourists who wish to have their mail sent to them in care of general delivery there is post office No. K-600, in the building of *National Hotel,* 1 Gorky Street, specially set up to serve foreign tourists visiting Moscow. If you like, you may leave the following forwarding address to friends: Moscow K-600.

You can be sure all correspondence will be waiting for you there.

Post office K-600 is open daily from 9 a.m. until 8 p.m. Tel. 29-72-32.

What the Pedestrian in Moscow Should Know

Traffic on Moscow streets is quite heavy, so it would be well to keep in mind the city's basic traffic rules:

—keep to the sidewalks, to the right side;

—cross streets only where indicated, on green light;

—remember that traffic moves along the right side of the road; crossing first look to the left and then, when you've reached the middle, to the right;

—cross streets only behind standing buses and trolley buses and in front of standing streetcars, otherwise you may not notice parallel traffic;

—remember that it is against the rules for a driver to blow his horn except in emergencies.

Helpful Hints for Finding Your Way About Town

Here are several signs frequently met on the streets which, if borne in mind, should help you find your way about town during your excursions and strolls:

hotel	Гостиница
restaurant	Ресторан
café	Кафе
barbershop, hairdresser's	Парикмахерская
post office	Почта
drug store, pharmacy	Аптека
grocery store, delicacies	Гастроном
store, shop	Магазин
books	Книги
Metro, subway	Метро
taxi stand	Стоянка такси
trolley bus stop	Остановка троллейбуса
motorbus stop	Остановка автобуса
public lavatory (L), (M)	Туалет (Ж), (М)
information office	Справочное бюро
news-stand	Союзпечать
public telephone	Телефон-автомат
street crossing	Переход
theatre	Театр
motion picture house, cinema	Кино-театр
museum	Музей

It will be helpful to remember that on all radial streets diverging from the centre of town, that is, from the Kremlin, the house numbers begin at the centre.

Automobile Service Facilities for Foreign Tourists

A-56 and A-70 petrol (gasoline)
is available (for cash) at:

Filling station No. 12, Novodmitrovskaya Ulitsa. Tel. 50-22-67.
Filling station No. 22, 44 Ulitsa Plyushchikha. Tel. 41-57-83.
Filling station No. 24, Leningradsky Prospekt near the Aeroport Metro Station. Tel. 57-77-64.
Filling station No. 41, 13 Volnaya Ulitsa. Tel. 69-10-63.
Filling station No. 42, Prospekt Mira, 4 Vtoroi Selskokhozyaist-venny Proezd. Tel. 1-81-13-73.
Filling station No. 63, 2 Nizhegorodskoye Shosse. Tel. 71-39-85.

A-93 petrol (gasoline) and diesel oil are available
(for cash or Intourist coupons) at:

Filling station No. 15, Metrostroyevskaya Ulitsa, Tretiy Zachatyev-sky Pereulok. Tel. 46-52-53.

A-70 and A-74 petrol (gasoline)
are available (for cash) at:

Filling station No. 18, Danilovskaya Ploshchad. Tel. 34-26-26.

A-56, A-70, A-93 and A-98 petrol (gasoline) are available
(for cash or Intourist coupons) at:

Filling station No. 42, Prospekt Mira, 4 Vtoroi Selskokhozyaist-venny Proyezd. Tel. 83-16-08.

Diesel oil (for Intourist coupons only):

Filling station No. 33, Khoroshevskoye Shosse, 19 Pervyi Magistralny Pereulok. Tel. 55-00-10, extension 3-73.

Automobile Service Station No. 7:

Prospekt Mira, 6 Vtoroi Selskokhozyaistvenny Pereulok. Tel. 1-81-06-31 ; 1-81-13-74. Open daily from 9 a.m. to 7 p.m. Saturdays and Sundays from 9 a.m. to 2 p.m.

Bus Service Station:

1 Pervaya Druzhnikovskaya Ulitsa. Tel. 52-21-28; 52-16-68. Open daily from 10 a.m. to 4 p.m.; Saturday from 10 a.m. to 2 p.m.; Closed Sundays.

Note: Bus drivers should make arrangements with the management in advance by telephone to have their machines serviced.

Useful information for Motorists in Moscow

Here are several suggestions that should help you drive confidently through Moscow.
While motoring in Moscow please remember:
—traffic moves along the right side of the street;

—strictly observe road signals and signs, traffic regulations and traffic lights, and comply with the directions of traffic officers;

—the speed limit in towns and other inhabited points is 60 km an hour (35 miles an hour);

—horns may be used only outside the city limits or in an emergency to prevent an accident;

—special service vehicles (fire engines, ambulances, etc.) have tne right of way; heed their sirens;

—traffic lights with 4 lights allow a left turn or a complete U-turn when the two green lights go on, a signal that should be awaited at the STOP (CTOII) line;

—never cross a solid white line running down the centre of the road: you may turn left or make a complete U-turn only where there is a broken line or a sign indicating that it is permitted;

—at crossings where there are stripes marked on the road and no traffic lights the pedestrian has the right of way.

Note: If you did not insure your car at the Soviet border, you may do so in Moscow at the office of the Foreign Insurance Agency (Ingosstrakh). This organization handles all accident insurance, both collision and liability insurance.

Insurance premiums are accepted in any currency. All claims are compensated in the currency used to pay for the policy. Ingosstrakh is located at 11/10 Ulitsa Kuibysheva. Tel. 23-49-27.

Handy Addresses and Telephone Numbers

Executive Committee of the Moscow City Soviet of Working People's Deputies, 13 Ulitsa Gorkogo. Tel. 94-09-90; 92-17-08; 92-19-74.

USSR Ministry of Foreign Affairs, 32/34 Smolenskaya-Sennaya Ploshchad. Tel. 44-16-06.

USSR Ministry of Foreign Trade, 32/34 Smolenskaya-Sennaya Ploshchad. Tel. 44-34-80 (Protocol Department); Tel. 24-19-47 (Information Office).

State Committee for Cultural Relations with Foreign Countries, 9 Ulitsa Kalinina. Tel. 41-95-43.

Union of Soviet Societies of Friendship and Cultural Relations with Foreign Countries, 14 Ulitsa Kalinina. Tel. 94-99-32.

All-Union Chamber of Commerce, 6 Ulitsa Kuibysheva. Tel. 21-08-11.

Soviet Peace Committee, 10 Kropotkinskaya Ulitsa. Tel. 46-94-36.

Soviet Women's Committee, 23 Ulitsa Pushkinskaya. Tel. 29-74-65.

Committee of Soviet Youth Organizations, 7/8 Ulitsa Bogdana Khmelnitskogo. Tel. 26-36-61.

USSR Slav Committee, 10 Ulitsa Kropotkinskaya. Tel. 46-07-23.

Union of Red Cross and Red Crescent Societies, 5 Ulitsa Cheryomushkinsky Proyezd. Tel. 36-57-61.

Soviet War Veterans' Committee, 10 Ulitsa Kropotkinskaya. Tel. 46-47-07.
Soviet Afro-Asian Solidarity Committee, 10 Ulitsa Kropotkinskaya. Tel. 46-07-28.
All-Union Znaniye Society, 3 Serova Proyez. Tel. 23-40-19.
Union of Sports Societies and Organizations of the USSR, 4 Skatertny Pereulok. Tel. 95-49-23.
State Bank of the USSR, 12 Ulitsa Neglinnaya. Tel. 23-20-38.
All-Union Central Council of Trade Unions, 42 Leninsky Prospekt. Tel. 32-95-00.
USSR United Nations Association, 19 Ulitsa Dmitriya Ulyanova. Tel. 36-05-50.
Sputnik Youth Travel Agency, 4 Lebyazhy Pereulok. Tel. 21-39-20.
House of Friendship with Foreign Countries, 16 Ulitsa Kalinina. Tel. 28-20-69.
Union of Soviet Architects, 3 Ulitsa Shchuseva. Tel. 28-25-79.
Union of Soviet Journalists, 30 Prospekt Mira. Tel. 81-55-07.
Union of Soviet Composers, 8/10 Ulitsa Nezhdanovoi. Tel. 29-35-21.
Union of Soviet Writers, 52 Ulitsa Vorovskogo. Tel. 52-21-46; 55-19-81.
Union of Soviet Artists, 25/9 Ulitsa Gorkogo. Tel. 99-22-89; 99-79-69.
Union of Film Workers, 13 Vasilyevskaya Ulitsa. Tel. 50-41-14.

Major Magazines and Newspapers Published in Moscow

Pravda, 24 Ulitsa Pravdy. Tel. 51-73-86.
Izvestia, 5 Pushkinskaya Ploshchad. Tel. 99-00-08, extension 200.
Trud, 18b Ulitsa Gorkogo. Tel. 99-39-06.
Komsomolskaya Pravda, 24 Ulitsa Pravdy. Tel. 53-30-56.
Vecherniaya Moskva, 8 Chistoprudny Boulevard. Tel. 95-20-53.
Les Nouvelles de Moscou, 2 Pushkinskaya Ploshchad. Tel. 29-12-66.
Moscow News, 2 Pushkinskaya Ploshchad. Tel. 29-12-66.
Novedades de Moscû, 2 Pushkinskaya Ploshchad. Tel. 29-90-00.
Neues Leben, 14 Bumazhny Proyezd. Tel. 53-32-26.
Literaturnaya Gazeta, 30 Tsvetnoi Boulevard. Tel. 94-04-62.
Moskovskaya Pravda, 8 Chistoprudny Boulevard. Tel. 23-17-50.
Sovietskaya Kultura, 19a Chistoprudny Boulevard. Tel. 97-36-22.
Sovietsky Sport, 8 Ulitsa Arkhipova. Tel. 23-43-97.
Sovietskaya Rossiya, 24 Ulitsa Pravdy. Tel. 53-37-72.

News Agencies
Telegraph Agency of the Soviet Union (TASS), 10 Tverskoi Boulevard. Tel. 29-80-53.

Novosti Press Agency (APN), 2 Maly Putinkovsky Pereulok.
Tel. 28-56-85.

Radio
State Committee for Radio and Television, 25 Pyatnitskaya Ulitsa.
Tel. 33-60-60.

Foreign Embassies

Afghanistan, 42 Ulitsa Vorovskogo. Tel. 94-17-87.
Algerian People's Democratic Republic, 1 Krapivinsky Pereulok.
Tel. 21-73-20.
Argentina, 8 Ulitsa Lunacharskogo. Tel. 41-33-88.
Australia, 13 Kropotkinsky Pereulok. Tel. 41-20-35.
Austria, 1 Starokonyushenny Pereulok. Tel. 46-32-00.
Belgium, 15 Khlebny Pereulok. Tel. 95-22-72.
Brazil, 54 Ulitsa Gertsena. Tel. 95-25-23.
Bulgaria, People's Republic of, 20 Leningradsky Prospekt. Tel.
51-25-85.
Burma, Union of, 41 Ulitsa Gertsena. Tel. 95-75-08.
Cambodia, 5a Sobinovsky Pereulok. Tel. 95-80-65.
Cameroons, 5 Ulitsa Obolenskogo, apt. 113. Tel. 46-88-97.
Canada, 23 Starokonyushenny Pereulok. Tel. 41-90-34.
Central African Republic, 7 Pereulok Vadkovskogo. Tel. 50-35-18.
Ceylon, 24 Ulitsa Shchepkina. Tel. 81-91-26.
Chad, Republic of, 3 Gruzinskaya Ulitsa, apt. 256. Tel. 53-29-14.
Chile, 4 Sadovo-Triumphalnaya Ulitsa, apt. 132. Tel. 99-75-74.
Chinese People's Republic, 6 Ulitsa Druzhby Lenin Hill. Tel.
46-13-09.
Congo, Republic of (Brazzaville). 5 Lopukhinsky Pereulok. Tel.
46-30-80.
Cuba, Republic of, 6 Pomerantsev Pereulok. Tel. 46-13-09.
Cyprus, Republic of, 51 Ulitsa Gertsena. Tel. 23-21-54.
Czechoslovak Socialist Republic, 12 Ulitsa Juliusa Fuchika. Tel.
53-75-07.
Denmark, 9 Ostrovsky Pereulok. Tel. 41-10-30.
Ethiopia, 35 Kropotkinskaya Naberezhnaya. Tel. 46-80-23.
Finland, 15 Kropotkinsky Pereulok. Tel. 46-45-40.
France, 43 Ulitsa Dimitrova. Tel. 31-85-06.
German Democratic Republic, 10 Ulitsa Stanislavskogo. Tel.
94-00-25.
German Federal Republic, 17 Bolshaya Gruzinskaya Ulitsa. Tel.
52-05-30.
Ghana, 12 Lopukhinsky Pereulok. Tel. 46-40-61.
Great Britain, 14 Naberezhnaya Morisa Thoreza. Tel. 31-95-55.
Greece, 4 Ulitsa Stanislavskogo. Tel. 29-22-74.
Guinea, Republic of, 13 Ulitsa A. Tolstogo. Tel. 94-40-02.
Hungarian People's Republic, 22 Ulitsa Vorovskogo. Tel.
95-20-06.
Iceland, 28 Khlebny Pereulok. Tel. 94-06-03.
Indian Republic, 6 Ulitsa Obukha. Tel. 97-08-20.
Indonesian Republic, 12 Novokuznetskaya Ulitsa. Tel. 31-95-49.

Iran, 7 Pokrovsky Boulevard. Tel. 97-23-30.
Iraq, Republic of, 8 Pereulok Ostrovskogo. Tel. 46-27-53.
Israel, 56 Bolshaya Ordynka. Tel. 33-86-13.
Italian Republic, 5 Ulitsa Vesnina. Tel. 41-15-34.
Japan, 12 Kalashny Pereulok. Tel. 94-25-30.
Kenya, 70 Bolshaya Ordynka. Tel. 33-86-17.
Korean People's Democratic Republic, 9 Ulitsa Stanislavskogo. Tel. 29-60-13.
Kuwait, 28 Lomonosovsky Prospekt. Tel. 14-30-77.
Laos, 18 Ulitsa Kachalova. Tel. 95-64-67.
Lebanon, Republic of, 14 Sadovaya-Samotyochnaya Ulitsa. Tel. 95-20-83.
Libya, 20, Merzlyakovsky Pereulok. Tel. 95-27-65.
Luxemburg, 3 Khrushchevsky Pereulok. Tel. 46-17-27.
Mali, Republic of, 11 Novokuznetskaya Ulitsa. Tel. 31-22-60.
Mauretania, the Islamic Republic of, 93 Leninsky Prospekt, apt. 12, build. 2-A. Tel. 13-93-816.
Mexico, 4 Ulitsa Shchukina. Tel. 46-79-32.
Mongolian People's Republic, 11 Ulitsa Pisemskogo. Tel. 95-30-61.
Morocco, 60 Ulitsa Gorkogo. Tel. 51-23-12.
Nepal, 14/7 Vtoroi Neopolimovsky Pereulok. Tel. 41-94-34.
Netherlands, The, 6 Kalashny Pereulok. Tel. 94-19-85.
Nigeria, Federative Republic of, 13 Ulitsa Kachalova. Tel. 94-25-00.
Norway, 7 Ulitsa Vorovskogo. Tel. 95-25-20.
Pakistan, 17 Sadovo-Kudrinskaya Ulitsa. Tel. 51-78-39.
Polish People's Republic, 30 Ulitsa A. Tolstogo. Tel. 99-00-04.
Rumanian People's Republic, 40 Mosfilmovskaya Ulitsa. Tel. 14-30-459.
Senegal, Republic of, 40 Donskaya Ulitsa. Tel. 32-28-65.
Sierra Leone, 3 Gruzinskaya Ulitsa, apt. 3. Tel. 50-17-93.
Somali Republic, 8 Spasopeskovskaya Ploshchad. Tel. 41-86-24.
Sudan, Republic of, 9 Ulitsa Vorovskogo. Tel. 21-69-50.
Sweden, 15 Ulitsa Pissemskogo. Tel. 23-22-26.
Switzerland, 15 Bolshevistsky Pereulok. Tel. 95-53-22.
Syrian Arabian Republic, 4 Mansurovsky Pereulok. Tel. 46-66-03.
Tanzania, United Republic of, 38 Lomonosovsky Prospekt. Tel. 14-33-876.
Thailand, 3 Yeropkinsky Pereulok. Tel. 46-13-61.
Tunisia, the Republic of, 28 Ulitsa Kachalova. Tel. 52-17-69.
Turkey, 43a Ulitsa Gertsena. Tel. 95-30-62.
United Arab Republic, 56 Ulitsa Gertsena. Tel. 52-05-37.
United States of America, 19 Ulitsa Chaikovskogo. Tel. 52-00-11.
Uruguay, 28 Ulitsa Zholtovskogo. Tel. 99-53-04.
Vietnam, Democratic Republic of, 13 Bolshaya Pirogovskaya. Tel. 45-10-92.
Yemen Arabian Republic, 22 Prospekt Mira. Tel. 84-49-71.
Yugoslavia, Federative Socialist Republic of, 21 Khlebny Pereulok. Tel. 94-79-02.
Zambia, Republic of, 3 Gruzinsky Pereulok, apt. 149. Tel. 53-22-49.

CONTENTS

                    I.C.C. (J. LONDON, IMPR.) PARIS
September 1967   *Printed in France*